GENERATION DEBT

How Our Future Was Sold Out For Student Loans, Credit Cards, Bad Jobs, No Benefits, and Tax Cuts for Rich Geezers—and How to Fight Back

Item #: AC2011-B05
Generation Debt
Price : $16.00

INCLUDES A NEW CHAPTER FROM THE AUTHOR

ANYA KAMENETZ

Praise for *Generation Debt*

"Partly prescriptive (beware credit cards, consider state schools) and partly indignant (we're not slackers, we're victims of government policies that favor older Americans)." —*Newsweek*

"Surveying the economic realities facing today's twenty- and thirty-somethings, twenty-four-year-old Kamenetz decides, 'It's not too dramatic to say that the nation is abandoning its children.' Thanks to skyrocketing tuition and changes in federal funding, college students are graduating with an average of almost $20,000 in loans at the same time that jobs have become scarcer, real wages have dropped, and the cost of health care has soared. Is it any wonder that kids are boomeranging home and racking up credit card debt? Kamenetz, who first wrote about these issues for the *Village Voice*, intertwines an analytical overview of the new economic obstacles with interviews of the financially strapped and descriptions of her own experience struggling to make ends meet as a freelance journalist. . . . Most interestingly, Kamenetz documents how our perception of the crisis is shaped by self-centered boomers who have lost touch with their children's plight. . . . It make[s] clear how imperative it is that we find solutions to these problems as quickly as possible." —*Publishers Weekly*

"Call[s] attention to financial problems that plague us: sizeable student loans, credit-card debt, a tight job market, and skyrocketing housing prices." —*BusinessWeek*

"It's no wonder those of us eighteen to thirty-five are finding it so hard to get ahead. . . . Kamenetz lays out a well-researched blueprint of the current economy. The numbers are staggering. The average college student has amassed $20,000 in student loans and $2,169 in credit card debt by the time they graduate. . . . Kamenetz walks us through the history of contributing factors, putting this into context." —*Buffalo News*

"[Kamenetz] has some good suggestions about how to address the problems she raises. But one thing Kamenetz can't do, even by publishing this thoughtful and rigorous book, is force her comrades to do something that might actually make politicians listen: vote." —*The Philadelphia Inquirer*

continued . . .

"Kamenetz makes a passionate argument for young people to take action, such as lobbying the government as a cohesive group and being practical and frugal about money matters." —*Booklist*

"Written by a twenty-four-year-old journalist, this book explains some reasons people age eighteen to thirty-four are doing so poorly with money, including high college debt, low-paying or temporary jobs, and limited access to health benefits. Through interviews with experts in economics, labor markets, the health-care industry, and education as well as young adults, the author reveals why it's harder for people to stay afloat and amass personal wealth than it was thirty years ago." —*The Seattle Times*

"Thankfully, the liveliness of Kamenetz's mind mitigates the bleakness of her portrait. A twenty-four page bibliography reveals her as a wide and careful reader, and she performs an energetic, if procedural, diagnostic on the decried, double-crossing system. She has a dizzying array of figures, but also an occasional flair for pithy description ('credit cards are the piranhas that swim behind the shark of student loan debt'), and a real commitment to a prosperous future. It will take some work." —*San Francisco Chronicle*

"Anya Kamenetz captures the common goals, frustrations, and unrelenting optimism of an entire generation for whom the promise that hard work and a college education will bring financial security may very well not come true. *Generation Debt* provides the hard numbers and serious research that puts their struggles in the context of the rapid economic and political shifts radically affecting the economic prospects of today's young adults, and thus also those of their retiring parents and future children. Anya's book is essential reading not only for millions of struggling young adults, but also for their parents, who want to understand the stark economic circumstances their children face upon entering the workforce." —Michael Dannenberg, Director, Education Policy Program, New America Foundation

DEBT
GENERATION

How Our Future Was Sold Out
for Student Loans, Credit
Cards, Bad Jobs, No
Benefits, and Tax Cuts for
Rich Geezers—and How to
Fight Back

ANYA KAMENETZ

RIVERHEAD BOOKS

NEW YORK

THE BERKLEY PUBLISHING GROUP
Published by the Penguin Group
Penguin Group (USA) Inc.
375 Hudson Street, New York, New York 10014, USA
Penguin Group (Canada), 90 Eglinton Avenue East, Suite 700, Toronto, Ontario M4P 2Y3,
Canada (a division of Pearson Penguin Canada Inc.) • Penguin Books Ltd., 80 Strand, London
WC2R 0RL, England • Penguin Group Ireland, 25 St. Stephen's Green, Dublin 2, Ireland
(a division of Penguin Books Ltd.) • Penguin Group (Australia), 250 Camberwell Road,
Camberwell, Victoria 3124, Australia (a division of Pearson Australia Group Pty. Ltd.) • Penguin
Books India Pvt. Ltd., 11 Community Centre, Panchsheel Park,
New Delhi—110 017, India • Penguin Group (NZ), cnr Airborne and Rosedale Roads,
Albany, Auckland 1310, New Zealand (a division of Pearson New Zealand Ltd.) •
Penguin Books (South Africa) (Pty.) Ltd., 24 Sturdee Avenue, Rosebank,
Johannesburg 2196, South Africa

Penguin Books Ltd., Registered Offices: 80 Strand, London WC2R 0RL, England

While the author has made every effort to provide accurate telephone numbers and Internet
addresses at the time of publication, neither the publisher nor the author assumes any
responsibility for errors, or for changes that occur after publication. Further, publisher does not
have any control over and does not assume any responsibility for author or third-party websites
or their content.

First Riverhead hardcover edition: February 2006
First Riverhead trade paperback edition: January 2007
Riverhead trade paperback ISBN: 978-1-59448-234-2

The Library of Congress has catalogued the Riverhead hardcover edition as follows:

Kamenetz, Anya, date.
Generation debt : why now is a terrible time to be young / Anya Kamenetz.
p.   cm.
Includes bibliographical references.
ISBN 1-59448-907-6
1. Young adults—United States—Economic conditions—21st century. 2. Young adults—United
States—Social conditions—21st century. 3. College graduates—United States—Economic
conditions—21st century. I. Title.
HQ799.7.K36   2006   2005044720
330.9730084'2—dc22

PRINTED IN THE UNITED STATES OF AMERICA

10 9 8 7 6 5 4 3 2

To my parents and to Adam, my future

CONTENTS

Why I Wrote This Book

What would you do if you grew up and realized that everything America has always promised its children no longer holds true for you?

I am twenty-four years old, and I was born into a broke generation. I look around and I see people who have borrowed more to go to college than they can repay, who can't find a good job, can't save, can't afford basic necessities like health insurance, can't make solid plans. Their credit card bills mount every month, while their lives stall out on the first uphill slope. Born into a century of unimaginable prosperity, in the richest country in the world, those of us between the ages of eighteen and thirty-five have somehow been cheated out of our inheritance.

I came of age at a precarious moment in American history. I

graduated from Yale in the spring of 2002. During the four years I was in school, the country rode more highs and lows than the Coney Island Cyclone. In 1998 and 1999, some of my classmates had their own start-ups, making million-dollar deals on their cell phones between classes. By the turn of the millennium, the NASDAQ had peaked, the Internet balloon was leaking fast, and a presidential election decided in the courts shook the timbers of our democracy. Then, in the fall of my senior year, four days before my twenty-first birthday, came September 11, 2001. My generation was forever marked by a catastrophe, our Pearl Harbor.

The dust of the World Trade Center was still hanging in the air when I moved to New York to find work as a journalist. Dot-com exuberance had deflated; the paper millionaires had blown away. The country was struggling through a long "jobless recovery," and the drums were beating for a new global war. It was not an auspicious moment to begin a career.

Like many of my peers, I interviewed without success for full-time jobs, and ended up freelancing as a writer and researcher. In the spring of 2004, I began to contribute to a feature series in *The Village Voice* called "Generation Debt: The New Economics of Being Young," conceived and named by executive editor Laura Conaway.

I started talking with dozens of people around my age from different walks of life. At parties, at clubs, at coffee shops, on campuses, at bars, at job-training centers, at political meetings, on Internet message boards, on the street, I'd have the same conversation over and over. I'd say I was writing about the economic obstacles facing young people. "You could write about me," they would respond. Then they would tell me about student loan debt in the tens of thousands of dollars. About working their way through college for six years at $9 an hour. About parents' divorces or job loss that derailed their own dreams. About mounting credit card debt that kept them up at night. Degrees, even advanced degrees, that led nowhere. Long searches for unsatisfying jobs. Layoffs. Underemployment. Flat incomes. No health insurance, no retirement plan, no paid vacation. Unaffordable housing. Moving back in with Mom. Turning thirty with negative savings and no assets. Putting off marriage or kids because they couldn't afford them.

After a few months, I knew that the problem was bigger than a series of articles could describe. I had to write a book to document the full situation, not to mention get answers for my friends and myself. Is student loan debt really that bad? Why has college gotten so expensive? What happened to all the good jobs? Are we really going to do worse than our parents?

Through research, I have realized just how lucky I am. Not only am I one of just 28 percent of the young population with a bachelor's degree, I am part of the one-third of four-year college graduates without loan debt. My parents, married for twenty-six years—rare in their generation—can give me help if I need it. They raised me in middle-class comfort, but with realistic expectations. Because of them, I spend no more than I earn and pay off my one credit card every month.

Still, I live my life in a Zen-like state of transience. No employer has yet offered me a full-time job with a 401(k), a paid vacation, or any other benefits beyond the next assignment. I have a savings account but no retirement fund. Settling down seems like an insurmountable achievement; I can't afford preschool fees or a mortgage anywhere near the city where I live and work. People usually suggest graduate school as a means of finding something more permanent, but $40,000 in loans, with no guarantees on the other end, seems like a bad deal to me. In short, I've been taught to expect the world on a plate, but I know that I'll be stuck with the check. If concerns like these are touching my life, they are touching everyone's.

Wait a minute, you say. If things are really going down the tubes for young people, why hasn't anyone noticed? Well, for one thing, money in America is more private than sex. My friends and I rarely discuss our financial anxieties, so we tend to see our situations as our own fault. "I'm just lazy," an unemployed nineteen-year-old told me. "I don't know why I was so restless," said a twenty-eight-year-old who's held six jobs in eight years.

Not only do we blame ourselves, our elders blame us, too. It makes me really angry to see the Boomers in charge of the media and other powerful institutions attributing the problems young people are going through to nothing more serious than a lack of initiative. In the early years of this decade, the mass media stamped an image of eighteen-to-thirty-four-year-olds as slackers, overgrown children, and procrastinators, as though we're intentionally dragging our heels to avoid reaching adulthood.

In December 2004, *The New York Times* published a roundup of the coinages and catchphrases of the year. Among them was the awkward hybrid "adultescent."

"The adult it describes is too busy playing Halo 2 on his Xbox or watching SpongeBob at his parents' house to think about growing up," wrote John Tierney, a *Times* op-ed columnist. In January 2005, *Time* magazine devoted a cover story, written by Lev Grossman, to "twixters," another ugly neologism. Again, twenty-somethings were portrayed as drifting through "a strange, transitional never-never land between adolescence and adulthood."

Rather than probe the underlying causes of this shift, journalists too often settle for cheap shots. Most articles, books, and TV segments about people my age note economic factors only in passing. The headlines and the titles strike accusatory notes: "Don't Let Boomerang Kids Derail Your Goals"; "It's the Kids—Lock Up the China!" As Tierney concludes: "One common explanation for the rise in adultescence is the cost of housing and education, which has made it harder for young people (especially in places like New York) to afford homes and children. Another explanation is that young adults now enjoy some pleasures of marriage without the consequences." Of course! It's the premarital sex that makes us want to go without full-time jobs or benefits! "But if you ask adultescents why they haven't grown up," Tierney goes on, "they may give you a simple answer: Because they don't have to." How about, because we can't?

This attitude is especially insufferable because it's arguably our elders who are taking far more than their fair share. As Nicholas Kristof, another *Times* op-ed columnist, wrote in May 2005, history will probably call the Boomers "The Greediest Generation": "I fear that we'll be remembered mostly for grabbing resources for ourselves, in such a way that the big losers will be America's children."

Kristof is right. Instead of saving enough for their own retirement, let alone for our future, the Boomers are going into deeper debt than any generation before them. Because of their projected retirement expenses, the entire nation is essentially bankrupt, with a total accumulated funding gap in the federal budget that's greater than our national net worth. Who's going to be around when that bill comes due? Young people.

Add to these material debts the ominous global legacy our parents and grandparents have left for us—environmental degradation, petroleum dependence, climate change, geopolitical instability—and the smugness starts to look downright cruel.

The New York Times might see a typical young man as a baseball-cap-clad schlub on his parents' couch. Well, his father probably just refinanced that house, which has appreciated ten times over since he bought it after graduating from a practically free state university. While the poor kid sits at home, seeking electronic distraction from the bleakness of his emasculated, dependent existence, Dad is rattling down the highway in a brand-new $40,000 SUV that gets twelve miles to the gallon and has a bumper sticker on the back that says, RETIRED—SPENDING MY CHILDREN'S INHERITANCE! Who's immature now?

In all seriousness, I ask my over-thirty-five readers to keep an open mind as they look at the evidence marshaled here that the deck is stacked against the young. If you still can't summon much sympathy, at least consider the country's bottom line. The United States' greatest resource for future prosperity and growth is its human capital, which is a fancy term for educated young people. Our young nation has a robust image of itself as bursting with opportunity and devoted to progress. Each generation is meant to outdo the last. The innovation we rely on comes from a youthful, adventuring spirit of self-reliance and fair play.

And yet the country has retreated from this forward-looking stance into a defensive crouch. It is abandoning its children to struggle, narrowing their opportunities, dampening their boldness by forcing them to put liens on their future to pay for the education they need to make a decent living. Our debt precludes us from taking the kinds of entrepreneurial risks on which American success depends.

As perverse as the current course is, as cruelly as it plays out in the lives of so many young people, I don't think it's America's self-image that is wrong. It's the gulf that has grown between ideal and reality. Mom, Dad, listen up: Things have changed. We're not doing as well as you did. And if something doesn't change soon, it's unlikely that we ever will.

ABOUT THE RESEARCH

The stories you read here are real stories, drawn from more than a hundred interviews with young people across the country—by e-mail, by phone, and in person. I conducted in-person interviews in New York, New Orleans, San Francisco, and Washington, D.C. There are no composite characters, and no details have been changed. For the sake of privacy, I refer to all subjects by their first names only. In addition, several of those quoted asked that their first names be changed; these are indicated by quotation marks when a name first appears. In all cases, the age given is the person's age when we first talked, in late 2004 or early 2005. Once again, I thank all my interviewees.

DEBT
GENERATION

ONE

Why Generation Debt?

The next generation is starting their economic race 50 yards behind the starting line.

—ELIZABETH WARREN,
HARVARD LAW SCHOOL PROFESSOR
AND COAUTHOR OF *THE TWO-INCOME TRAP*, 2004

My maternal grandparents' house is down a country road in what was once quiet, rural eastern North Carolina. The last time I drove down there for a visit, alone, at night, in the rain, I had a nasty surprise. No one had warned me that a big highway had replaced the old route through Wayne County. Once the only industry around was a slaughterhouse; now there were floodlit signs for mobile home dealerships and strip clubs. Every exit had become a confusing cloverleaf. I drove back and forth three times before I saw the tiny street sign for their turnoff.

In America, progress is not to be argued with, though it often takes the form of sprawl. The point is to get where you're going faster, with more choices along the way. If simple paths get paved over, and unprepared people get lost, so be it.

So it is with the old route to adulthood. The primary cause for our generation's delay in reaching the promised land of independence, scholars agree, is economic development. The U.S. economy today is faster-moving than ever before, more competitive, more global. Outcomes are far more unequal and income more volatile than they were a generation ago. All this up-and-down motion raises the stakes for individuals. The rewards for success and the penalties for failure are much higher. And the requisite for competition—the college diploma—is getting economically further out of reach every year.

The simplest definition of a "generation" is those people who pass through a specific stage of life at the same time. We tend to think of human life stages as natural demarcations of growth, like the rings on a tree. Yet social and economic structures also determine the divisions between infancy and old age. Since 1960, when historian Philippe Aries published the book *Centuries of Childhood,* scholars have been writing about how childhood was "discovered" for sentimental and moralistic reasons in eighteenth- and nineteenth-century Europe. Before this historical turning point, infants were often farmed out to indifferent wet nurses, and seven-year-olds herded sheep.

Likewise, for most of human history, sexual maturity occurred just a year or two before marriage, and adolescence, as we know it, didn't exist. As Thomas Hine chronicles in *The Rise and Fall of the American Teenager,* when the United States was industrializing in the nineteenth century, people thirteen and up were the backbone of the semiskilled workforce. Teenagers came to America alone as immigrants. They ran weaving machines, dug mines, herded cattle, picked cotton, and fought wars. If they weren't slaves or indentured servants, they contributed their earnings to their families of origin until they got married and started families of their own.

American psychologist G. Stanley Hall popularized the term "adolescent" in 1904, as the rise of compulsory schooling and the move away from an agricultural economy began to lengthen the expected period of youthful preparation. It wasn't until the Great Depression, though, that teenagers' economic life assumed the limits it has today. Hine points out that Roosevelt's New Deal was explicitly designed to take jobs away from young people and give them to heads of households. Teenagers were thus compelled to enroll in high school in much larger numbers than ever before. Young people's secondary economic role has persisted ever since. The affluence and restiveness of postwar America gave new cultural prominence in the 1950s to the modern version of teenhood, a distinct stage of life, a subculture, and a commercial market, funded ultimately by parents. The accepted age of independence for the middle class and above was pushed forward to twenty-one.

Now the postmillennial years are bringing in an entirely new life stage: "emerging adulthood," a term coined by developmental psychologist Jeffrey Jensen Arnett in a 2000 article. The Research Network on Transitions to Adulthood at the University of Pennsylvania is a group of a dozen or so experts in various fields: sociologists, policy experts, developmental psychologists, and economists. Their 2005 book *On the Frontier of Adulthood*, a 591-page scholarly work, explores emerging adulthood in depth.

"More youth are extending education, living at home longer,

and moving haltingly, or stopping altogether, along the stepping stones of adulthood," Frank F. Furstenberg, chair of the network, has written. "A new period of life is emerging in which young people are no longer adolescents but not yet adults. . . . It is simply not possible for most young people to achieve economic and psychological autonomy as early as it was a half century ago." The underlying reason, once again, is an economic shift, this time to a labor market that rewards only the highly educated with livable and growing wages.

In 2002, there were 68 million people in the United States aged eighteen to thirty-four. The social and economic upheaval of the past three decades, not to mention that of the past five years, affects us in complex ways. We have all come of age as part of Generation Debt.

The Penn researchers use five milestones of maturity: leaving home, finishing school, becoming financially independent, getting married, and having a child. By this definition, only 46 percent of women and 31 percent of men were grown up by age thirty in 2000, compared with 77 percent of women and 65 percent of men of the same age in 1960.

"I went from being a child to being a mother," says "Doris," now in her fifties. "I was married at twenty. By thirty I had four children and was divorced." Doris completed college and a master's degree while keeping house and raising her children, then supported her family as a medical physicist.

Doris's youngest daughter, "Miriam," graduated from Southern Connecticut State University in 2000, after six years of work and school, with $20,000 in student loans and $5,000 in credit card debt. Now, at twenty-nine, she is living in Madison, Wisconsin, and training to be a commodities broker, a job she could have pursued with only a high school diploma. Her mother, who bought her first house with her husband in her early twenties, helped Miriam pay off her credit cards and gave her the down payment on the condo she lives in. Miriam earns $28,000 a year and just manages the minimum payments on her loans. She is single. She hasn't passed the five milestones of adulthood; she is barely out of the driveway.

Young people are falling behind first of all because of money. College tuition has grown faster than inflation for three decades, and faster than family income for the past fifteen years. Federal aid has lagged behind. An unprecedented explosion of borrowing has made up the difference between what colleges charge and what families can afford. Between 1995 and 2005, the total volume of federal student loans rose 249 percent after inflation, to over $61 billion. Two-thirds of four-year students are graduating with loan debt, an average of up to $19,200 in 2004 and growing every year. Three out of four college students have credit cards, too, carrying an average unpaid balance of $2,169 in 2005. Nearly a quarter of all students, according to a 2004 survey, are actually putting their tuition directly on plastic.

Even as the price has risen, more young people than ever aspire to college. Over 90 percent of high school graduates of all backgrounds say in national surveys that they hope to go on to college. Yet the inadequacy of aid shoots down their hopes.

As a direct consequence of the decline in public investment in education at every level, young people today are actually less educated than their parents. The nationwide high school graduation rate peaked in 1970 at 77 percent. It was around 67 percent in 2004. According to a recent study cited in the 2004 book *Double the Numbers,* by Richard Kazis, Joel Vargas, and Nancy Hoffman, of every 100 young people who begin their freshman year of high school, just 38 eventually enroll in college, and only 18 graduate within 150 percent of the allotted time—six years for a bachelor's degree or three years for an associate's degree. Only 24.4 percent of the adult population has a B.A., according to the 2000 Census, and those twenty-five to thirty-four years old are a little less likely to have one than forty-five-to-fifty-four-year-olds. Sociologists call non-college youth "the forgotten majority."

Statistically, the typical college student today is a striving young adult; nearly half are twenty-four or older. She (56 percent are women) is spending several years in chronic exhaustion, splitting her days between a nearly full-time, low-wage job and part-time classes at a community college or four-year public university. She uses her credit cards to make ends meet—for books, meals, and clothes—and barely manages the minimum payments. Overloaded and falling behind, she is likely to drop out for a semester or for good. Almost one in three Americans in his or her twenties is a college dropout, compared with one in five in the late 1960s.

What happens to the three out of four young people who don't get a four-year degree? They are much more likely to remain in the working class than previous generations. Youths eighteen to twenty-four are the most likely to hold minimum-wage jobs, giving them a poverty rate of 30 percent in 2000, according to the U.S. Census; that's the highest of any age group. For those aged twenty-five to thirty-four, the poverty rate is 15 percent, compared with 10 percent for older working adults.

As policy analyst Heather McGhee, formerly of the think tank Demos, points out, when the Boomers were entering the workforce in 1970, the nation's largest private employer was General Motors. They paid an average wage of $17.50 an hour in today's dollars. The largest employer in the postindustrial economy is Wal-Mart. Their average wage? Eight dollars an hour. The service-driven economy is also a youth-driven economy, burning young people's energy and potential over a deep-fat fryer. McDonald's is the nation's largest youth employer; workers under twenty-four make up nearly half of the food service, department store, and grocery store workforce nationwide. The working world has always been tough for those starting out, but today's economy relies on a new element—a "youth class." The entire labor market is downgrading toward what was once entry level.

Some of you might be thinking, That's too bad for *those* kids, but what about my child? For better-off, college-educated sons and daughters, it's the same song, different verse. An astonishing 44 percent of dependent students from families making over $100,000 a year borrowed money for school in 2002. Credit card debt is higher for the middle class than for the poor. Unable to find good jobs with a bachelor's degree, young people are swelling graduate school classes, only to join the ranks of the unemployed or the underemployed, after all.

The middle class has been shrinking for two decades. On a family-by-family basis, this means that many people my age who grew up in comfort and security are experiencing a startling decline in their standard of living. Median annual earnings for male workers twenty-five to thirty-four sank nearly 20 percent in constant dollars between 1971 and 2002. We start out in the working world with large monthly debt payments but without health insurance, pension benefits, or dependable jobs. It is impossible to predict whether we will be able to make up these deficits with higher earnings later on, but the evidence suggests that most of us will not.

In the 1960s, the phrase "midlife crisis" captured the malaise of the educated middle-class man confronting his mortality and an unfulfilling job or family life. Today "quarterlife crisis" has entered the lexicon for a generation whose unbelievably expensive educations didn't guarantee them success, a sense of purpose, or even a livable income.

When we talk about economics, we are also talking about ambition, responsibility, trust, and family. The new economic realities are distorting the life paths and relationships of the young. We are spending more time moving in and out of school, finding and losing jobs. Some of us move back home, and we put off marriage, children, and home buying. The older generation's response to these changes has been a chorus of disapproval and dismay.

While potential readers my age have been overwhelmingly responsive to the ideas set forth here, those in another demographic—

from my editor to my parents—have advised me that the most formidable obstacle this book will have to overcome is the incredulity of educated, affluent readers in their fifties and sixties. "I gave my child absolutely everything," they will say. "Now you're telling me I didn't do enough?"

This book is not about blaming parents. The main problems confronting young adults are economic and social, much bigger than individual family dynamics. My desire is precisely for people my age to be able to become adults, to leave the orbit of their families, to make a living and make a life in a supportive society. After all, independence is the one gift you can't give your own offspring, no matter how hard you try.

Older writers, and some younger ones, too, have unduly personalized the public conversation about emerging adulthood. Most of the popular works published on the topic are actually parenting books, directed to the bewildered caretakers of that oxymoron the "adult child." My favorite tome on the shortcomings of my generation is *When Our Grown Kids Disappoint Us: Letting Go of Their Problems, Loving Them Anyway, and Getting On with Our Lives.* Jane Adams, a Seattle-based psychologist, compiled the complaints of hundreds of parents for this 2003 book. Many of the "adultolescents" she writes about are merely having routine problems with finding a job or a life partner. She addresses the book to "parents of kids who've let them down."

"That sounds like a self-centered way to describe those parents and the choices their kids have made, doesn't it?" Dr. Adams asks in the first chapter, hitting it right on the nose. "After all, whose life is it, and who are we to judge how they should live it? . . .

Only their parents, for whom coming to terms with our adult children's limitations also means facing our own." No doubt Adams is describing a psychologically necessary process, but what does it have to do with the price of college, the youth poverty rate, the bear market in opportunity?

Linda Perlman Gordon and Susan Morris Shaffer, coauthors of the 2004 book *Mom, Can I Move Back In with You?*—billed as a "survival guide" for parents—hit similar notes. Shaffer characterized those aged eighteen to thirty-four to *The Washington Post* as "kids with a sense of entitlement, a lack of long-range goals, a lack of persistence. . . . And they tend to see us as their personal concierges."

A sense of entitlement? Maybe, except that we're missing entitlements like health care, and can look forward to missing the Social Security and pensions enjoyed by our parents and grandparents. A lack of long-range goals? Unless you call making thirty years' worth of debt payments a goal. A lack of persistence? College enrollment (if not completion) has grown steadily in the past three decades, even as the hours students work outside of class have doubled and tripled. Seeing parents as their servants? Kids growing up these days are just as likely to see a divorced dad on the weekends or not at all, and Mom as she goes from the day shift to the night shift.

When I talked to Shaffer, she backpedaled, saying that her *Washington Post* quote sounded "very blaming" and didn't capture her real view of twenty-somethings. She wrote the book about her own feeling that she had overindulged her children and failed to set boundaries. "We were much more heavily involved in the everyday lives of our children, so all of a sudden to cut that off would not make sense," she told me. "What the book does is I think it allows parents"—not twenty-somethings—"to not feel shamed by what's going on or feel like failures. You always feel better to know you're not alone." With this kind of public blaming, young adults are guaranteed to feel more alone.

These writers assuage very real feelings of parental guilt, confusion, and disappointment. It's unfortunate that they do this by tarring my whole age group with the same brush. It's doubly unfortunate that they speak overwhelmingly to a thin slice of affluent parents with college-educated offspring, and that their disparagements obscure the real issues.

It doesn't help that nearly all the writers I have seen published on this topic, like Shaffer and Adams, have left their twenties far behind and are judging a generation to which they don't belong. Our parents, who have been used to hogging the cultural spotlight since they themselves were young adults, continue to dominate the conversation, naming and categorizing young people as they choose.

The scholars of the Research Network on Transitions to Adulthood, relying on hard data, make the point that economic factors far outweigh psychological ones in explaining what has happened to young adults. "The changing timetable of adulthood has given rise to a host of questions about whether current generations of young people are more dependent on their parents, less interested in growing up, and more wary of making commitments," they write. "We do not think any of these psychological explanations fit the facts described in the chapters of this book." Yet the self-appointed pop culture experts do seem mostly interested in psychology. Our generation's delay in entering adulthood is often interpreted as a reflection of the narrowed generation gap, as if we just loved our mommies too much to leave the nest.

In the 1980s, President Ronald Reagan began to dismantle the welfare state and put to rest the liberal dream of ending poverty on a large scale in America. His rhetorical ace was the Cadillac-driving, government-cheating "welfare queen." Creating this infamous bogeywoman blamed the poor for their own problems, and made taking away their means of support into the morally right thing to do.

The lazy, irresponsible, possibly sociopathic "twixter" is this decade's welfare queen, an insidious image obscuring public perception of a real inequity. If you look at where public resources are directed—toward the already wealthy, toward building prisons and expanding the military, away from education and jobs programs—it is easy to see a prejudice against young people as a class.

This is not to say that the phenomenon of emerging adulthood in and of itself is exclusively bad. It's a fact of history, like the so-called discoveries of childhood and adolescence before it. This change in the way we experience the life cycle brings upsides and downsides that we may not realize for decades to come. My friends, my interviewees, and I overwhelmingly relish the time that we have, as postmillennial young adults, to try out prospective jobs, travel, volunteer, study, and form strong friendships before settling down into career and family responsibilities. Young women, especially, tend to appreciate the way their options have widened, and the chance that medical science gives us to possibly delay motherhood into our thirties and forties. The more money and education you start out with, the better this time of uncertainty starts to look. The problems arise because our society does not yet recognize this new stage of life, and is instead withdrawing resources from young people. Therefore, the majority of us face obstacles that make it harder to see the bright side of emerging adulthood.

Nor am I trying to cast my cohort as hapless victims. Although I haven't come face-to-face with any real live slackers, some of the people I've met in the course of my research seem overwhelmed and unable to move forward under their own steam. I'm willing to believe that some of us are indeed dilettantish, irresponsible, apathetic, vague, afraid of commitment, or just plain spoiled, perpetually dissatisfied with the gap between reality and reality TV. I've felt this petulance myself at times. It's a natural result of our circumstances.

For our critics are right about one thing: Generation Debt's sea of troubles isn't just economic or political. It approaches the spiritual. We are restless as well as strapped. The common thread joining all members of this generation is a sense of permanent impermanence. It's hard to commit to a family, a community, a job, or a life path when you don't know if you'll be able to make a living, make a marriage last, or live free of debt. It's hard to invest in ourselves when our nation isn't interested in investing in us. It's hard to be hopeful in a time of global warming and global war.

. . .

In the past few decades, the trend in the United States has been toward smaller families and looser kinship ties. The bonds of kinship in our national family are weakening, too. It's not too dramatic to say that the nation is abandoning its children. In everything from national budget deficits to the rise of household debt to cuts in student aid and public funds for education, Americans are living in the present at the expense of the future.

In a short ten or fifteen years' time, our whole generation, haves and have-nots, will take our place as the smallest group of workers staggering under the largest proportion of retirees our nation has ever seen. We will come into the prime of life in a nation as gray as Florida is today, where people born far back in the twentieth century set the public agenda.

We have little practice in speaking up for ourselves. Eighteen-to-thirty-four-year-olds may be one-quarter of the electorate, but after years of scandal and cynicism, we vote less often than any generation alive. And just as we have turned our back on politics, the nation has turned its back on us. Education, health care, Social Security, Medicare and Medicaid, and giant budget deficits bear directly on our chances of a secure life, yet our voices have been largely left out of these debates. If we young people are to overcome our disadvantages and have a hand in shaping these decisions, we must come together now as a broad political constituency. It's past time for us to wake up and realize that we're drifting toward a precipice; not only our own fates but the whole country's future is at stake.

TWO

College on Credit

*Let our countrymen know that the people alone can pro-
tect us against these evils, and that the tax which will be
paid for this purpose is not more than the thousandth part
of what will be paid to kings, priests and nobles who will
rise up among us if we leave the people in ignorance.
Preach, my dear Sir, a crusade against ignorance; establish
and improve the law for educating the common people.*

—THOMAS JEFFERSON,
LETTER TO GEORGE WYTHE, 1786

*No qualified student who wants to go to college should be
barred by lack of money. That has long been a great American goal; I propose that we achieve it now.*

—PRESIDENT RICHARD M. NIXON,
SPECIAL MESSAGE TO THE CONGRESS ON HIGHER EDUCATION, 1970

Kids of all backgrounds now aspire to a college
diploma. Yet the parchment's promise to our parents,
of a steady middle-class living, goes increasingly

unfulfilled for us, replaced by burdens of debt. "Stella," thirty-one, is one of millions of young people in the United States knocked down by the one-two punch of student loans and credit card debt. Here is her story, in her own words.

I was tired of living at home with Mommy. When I filled out my Free Application for Federal Student Aid [FAFSA], I found out I didn't qualify for any grants at all, since I was working and they thought I made too much money. I qualified for $5,000 in loans each semester for two semesters. The funny thing is, I only needed about $1,000 to cover the actual schooling. The rest of the money they included was for expenses. Since I had none living at home with Mom, I got it into my young, uneducated brain that I could use the money to move out of her house and become independent.

I don't need to tell you what a mistake that was . . . or what easy prey I was for all the credit companies with their tables of free pizza coupons, day planners, gift cards for music stores, T-shirts, and so on. My first credit card was a Citibank Visa with a $900 limit, which I maxed by taking a trip to San Diego on my semester break. Duh . . .

I am now 31 years old and *still* in debt from those days. Do I still charge to my cards? Yes. But only when I need a car repair or something that my emergency cash reserve won't cover. I consider bankruptcy every day.

What started out as $10,000 in student loans and about $2,000 in credit card debt has ballooned to a total of $33,000.

But after all this, whom do I blame?

Myself, mostly. My mother (a single mom) next . . . for not teaching me about money before I took that crazy leap all those years ago. You'd think I would have learned by osmosis, watching her struggle to raise my sister and me. But some people (such as myself) don't learn just by watching others. Some of us need it spelled out in a lecture.

I cannot save for retirement because I am too busy paying as much over the minimums as I can to the $%#@ cards in hopes that one day I will finally be debt free.

Ironically, I now work for Discover Card. What I know about money and credit now feels like a knife in my back most days. The "Oh, God, I was just like you" feeling hits me so often when I talk to our 18-year-old card members who have exceeded their credit lines and have missed payments. I want to scream at them: "RUN! Next time you see our table on campus, RUN the other way!!"

I actually went home and cried recently after I had to spend $711 on a car repair.

I dream of ocean vacations, a good steak dinner, clothing that isn't faded by numerous washings. I dream of winning the lottery or opening the door to see Dave Sayer, the Publishers Clearing House guy, standing there with the first of many checks. I dream many things, but I can't do most of them for lack of funds.

I hope you reach the right target audience, Anya. If I could help just one person avoid the nightmare that I'm living, I'd consider this e-mail I just wrote you well worth it.

Stella's debt nightmare speaks to a massive shift in the way our nation finances higher education and thus prepares young people for life. The deal offered to kids has changed in one generation, with little public debate.

In 1981, 45 percent of all federal undergraduate student aid dollars came in loans, 52 percent in grants. By the end of the 1990s, the proportion was more than reversed; loans made up 58 percent of federal financial aid, and grants just 41 percent. Two-thirds of the nation's college students are now borrowing to pay for school. Although the government doesn't issue an official figure, independent studies put the average student loan debt for graduates of four-year colleges at $19,200 in 2004.

Credit cards are the piranhas that swim behind the shark of student loan debt—smaller but even more rapacious. Nearly all the students I talked to, like Stella, compounded their problems with credit card debt.

Twenty years ago, most companies required a cosigner for those under twenty-one to get a card, and sophomores with credit card debt were rare. No more. In the 1980s, as detailed in Robert Manning's 2000 book *Credit Card Nation*, banks escaped usury laws in many states. They sought out high-risk, low-income customers, charging annual percentage rates of 20 or 30 percent. College students, on their own for the first time and forming brand loyalty, have been ideal targets for aggressive marketing. An employee of a major credit card issuer revealed to me that the student market accounts for 25 percent of their annual new-account goals. According to student lender Nellie Mae, 76 percent of students overall and 91 percent of final-year students had at least one credit card in 2004. Their average balance was $2,169, and barely one in five paid off their cards each month.

Each of the players in the education game—institutions, government, families, and students—bears some responsibility for the growth of student debt.

The most obvious cause of debt is the increase in college tuition prices. Tuition has been rising two or three times faster than inflation for three decades. But increases in dollar amounts were much higher in the 1990s. With incomes growing more slowly, middle-class families started feeling the hit. Tuition at public colleges, where 76 percent of American students are enrolled, went up 59 percent after inflation between 1994 and 1995, and 2004 and 2005; median family income went up just 2 percent.

I saw this effect firsthand in May 2005, when I flew home to New Orleans for my younger sister's high school graduation. Both of us attended Benjamin Franklin High School, an exceptional public magnet school. My sister, a budding fiction writer, was following me to Yale.

At the seniors' brunch, held on a sweltering morning in a hotel ballroom in the French Quarter of New Orleans, Principal Carol Christen, a square-shouldered woman with close-cropped gray hair, recited the graduating class's statistics. Of 186 seniors, every last one was headed to college, 104 of them out of state. Collectively, the class had been awarded more than $18 million in scholarships, many from the state TOPS Scholarship offered to all Louisiana seniors who met academic criteria.

The love and pride among the Franklin families that morning was palpable. Yet beneath the excitement of the day, even in such a successful group, ran a buzz of anxiety. One of the speakers, a retired coach, alluded to it. "Eighteen million divided among a hundred eighty students—that'll just about get you to Thanksgiving," he said. Few people laughed.

While I was born toward the end of the 1970s "birth dearth," my sister's class is part of the "echo boom," an upturn that will lead to the largest high school class in history in 2009. Accordingly, the admissions market is bigger and more competitive than ever. The cost of college and the availability and amount of financial aid weighed in the plans of almost every student at that brunch. My own parents, college professors, were reeling at how much Yale's sticker price had risen in just the seven years since I was a freshman—from $31,030 to $38,850. "How can they justify it?" my father asked me. (Never mind that when my father attended the same school, on scholarship, the price was $3,000.) They considered sending my sister to Tulane University, just around the corner from our house, which had offered $20,000 in scholarship money. They even joked about handing her the $160,000 up front, maybe buying her a condo and letting her figure things out from there. In the end, though, they really wanted her to go to the best school she had gotten into. "We think that the name will be worth something," my mother said. Whether the name will ultimately be worth 16 percent, after inflation, more to my sister than it was to me—twice as much for us than for our father—remains to be seen.

. . .

Why has college gotten so goddamn expensive, as my uncle would say? There are many reasons, varying in importance according to whether the school is large or small, private or public. One major factor is the decline in state appropriations to public colleges and universities. The late '90s brought fiscal crises to forty-one states; in a cruel double whammy for families, tuition hikes tracked closely with downturns in local economies. Higher education was known as the "budget balancer" for states cutting essential services. At UC Berkeley, for example, state funds provided 60 percent of the budget in 1980; in 2000, they provided just 34 percent. Private philanthropy, commercial investment, and higher tuition are making up the difference.

New expenses, especially for technology, have contributed to price hikes. From an economic point of view, education is unusual among modern industries, because technology has brought it lots of new costs without appreciably improving productivity. At most schools, the majority of classes still consist of professors lecturing before a group of students, as they have since the twelfth century. Only now they need PowerPoint.

The factor in college prices that probably gets the most attention is spending caused by increasing competition among schools. Those *U.S. News & World Report* rankings pressure schools to raise their national profiles to attract out-of-state students and others who pay full tuition. The media cover novelties like state-of-the-art stadiums, food courts, and gyms. "They are mansions of muscle tone, Taj Mahals of taut abs, Biltmore Estates for those who want to be built more firmly than their sluggard peers," drooled one newspaper story about the University of South Carolina's Strom Thurmond Wellness & Fitness Center. In fall 2004, Richard Brodhead, the new president of top-rated Duke University, announced that he would present each incoming freshman with a brand-new iPod.

Besides paying for new perks, pricing itself can be deployed as a marketing technique. John, a student at the Albertson College of Idaho in Caldwell, Idaho, explained the theory when he called in to an NPR program on tuition prices in 2004. His tiny private school had raised its sticker price to $26,000 "to make it look like we were more prestigious, because everyone was asking us, 'Why is your college so cheap?' . . . But then we increased our price and people said, 'Oh, you are as good as those other schools,' but we couldn't afford to go there anymore. So we just recently decreased it back down [to $14,550]. When we had the price up higher, only about three people actually ever paid the full price."

As John suggested, an inflated sticker price leaves more room to give incentive discounts, just as it does at a car dealership. During the 1990s, tuition grants themselves became the fastest-growing expenditure for most four-year private colleges and universities. This phenomenon justified a masterpiece of circular reasoning: increased financial aid appropriation is driving the explosion in tuition prices!

Expensive technology, new perks, and lower state funding aren't the whole story, though. Sticker prices increased more than twice as fast as the actual cost of an education per student at public four-year schools in the 1990s. While the cost of higher education remains highly subsidized with public and philanthropic money, universities are choosing to shift more of the burden to students.

The most compelling explanation for the steep jump in costs is simply that the market will bear it, as my parents' decision suggests. A college education is worth more than it was in our parents' time. It is now seen as a prerequisite for making a decent wage. So families that can afford it, and a lot that can't, are willing to pay more for that diploma. Enrollment in higher education doubled from 7 million in 1970 to 14 million in 2002, while the total population of young people barely budged from 36 to 39 million.

True, up to half of these students don't persist to graduation, but they stay enrolled long enough to cause overcrowding at state universities nationwide. Even as more students apply to college each year, the number of classroom seats has not increased significantly since the 1960s. The supply of prospective students will rise even more in the coming years. More students will be enrolling, and they're likely to continue paying even more for the privilege.

Colleges alone did not cause the student loan explosion; it would not have been possible without a change in federal policy. The sixth reauthorization of the Higher Education Act, which covers federal student aid programs, happened just as Bill Clinton first took office in 1992. President Clinton chose not to significantly raise the maximum Pell Grant, the largest federal student grant program. With the country coming out of a recession, the budget was tight, and offering loans was cheaper than handing out grants. Moreover, Clinton ran as a New Democrat, positioning himself as the champion of the middle class, not the defender of the poor. So he raised student loan maximums, made subsidized federal loans available to higher-income families for the first time, and created a new unsubsidized loan program for students of any income. Subsidized loans are cheaper for the borrower because the federal government pays the interest while students are enrolled; with unsubsidized loans, the interest that has accumulated is tacked on to the principal after graduation. Clinton also created a new direct loan program where the federal government lends money right to students, cutting out financial middlemen. Federal student loan borrowing climbed by 50 percent in just the next two years after 1992, and doubled by the end of the decade.

The EZ-credit approach to the growing need for federal student aid marks a sea change from most of our nation's history. Higher education policy in the United States was founded on sweeping federal legislation that defined education as a requisite of citizenship and the right of a free people. First came the land-grant colleges, created by the Morrill Acts in 1862 and 1863 to "promote the liberal and practical education of the industrial classes." Vermont Senator Justin Smith Morrill was self-taught, since his farm family could not afford to send him to one of the nation's few private seminaries or colleges. Morrill spent his career as a champion of universal higher education, even for women and former slaves. The two Morrill Acts founded the public higher education system: the great state universities and the historically black colleges. They supplied the heartland with teachers, scientists, and agricultural engineers, subsisting then as they do today on a shifting mix of state and federal funds, private philanthropy, and tuition.

Despite Morrill's egalitarian vision, higher education remained largely a privilege of the social elite for the next eighty years, until the GI Bill. Franklin Roosevelt signed the Servicemen's Readjustment Act on June 22, 1944. It provided full-tuition grants and family stipends to nearly 8 million Americans who had served their country in World War II and were returning home, starting families, and seeking employment at high-tech companies like Boeing, IBM, or General Motors. The GI Bill was good politics and sound economic policy. It's estimated that for every dollar spent on it, six were returned to the Treasury because of higher lifetime earnings for the graduates of the 1950s.

With many more Americans than ever before heading to college, the post–World War II era saw the second great expansion of the public higher education system. Flush with wartime research grants, state universities built new campuses. The Truman Commission Report in 1947 proposed a "community college within commuting distance of every American." These "junior colleges" would focus on the first two years of preparation for a baccalaureate program, as well as vocational training and continuing education for adults.

When the Baby Boom began, then, higher education stood as an acknowledged national policy priority. Passed in response to the Soviet Union's coup with Sputnik, the little space engine that could, the National Defense Education Act of 1958 provided loans to students who pursued valuable technical and engineering occupations. The Economic Opportunity Act of 1964, in step with the civil rights movement, offered education grants to poor kids—the first need-based federal student aid. Leaders justified higher education aid as an investment in our country's competitiveness, not to mention political gravy for the growing middle class.

In this climate, the Higher Education Act (HEA) of 1965, which laid an entirely new foundation for federal student aid, was, according to the historian Bruce Schulman, among the least controversial and most widely supported of President Lyndon Johnson's Great Society programs. As a result of the programs in Title IV of the HEA, between 1965 and 1968 the number of college students receiving federal aid more than doubled and the total amount more than tripled, to over a billion dollars. The 1960s also brought the country's last major expansion in college capacity. Throughout the decade, public universities grew, and new two-year colleges opened at an average of one per week, serving minority populations, immigrants, and nontraditional students of all kinds.

The '60s were the heyday of big, beautiful, liberal dreams like the War on Poverty and civil rights. Higher education for all was one vision that seemed within reach. The number of individuals receiving university degrees doubled in just ten years.

LBJ often referred, with misty eyes, to his early experiences as a teacher of impoverished Mexican schoolchildren in Texas. With the Higher Education Act, he announced, "a high school senior anywhere in this great land of ours can apply to any college or any university in these great fifty states and not be turned away because his family is poor." It took just twenty-five years for that promise to expire.

Although most college students now receive some form of federal financial aid, it is not enough to equalize access to education for students of all income levels. Both regulatory issues and a lack of political will keep HEA programs from being as effective as they could be. For example, Pell Grants and other aid programs are not entitlements, meaning that their amounts are not automatically tied to inflation or to college prices and must be adjusted each time the acts are reauthorized. For this reason, the buying power of the Pell Grant has declined steeply over the years. In 1976, the maximum Pell covered 72 percent of costs at the average four-year public school; in 2004 it paid just 36 percent of a much bigger bill.

Moreover, as Stella found out when she filled out her Free Application for Federal Student Aid, the financial aid program can be as inflexible as any other federal bureaucracy. Many students I have talked to find that their Expected Family Contribution (EFC) is higher than their families are able or willing to pay. Because financial aid assessments are based on the previous year's income, they don't take into account sudden changes like a job loss or divorce that can leave students high and dry. You are automatically considered a dependent student for the purposes of aid assessments until the age of twenty-four, even if your family won't or can't help you out. And small changes made to the aid formulas can have big consequences. In December 2004, President George W. Bush announced that the Department of Education would change the way it calculated state and local taxes for the EFC. This quiet regulatory change cut an estimated 90,000 students out of their Pell Grants.

When I met "Fred" at City College of San Francisco in November 2004, he was funny, personable, stylishly dressed in a Kangol fedora, and frustrated as hell. Then twenty-six, Fred aspired to be a classic first-generation American, climbing the status ladder, improving on his parents' education, earnings, and accomplishments. But the way things were going for him, it looked as though his older brother, a bouncer and auto mechanic who skipped college, had made a smarter choice.

Fred's parents, Filipino immigrants, had brought the family up in middle-class security. His father was a military reservist and a warehouse foreman at an army hospital, his mother a registered nurse. With seemingly stable jobs and good benefits, they sheltered Fred from all worry about money and saved something for his college education.

Using his considerable charm, Fred wangled himself a full scholarship to an elite private prep school despite B average grades. He graduated in 1996 and was headed to UC Santa Cruz. Then everything changed. His parents separated, the hospital where his father worked closed because of military cutbacks, and his mother was injured on the job and was unable to resume work for two years.

"So we went from this stable and comfortable life to stuff going downhill," he says. "I was eighteen years old, and for the first time I could not count on my parents. It was a big shock for me. Based on their tax return I could not get aid. So I liquidated all my CDs, savings, money my parents had socked away for me to have after I graduated. That paid for my first year, and I had nothing left. The second year they offered me $2,950 in financial aid for $13,000 tuition. I said, Okay. We're only getting $3,000. We need help and it's not there.

"I registered for classes, showed up, and I wouldn't be on the roll. They drop you from classes if the check doesn't come. So I would crash classes to try to get in. I called my mother and said, 'Did you send the check?' And she tells me in tears, 'I didn't have the money.'"

Federal student loan limits were $3,500 for second-year students in the late 1990s, meaning Fred would have had to come up with another $6,500 through work, private loans, or credit cards to stay at Santa Cruz. That's without living expenses. Reluctant to take on that kind of debt, Fred decided to leave Santa Cruz after his sophomore year and work full-time in retail until he turned twenty-four and would be considered an independent student, which means higher financial aid awards. A lot of working-class students are putting the brakes on their aspirations because of this cutoff.

Fred still lives at home and has at least two more years and one more transfer left to finish his bachelor's degree. Then he hopes to go to law school to earn some real money to make up for all that lost time. "If I had gone on the 'straight track,' I'd be just like the rest of my friends, making forty, fifty, sixty thousand," Fred reflects, referring to his old classmates from UC Santa Cruz. "Kids [like me] are scraping by, bloody knuckles on the ground, working their butts off, and they get nothing."

In contrast to the grandeur of our nation's large student aid bills, the federal student loan program sprang up haphazardly in the past thirty years, like a ramshackle student union with additions built on in the '70s, '80s, and '90s. The program began almost by accident. During the first amendments to the HEA, in 1968, Congress debated a tuition tax credit for middle-income families. To save government money, the Guaranteed Student Loan program was proposed as a last-minute alternative. The loans aimed to help

middle-class families with temporary cash-flow problems in paying for tuition, particularly if they had more than one child in
school. As the name suggests, the federal government guarantees
the loans, through subsidized guaranty agencies, instead of any
collateral or cosigner, while banks lend the money. Typically, a
school's financial aid office steers students to specific "preferred
lenders," whose relationship with the university can include various fees and rewards.

In 1972, Nixon established Sallie Mae, the Student Loan Marketing Association, as a publicly chartered private corporation to
offer a secondary market for student loans, buying and selling the
portfolios of private lenders. Sallie Mae was the second most profitable company in returns on revenue in the entire 2005 Fortune
500. Late in 2004, posting profits in the billions from the secondary
market and from its own private "alternative" student loans, it
became a fully private corporation. It was already the largest broker of student loans, and it is now poised to expand even more.

Federal student loans differ in many ways from commercial
loans. The government sets a top interest rate and pays the interest
on subsidized loans while you are in school. For both subsidized
and unsubsidized loans, after graduation, there is a six-month
grace period before repayment begins, usually on a ten-to-twenty-
year schedule. You can apply for a deferment or forbearance on
your loan to put off payments further, extend the repayment time
frame, or go on an income-contingent repayment plan where you
pay a fixed percentage of your income each month rather than a
dollar amount. Deferments are granted to people enrolled in grad-

uate school, for unemployment, or for other economic hardship; the federal government pays the interest on subsidized-defined loans while you are exempt from payments. With forbearance, the interest still builds up during a period of nonpayment and is later added to the principal of the loan. Having a student loan canceled or forgiven, however, is nearly impossible. Defaulting means missing payments for nine consecutive months, which leads to legal proceedings to recover the full balance of the loans. It can ruin your credit for several years, and the federal government, not surprisingly, has unusual powers to recover its money.

Deferments and forbearance can be lifesavers, shielding people from the harsh penalties imposed on defaulters. But some of the cash-strapped borrowers I've talked to are making such low monthly payments that the total amount owed barely goes down, or even increases, from year to year. A half step behind compounding interest, they're on a treadmill of debt scheduled to last from thirty years to eternity.

The student loan system currently does a great job of delivering billions in profits to lenders while amply protecting them from risk through generous federal subsidies and guarantees. For borrowers, the picture is not so rosy. There are no disinterested actors to guide borrowers through the system. Students with no credit history and no experience making financial decisions for themselves are apt to leave the borrowing decisions to their parents, who in turn place trust in the hands of the college financial aid office, which may not be fully disclosing its relationship with the commercial institutions that actually become the creditors. By

the time graduation rolls around, the student, who has managed
not to think about her loans for the past four or five or six years,
usually doesn't even know how much money she owes, or to
whom. Surveys show that college students ebulliently overestimate their future incomes and underestimate their loan payments. The higher the loan amounts, the further off the students'
estimates tend to be. It's hard to make the case that this is the best
way for anyone to begin a responsible financial life.

For kids like me, reared in the Reagan era, the generous days of
'60s and '70s student aid seem too far away even to imagine. The
campus upheaval of those decades drove a wedge between university and society, weakening public support for higher education.
Americans used to think of higher education primarily as a public good, advancing values like national defense, peace, freedom,
and justice. Ronald Reagan inaugurated a shift in higher education policy from investing in our nation's prospects to borrowing
against those prospects.

In the mid-1960s, Reagan became governor of California in
part on a promise to crack down on the "freaks," "brats," and
"cowardly fascists" who made up the student protesters of the
Free Speech Movement at UC Berkeley. While governor, he declared, "The state should not subsidize intellectual curiosity."
Continuing his vendetta against eggheads, Reagan campaigned
for president on a proposal to abolish the U.S. Department of
Education, which had just been established under Carter. To the
preacher of open markets and free enterprise, a college diploma

was primarily a private investment, like a house, which provides its main advantages to the individual and her family, and should therefore be financed with personal loans, at no small gain to the financial services industry. During Reagan's two terms, the proportion of the federal budget spent on education fell from 12 percent to 6 percent. Loan limits were raised.

In 1983, Reagan introduced loan consolidation. Like refinancing a mortgage, consolidation allows students to make lower payments over a longer period on one new large loan, which can be locked in with a fixed interest rate. It can also add up to more interest paid in the end. Loan consolidation skyrocketed between 2000 and 2005 as interest rates plunged to record low levels. Consolidation loans totaled $32 billion in 2004, of a total $84 billion in new student loans.

In the late 1980s, default rates on federal student loans started rising, peaking in 1992 at an incredible 22 percent after two years. Proprietary (for-profit) schools were the major culprit in the default explosion. Hundreds of these fly-by-night academies registered unqualified or even indigent students, collected their tuition, and then vanished. More than half of students thus victimized—tens of thousands in all—were defaulting on their loans. Reams of federal regulations were written into the 1992 HEA reauthorization to deal with proprietary schools, hundreds of which were disaccredited, and the penalties for defaulting increased. In 2004, the student loan default rate hit a record low of 5 percent, meaning that most students were managing to keep up with their loan payments—but at what cost?

·   ·   ·

The increased penalties for defaulting tightened the screws on student borrowers. Ben, a consumer debt counselor, settles with banks on behalf of clients overloaded with credit cards, auto loans, and mortgages, often by their early thirties. When clients come in with heavy student loans, though, Ben can't help them. "The first thing I tell them is that student loans are unsettleable and for the most part even undischargeable," he says, meaning that they can't be written off in bankruptcy. "The most you can do is fill out the forms for deferment and try to get refinancing or a payment plan through the federal government."

If student loans go into default, the government can garnishee 15 percent of your wages without taking you to court. Under a 1996 law upheld in 2005 by the Supreme Court, the feds can seize your Social Security, tax refunds, or even emergency and disaster relief payments to pay off old student loans. Unlike credit card debt, medical bills, auto loans, and virtually every other kind of personal debt, student loans are not forgiven if you declare Chapter 7 bankruptcy. (A law drafted by the financial services industry and passed in early 2005 makes it much harder for middle-class people to declare Chapter 7 and fully discharge debts.) For student loans, an extremely tough legal standard of "undue hardship" must be met in order to get a loan canceled, a standard covering permanent disability, death, or "the certainty of hopelessness" about one's means of survival.

Ben, thirty-six, knows something about hopelessness. Even as he counsels others, he himself carries a whopping $55,000 in student loan debt from an unfinished bachelor's degree at Kent State

University in Ohio, along with over $1,000 in credit card debt. He ran into a common problem at overloaded state universities: the classes he needed for his major were overcrowded and sometimes he was shut out. He quit school after four years in 2003 when he found he'd have to borrow even more money to complete a six-month, full-time, unpaid internship in order to get his degree. Today Ben earns the minimum wage, plus commissions; his student loans are in temporary deferment because of his low income. "If I had known then what I know now . . . Famous words," he says in his smooth salesman's voice.

Like any other sector of our nation's economy, the quickly growing student loan market has its own profit seekers, hawking private-label, or "alternative," student loans. Private loans, marketed by big national banks and trusted student loan providers, including Sallie Mae, are really not much better than putting tuition on your credit card. They generally offer no deferments, no grace periods, and fewer repayment options. Interest rates are higher than those on federally guaranteed loans and sometimes higher than those on regular commercial loans. While such loans used to go mainly to professional-school students, who can expect much higher incomes from their degrees, now lower-income undergraduates are increasingly resorting to them. The volume of these loans grew from $1.1 billion in 1995–96 to $15 billion in 2005. In 1999–2000, the average holder of private student loans owed $6,206. Forty percent of Sallie Mae's revenue comes from private loans; now as a private company, it is free to expand and market these higher-profit loans even more aggressively.

These marketers are taking advantage of the fact that most students and parents are daunted by the student loan system, and may not understand the difference between federal and private student loans.

Jerry Davis recently retired after thirty-eight years in the field of higher education finance, working for three of the biggest student loan companies: Sallie Mae, USA Group (now part of Sallie Mae), and the Pennsylvania Higher Education Assistance Agency. Davis worries a lot about the growth of student debt and the decline of grant aid. He says that parents, wanting to do the best for their children, are choosing pricier private schools that may not be a better value when the increased debt is factored in. And he thinks private-label student loans, especially, are being made for the wrong reasons. In 1999–2000, he says, 85 percent of all private student loans made by Bank One originated in the month of August. "Parents didn't want to have to deal with the student aid application process, but they could pick up the phone and get a [commercial] student loan with no difficulty," Davis said. "That's just not very smart. It's a sad comment when our market depends on the stupidity of the consumer."

The growth of the student loan business also means that the secondary market has expanded. For students, this can mean their loans are bought and sold without their knowledge as part of huge portfolios, and they are then subject to competing claims for payment from unfamiliar companies; they can even go into default without realizing it if the companies lose track of them or they send their payments to the wrong place. "I have six people calling me telling me I owe money," said Deb, who owes $15,000 and says she has never missed a payment. "My credit is ruined because they say I'm not paying, but I am."

Despite higher prices and decreased federal support, kids like Stella might still be shielded from taking on tens of thousands of dollars in debt if their parents could or would contribute more. Yet there's some evidence that middle-class and wealthy families actually saved proportionally less for college in the 1990s than in previous years, as borrowing got easier and families racked up record-high levels of consumer debt. State governments have introduced a special tax-deferred college savings plan called a 529, but 77 percent of investors in a 2002 survey knew little about it. Several surveys between 2002 and 2006 found that half of parents who planned to send their kids to college have not yet saved Dollar One. (Financial planners say you can't start saving too early.)

Even if they don't have the money on hand, parents have the option of taking out special federal student loans, called PLUS Loans, in their own names to pay for the full cost of their children's education. Although average loan amounts are higher, only one in ten parents with offspring in college in 2003–2004 took out a PLUS loan. This could be because their interest rates are slightly higher than other student loans, because parents think it's appropriate to place the responsibility for tuition in the student's name, or once again, because families are not fully informed of all their options.

One reason more parents may not be in a position to help is that the rise in student loans is just a detail in a larger American picture of soaring household debt. Consumer debt doubled from

1992 to 2002, from just under $1 trillion to just under $2 trillion. At the end of 2004, the American savings rate hit zero, and the average household owed 113 percent of its annual take-home pay, an all-time high. Between 1996 and 2003, the number of personal bankruptcies every year exceeded the number of people who graduated from college.

The Fragile Middle Class: Americans in Debt was a major study of 1990s bankruptcy filings. The writers, Teresa Sullivan, Elizabeth Warren, and Jay Lawrence Westbrook, found that the rising tide of bankruptcy was largely a middle-class phenomenon, spurred by new and seemingly permanent features of our society: divorce, health care costs, credit card debt, downsizing. Their conclusion singled out student loans as a possible addition to the litany. "One additional financial factor is rarely mentioned in our data but may emerge as an important middle-class frailty in the next study of economic failure: student loans. . . . The impact of burdening so many young people with high levels of educational debt at the outset of their adult lives is just beginning to be felt."

Anna Griswold is at the front lines of student borrowing. She is assistant vice president for Undergraduate Education and executive director for Student Aid at Penn State University, a first-tier flagship public school with an enrollment of around 30,000. Tuition in 2005 was around $11,000 for in-state and $21,000 for out-of-state students. For over twenty years, Griswold has been a legislative advocate on growing student loan debt. Each year, her office holds more tutorials, workshops, and counseling sessions, trying to make students fully aware of their obligations. Nevertheless, she says, most students and families still borrow the maximum amounts available under federal rules, and more each year sign up for private loans on top of that. "We'd like to not see students borrow more, but grant funds are inadequate, so students have no other choice." Griswold and her fellow financial aid professionals advocate the lesser-evil position of increasing federal student loan limits to reduce the growth of private loans.

Griswold also has a novel proposal: she would like to see borrowing tied to students' chosen fields of study. Her office maintains an online calculator where Penn State students can compare their likely income to their loan payments. "A student going into a higher-paying career field—say, engineering—may be able to borrow a little bit more," she says, "but I'm worried about students in specific fields: in the humanities, liberal arts, teaching, social work, in which the salaries are not always that great. If I had a way to control how much they'd borrow and I could make up the difference with grants, I would."

It's clear that college students from all classes are taking on far more personal debt than at any other time in our nation's history. It's good debt, though, right? Money guru Suze Orman says so. A bachelor's degree now brings a $1 million average difference in lifetime earnings. The relative power of the degree has grown as unionized blue-collar jobs have declined and low-wage service jobs have taken up the slack.

Why shouldn't an investment in your mind be financed the same way you finance a car? Well, there are a few reasons. First of all, higher education is more than a private investment. It's a public good, and the trend toward expensive educations financed with loans is doing nothing good for democracy. Second, even if you look solely at the advantages to individuals of a college diploma, the current level of borrowing carries unacceptable risks.

"Cindy," age thirty-one, has a typical story of why loans aren't working to improve educational access. She grew up in Arkansas, one of five children of a single mother on welfare. At the age of seventeen she left home and moved to Atlanta, where she eventually enrolled at a four-year public university. Still under twenty-four, she was officially considered a dependent student, and therefore qualified for less federal aid. Her mother, who had by that time managed to attend college using special state benefits and to get a job, offered her no help. So Cindy initially borrowed about $6,500 in student loans, and she worked two jobs, forty-five hours a week, while studying full-time for a bachelor's in business administration. After nearly two years of this grueling schedule, stress-related ailments landed her in the hospital, and without health insurance from either of her jobs, she ran up thousands of dollars in medical expenses. Meanwhile, she missed a semester of college, and her unpaid student loans went into default. "I pretty much gave up at that point and got married instead," she said.

Today, Cindy has moved back to Arkansas. Divorced, she manages a small business, earning around $20,000 a year. Her original $6,500 student loan, after ten years in default, has accumulated to $10,000-plus with interest and fees. She says she "lives in fear" of having her wages garnisheed, and she often gets nasty calls from collectors.

"I regret with all my being having ever gone to college," she told me. "I just ask that you not use my real name. There is a certain feeling of shame at having defaulted on my student loans. After all, it's the taxpayers' money—something a collections agent didn't hesitate to point out to me in a very demeaning way. His exact words were, which I have not forgotten years later, 'Good honest taxpayers have to foot the bill for deadbeats like you who refuse to pay their student loans.' My purpose for going to college was to avoid just that and not end up, like my mother, on public assistance. Unfortunately, it didn't work out as I had planned."

Low-income students like Cindy suffer the most from the trend of high tuition and high debt. And the response by governments and institutions has hurt these students even more. Incredibly, poor families are now getting a smaller proportion of the grant-aid pie than before tuition started its most recent climb.

Just as the "college cost crisis" was first grabbing headlines, the hurt put on the middle class started to abate. At the last HEA reauthorization, in 1997, borrowing limits weren't increased. Instead, Congress passed the Taxpayer Relief Act, providing $41 billion in tax credits for higher education and a tax-free "Education IRA" for college savings. In subsequent years, the growth in volume and number of new loans slowed considerably. Both new benefits, however, were designed to offer help to the middle class, not the poor or working class. Savings accounts and tax credits are for people who have the money to spare in the first place.

Higher costs also mean more families competing with the poorest for limited grant aid. The median family income of Pell Grant recipients rose 59 percent from 1990–91 to 1997–98. The higher-income families became eligible because tuition jumped, while the poorest families were priced out of the market altogether.

At the same time, merit-based grants have been growing. Attempting to address the "brain drains" of college-educated workers, a dozen states, including my home state of Louisiana, followed the lead of Georgia's HOPE Scholarship, offering free admission at state universities to all in-state high school graduates with certain grade point averages, regardless of need. Studies show these programs are disproportionately serving students who could afford full tuition. The increase in merit-based aid means students who don't really need them are often getting discounts, while low-income students, for whom small grants might determine whether they attend school at all, aren't getting them. At the nation's most selective colleges, meanwhile, economic diversity has decreased since the 1970s. Just 10 percent of students there come from the lower half (that's right, half) of the economic spectrum.

When the federal government gets out of the grant business, no one else looks out for equal access. The money distributed by colleges themselves has grown laughably lopsided. In the second half of the '90s, institutional awards to families making $100,000-plus grew by 145 percent, while awards to families earning less than $20,000 grew by just 17 percent. Need-blind, indeed!

It's not that institutions are intentionally discriminating. Financial aid officers give out money case by case, considering the goals of the university just as much as the needs of the students. They would rather entice a violin-playing math whiz from the middle-class suburbs with a merit-based grant than enroll a poor student with unexceptional test scores who may need intensive help to succeed.

. . .

Donald Heller, associate professor and senior research associate at the Center for the Study of Higher Education at Penn State, has testified several times before Congress on higher education financing. Over the past decade, he's become increasingly concerned with the problem of college access for lower-income students. Dr. Heller draws a distinction between making college affordable—that is, attractively priced, like the discount goods at Wal-Mart—and making it accessible, a bottom-line issue of whether poor yet qualified students can get in the door. "In the last decade or so there's been more focus in terms of policy on making college affordable for middle- and upper-middle-class students," he says. "And if you go back to the creation of the HEA in 1965, the focus was on making college accessible for kids who wouldn't otherwise have been able to go. The primary focus has really shifted. And from my perspective it makes little sense to be spending public money to subsidize the cost of college for kids who are going there anyway."

To repeat a phrase, there are two Americas when it comes to higher education opportunity. As Dr. Heller points out in his presentations, the lowest-achieving rich kids attend college at about the same rate (77 percent) as the smartest poor kids (78 percent). In 2000, the gap between whites and blacks in college attendance was 11 percentage points; back in 1972, the gap was only 5 points. The disparity between Hispanics and whites was 13 points in 2000, compared with 5 points in 1972.

And those two Americas don't have much to do with each other, which is a problem for policymaking. Two years ago, I didn't have the foggiest idea that less than one out of three people in my age group have a four-year college degree—among my friends and acquaintances the figure is more like 95 percent. Nor did I realize that nearly half of the nation's college students were enrolled in community colleges, while barely one in ten resembled me as a former student—a teenager, dependent on my parents, living on the campus of a private university.

There were certain assumptions I shared with my class and my family about the centrality, first, of college, and second, of a "good" college—that is, one with a known name. I confess that I am still grappling with the unseating of these assumptions. I certainly accept the argument that the rise of feverish competition for selective college admissions among an increasing number of Americans, which has helped drive up the price at the highest end, is no more than a mechanism for the reproduction of privilege. In this understanding, the so-called meritocracy that I was so proud to be a part of has really come to measure SAT tutoring, museum trips, music lessons—and, not least, the property taxes that parents are able to fork over to live in good school districts or tuition for private schools. With the decline in need-based financial aid, academic competition is becoming a game that the ruling class plays largely against itself, like tennis.

Jessica, a nineteen-year-old, blond, blue-eyed junior at the University of Georgia, has been caught in the middle of this shift. Her middle-class parents could not afford today's private college tuition, so she opted to accept the HOPE Scholarship. "It's hard, because I and all my friends grew up thinking if you work really hard you can go to Yale. We were in International Baccalaureate—

we did everything you could. And we found out it wasn't like that. It was a big disillusionment. We're not poor, so I couldn't get financial aid. I didn't even apply. And UGA is not a bad school, but that wasn't the dream."

There is a part of me that, like Jessica, buys into the mystique of Old Blue and its ilk. After all, I got a top-notch education there, one bound to enrich my quality of life for the long haul. And I learned to smoke a clay pipe and drink from a silver trophy cup, just like some parody of an English aristocrat.

At the same time, I now understand that an overemphasis on "name" schools distorts our national discussion about the value and purpose of higher education. Plus, I've been out here in the job market for a few years, and I've found that even the most prestigious liberal arts degree won't cover my rent or buy me health insurance.

The problem in our education system is not that there aren't more Ivy League universities. It's that the public colleges most students attend are undersupported.

From Franklin's class of 2005, students headed to local, public colleges with serious public assistance greatly outnumbered those borrowing their way into expensive private institutions. And if public universities are the answer, increased taxpayer support of higher education, enough to relieve the burden on families and kids, is the only plausible way to get there.

What about the centrality of four-year college itself? I don't think anyone would be willing to say what percentage of America's population should ideally be earning a bachelor's degree, though we can certainly agree that the current number is too low.

After a decade that saw a 47 percent jump in public tuition in constant dollars, the Senate held hearings on the "college cost crisis" in 2003. They warned that half of all students who qualify for college cannot afford a four-year institution; 2 million qualified students by the end of this decade will give up on the idea of college completely because of funding shortages. The idea that hardworking, capable students should be denied the chance to better themselves simply because of money is a travesty.

Still, the reality is that universal access to higher education probably also means more high school graduates going into programs at the associate's degree or certificate levels. Compared with students three decades ago, those today are older, working more hours, and taking more time moving from high school to college. Most of these new nontraditional students need more financial aid. They also require child care, courses offered at night and on weekends, and specialized counseling services in order to have a decent chance at graduating. Instead, they get loans and longer hours at low-wage jobs. Shorter programs can provide the less expensive, more flexible options that these older, working students need.

Young people arriving on campuses today have little idea of how financial aid has changed over the decades, still less of the consequences of long-term debt. "Oh, man, I really don't know the exact price, my parents send in my loans for me," said "John," a senior at La Salle University in Philadelphia. La Salle is a third-tier private school at the price of an Ivy—$32,940 a year in 2004, with a higher-than-average graduating debt of $21,364. John, with an unemployed father and schoolteacher mother, worked his way through college as a bouncer, paying for his own books, food, clothes, and rent. Nevertheless, eight months before graduation, he had very little idea of his obligations; he was planning on deferring his loans, anyway, by going straight to law school.

"It's an education at Cornell, which you can't really put a price on," says Kyle, twenty-five, who has a degree in marine biology, owes $23,000, and makes $20,000 a year at an animal preserve in North Carolina, taking care of tigers and jaguars. "If I had known, I might have put more money towards my tuition while I was in school, I might not have had a car, but I wouldn't have not borrowed. Still, money affects what I'm doing now. It's the facts of life. I hate it."

Lagusta, twenty-seven, who operates her own vegan catering business in upstate New York, thinks college is a "scam." She owes $45,000 from a combination of college loans and putting her culinary school tuition on credit cards. "I was an English and women's studies major, and now I'm a cook. I'm happy I went to college, but if I'd known I would come out with so much debt and wouldn't be making money from my degree, I wouldn't have gone."

The ideal of making it possible for every young person to pursue advanced studies dates back nearly to our nation's founders. Yet young people today live in a different dimension from the past, with its sweeping promises. A renewed commitment to higher education for all would require an investment on the scale of a New Deal or a Great Society program.

Without action, the higher barriers to higher education will continue to reinforce social divisions. Many lower-income students are the children of immigrants or the first person in their family to go to college. They understand the financial aid game imperfectly and are deterred by high sticker prices. On average, Americans of all incomes overestimate the cost of a year at a public university by 70 percent. Studies show concerns about money help dissuade poor kids, especially blacks and Hispanics, from preparing for college, starting as early as the eighth grade.

Donald Heller says the best we can do right now for access is convince working-class families to borrow more than they are currently inclined to. "One concern I and others have about loans becoming the foundation of student aid is aversion to debt. There's some evidence that lower-income students have an aversion to borrowing." When asked if it isn't perverse to encourage high levels of debt among people coming from public assistance and minimum-wage jobs, he sighs. "In the best of worlds, we would shift the system back, and rely on grants like back in the '70s. Realistically, we're not going to be able to return to an era like that."

Graduate school is an increasingly popular next step for people who manage to graduate from college, with or without loans, only to face an uncertain job market. Graduate enrollment—excluding law, medicine, and business schools—rose a third between 1985 and 2000, after holding steady through the 1970s and early 1980s. The National Center for Education Statistics projects that enrollment will be up another 20 percent by 2013. In 2002–2003, there were 2.7 million graduate students across the country, with an average age under thirty. Almost half were in master's programs in arts, sciences, or education. Thirteen percent were pursuing Ph.D.'s. Twelve percent were getting MBAs, and five percent, law degrees.

Amped-up competition fuels the rising popularity of grad school. Ask Kyle, not the Cornell grad but a tall, driven twenty-one-year-old senior at Western Illinois University. When I met him, he was spending the summer before his senior year in Washington, D.C., interning thirty-five hours a week, taking fifteen hours of classes, and working another thirty-five hours nights at a restaurant. He hoped to go on to earn a combination law degree/MBA. "I really think the bachelor's degree is like the new high school diploma," he says, "and the master's is the new bachelor's. You need it to stand out." Grad school can be a way of hedging your bets in a world of uncertainty, sitting out what you hope is a temporarily bad job market, and most of all, increasing the chance of getting one of those elusive good jobs. When I asked interviewees what they thought they could do to increase their chance of success, going to grad school was the number-one answer.

It's true that persevering beyond a bachelor's degree has a measurable effect on earnings—on average. The median income of people aged twenty-five to thirty-four with a master's degree was $42,800 in 2004, compared with $36,429 for those with a B.A. Professional-school grads—doctors, dentists, lawyers, and MBA execs—can earn $90,000 to $100,000 just out of school. Yet just as college majors can result in very different income levels, different grad school programs can have wildly different, even negative, effects on income. Ironically, job prospects are worse within the academy than outside it, as the economics of higher education are currently undergoing a major upheaval. Tenure-track positions are much harder to find, increasingly replaced by underpaid, low- or no-benefit, temporary postdoctoral and adjunct posts.

More subtly, our generation's restless relationship with employment increases the chances that graduate degree holders will be out some time and a lot of money, working in an area that doesn't at all fit their degree or their income expectations. Add the uncertainty of payoff to the reality of newly outsized debt burdens, and lots of graduate students are wishing they had never seen their library carrels.

Debt is a fact of life for the majority who pursue a graduate education. As of 2002, the graduate student debt burden averaged above $24,000 for master's degree holders and a staggering $100,000-plus for law and medical students. Loan debt among grad students increased seven times faster than undergraduate debt in the 1990s. Many applicants believe graduate programs, especially Ph.D. programs, will offer them funding. Yet fellowship or no, a majority of all graduate students borrow to finance their educations.

Graduate program tuition has grown at rates similar to undergraduate tuition, but starting from higher levels. Graduate students are older and more likely to be self-supporting or have dependents, and to earn incomes that make them ineligible for federal student aid. So they take out more private-label loans and rely on credit cards for the rest.

In 2003, grad students carried an average of six credit cards, according to student lender Nellie Mae. And grad students are using that plastic. Their average credit card debt in 2000 was $7,831, an increase of almost $3,000 just from 1998. (The average credit card balance held by all indebted Americans twenty-five to thirty-four in 2001 was $4,088.)

Ph.D. students have always resigned themselves to relative poverty in anticipation of a cushy tenured payoff. But in the past decade, the rules have changed. They've gone from being members of the intellectual elite to what one of my interviewees called "the intellectual lumpenproletariat." Tuition has gone up. Time to degree has lengthened. Budget pressures have spurred universities' increasing dependence on non–tenure-track teachers, which damages both the working conditions of graduate students and their job prospects. Graduate teaching assistants and adjuncts, short-term appointees, now log over half of the teaching time at major universities.

According to national surveys, humanities graduate students experience the highest median debt burdens and are the most likely to be dissatisfied with their choice to go to school in the first place. The Modern Language Association projected that students who entered an English Ph.D. program in 2003 had a 25 percent chance of coming out with a tenure-track position and a 50 percent chance of dropping out.

One professor at a small Midwest liberal arts college wrote a series of cautionary columns on the fate of the Ph.D. under a pseudonym for the *Chronicle of Higher Education*. "The premise of graduate education in the humanities is a lie: Students are not apprentices preparing for a life of scholarship and teaching," "Thomas H. Benton" told me. "They are a cheap source of labor and status for institutions and faculty and, after they earn their degrees, most join the reserve army of the academic underemployed."

. . .

Future lawyers, of all people, exemplify the plight of grad students. Many lenders have reported over the past decade that law students default on their loans more often than any other grad students, up to 20 percent of the time. How can this be? Well, fat corporate paychecks are not awaiting everyone who passes the bar exam. Debt load went up 400 percent between 1987 and 2002. In the same time period, private salaries doubled, but public salaries, like those at New York's Legal Aid Society, barely kept pace with inflation. Average monthly payments over $900 put an unacceptable debt burden on all but the highest-paid attorneys.

Skyrocketing student debt is affecting the altruistic intentions of young law students. According to the National Association for Law Placement, which tracks law graduates nationwide, the proportion of new lawyers who enter public service has declined from around 5 percent to less than 3 percent in the past twenty years. The American Bar Association (ABA) reported in 2003 that legal aid societies and other public interest practices are having trouble recruiting the best students because of high loan burdens. Too often, new recruits leave after a few years, when marriage, children, and other adult concerns make it impossible for them to manage their loans on a public-sector salary. "The retention problem is severe," says Terry Brooks of the ABA. "And a substantial investment in training is then lost when those people can no longer afford to stay in the public interest field."

Sixteen out of 187 law schools nationwide have established scholarship programs for students planning public service careers. At least 50 law schools have loan repayment assistance programs (LRAPs), offering partial or complete loan forgiveness for those who stay in public interest jobs for a specified period. Some state governments, state bar associations, and nonprofits also run LRAPs, but with smaller budgets.

But it's not only public defenders who are having a hard time making their loan payments. According to Terry Brooks, high loan burdens also put the squeeze on reasonably priced lawyers in small firms who serve the middle and working class for routine events like divorces.

Eric could tell you that. He grew up in Indiana, graduated from Indiana University in 1992, and planned to travel overseas to teach English. His parents wanted him to do something more stable and lucrative. "My father, at the time, was making nearly $500,000 a year. He said that if I could get through law school and pass the bar exam, I could work for him and be set for life."

Eric's conservative father insisted he attend Regent University, a small, private Christian law school. Eric borrowed $90,000 from a private lender. While he was in school, though, his father was sued and dissolved his firm. Eric's plans evaporated. He graduated at twenty-six and found his fourth-tier law degree to have little cachet on the national job market.

Over the past few years, Eric worked as an assistant DA, for $29,000 a year, and at a small private law firm, and then hung out his own shingle. "I take whatever comes through the door," he says. Eric rents a small apartment, drives a ten-year-old car, and steers away from dating because he can't imagine supporting a family. He estimates his income at about $2,400 to $3,000 a month, which means he often ignores his several-hundred-dollar loan payments, even though defaulting would mean losing his license to practice law.

"I don't know why school is so expensive now," he says. "Maybe because we are suckers who are willing to borrow the money just to put a few letters on the end of our name because that is what we think we need to make it."

When reckoning the current and future social impact of high and growing student loan debt, it's important to distinguish between the raw amount of debt on the one hand and debt burden—debt as a percentage of income—on the other. Economists generally estimate that a "manageable" debt burden means payments that are 8 percent or less of monthly income—an outlay of a third as much in debt payment as on rent. Thirty-nine percent of student borrowers now graduate with unmanageable debt by this measure. That includes 55 percent of African-American grads and 58 percent of Hispanics.

Debt burden, for both graduates and undergraduates, is increasingly affecting young people's decisions and life paths. In one 2004 national survey of college graduates, 59 percent said that student loan debt makes it difficult for them to fulfill their financial goals, like buying a house or a car or saving any money. In a 2006 Internet poll, 42 percent of indebted graduates up to age thirty reported living paycheck-to-paycheck, compared to 24 percent of the debt-free. Debt led 44 percent to put off buying a home and 43 percent to shelve grad school. Almost half reported that the student loans contributed to feelings of anxiety and depression, and those with student loans were 30 percent more likely to say that they were below where they had expected to be financially at this point in their lives. "Realistically, I'll be paying off my student loans for another ten to fifteen years, and that affects how I make decisions," says "Lawrence," twenty-four, who graduated after six years from John Jay College in New York City, makes less than $20,000 a year, and owes $20,000. "I definitely want to settle down and have kids. Although it's tough to be thinking about how many kids I want versus how many I'll be able to afford."

One small policy change that could potentially put billions into student aid without spending a taxpayers' dime was first introduced as a bill in the House and Senate in March 2005. When President Clinton created the direct loan program, where the government makes loans to students directly from the Treasury without banks as middlemen, he tried to do away with guaranteed loans altogether in favor of direct loans. But the financial services industry fought hard, and so the two programs have existed side by side since then. Over ten years later, the numbers are in. For every $100 lent to students, the federal government pays $12.09 in subsidies to banks on guaranteed loans; direct loans cost just 84 cents per $100. Currently, one-quarter of universities use direct loans. If just 40 percent participated in the voluntary program, the Department of Education would save $17 billion over ten years, enough to raise the Pell Grant by a thousand bucks— again, without any cost to taxpayers. But this change would require defying the profitable financial companies, which donated hundreds of thousands of dollars to members of the House Committee on Education and the Workforce in the most recent reauthorization cycle.

. . .

Richard Fossey, a professor of education law at the University of Houston and coeditor of the 1998 book *Condemning Students to Debt,* says nothing less than a giant federal bailout, on the scale of the 1980s savings-and-loan debacle, will save the higher education funding system. "It seems to me ultimately we're heading for disaster. We can't finance higher education this way forever. There's going to be a reckoning."

What's certain is that the problem of student debt is not going anywhere. Between 2000 and 2015, the college-age population will increase by 16 percent, more than in the previous thirty years. Compared with today's high school students, studies say, more of these students will be applying to college. Eighty percent will be nonwhite, belonging to a population that is more likely to need financial aid.

America's promise of opportunity for all has assumed a collision course with the charge-now, pay-later habits of government and families alike. The student loan detonation is only one example of a political climate that shifts risk to individuals and favors instant gratification over long-term investment. The message to young people from all backgrounds is: You're on your own. Good luck!

Low-Wage Jobs

Sittin' in the hood like community colleges
This dope money here is Lil Treys scholarship
Cause ain't no tuition for havin' no ambition
And ain't no loans for sittin' your ass at home
So we forced to sell crack rap and get a job
You gotta do something man your ass is grown

—KANYE WEST,
"WE DON'T CARE," FROM THE 2004 ALBUM *COLLEGE DROPOUT*

I met "Jerome" at my local café in the East Village. A chubby guy in regulation oversized hip-hop gear, he was listening to headphones while filling out a job application. Like half of the black men in New York City, Jerome, nineteen, was unemployed. "I've been looking for a job everywhere for a year—I mean *everywhere*," he told me with a self-deprecating smile.

Jerome, the youngest of five, lost his father two years before we met. The rest of his siblings are out of the house. He graduated all right from Harry S Truman High School in the Bronx, but his

momentum got stalled sometime last year when a good friend of his
was shot and killed.

His mother moved them to Harlem to get away from bad influ-
ences. Jerome soon lost touch with his old friends. "It just be me
and my girlfriend," he says. He's been with his girlfriend for eight
years; they met as schoolkids sneaking into nightclubs. These
days, Jerome is a self-described mama's boy and stays out of trouble, filling the days playing basketball and video games and writing raps. His mother's job at a hospital keeps him in room, board,
cell phone, Walkman, clothes, and sneakers.

Jerome's employment search hasn't gone so well. "I looked for
a job right away after school. I worked two months at McDonald's. Then I left 'cause of the death of my friend." Jerome has
applied for mostly low-wage retail and food service jobs, plus one
in construction. "I don't know why I'm not getting hired. I feel
like I have the qualifications. They don't want to hire people
sometimes. Sometimes positions be taken."

Jerome was a B student in school, with history a favorite subject. His girlfriend, a customer service rep at Sprint, and his
mother both nag him to further his education. "[My mom] tells
me every night, 'You should go to college. Try it. You can't knock
something until you try it.'" Jerome accepts the idea, to some extent. "If I want to go on and be a rapper, I need to learn more
words." But he doesn't know where to start with the application
process. When I ask him, he can only think of one current college
student he knows, a neighbor.

Reflecting on his life, Jerome radiates a bemusement cut with flashes of exasperation. He is trapped by inertia, yet not quite resigned.

"I don't feel like I really accomplished anything yet besides getting out of high school. That's just one step, but I have to focus to take the steps. It's quite easy but I'm just so lazy. I don't know. . . . With all the time that I use looking for jobs I could be enrolled in a school and getting my education." Jerome ended up getting the job as a porter at the café where we met. College remained in the back of his mind.

I found this chapter especially difficult to write. For all the other issues in this book—the rising cost of education, the growth of debt, the decline in employment benefits, budget deficits, and changing families—I can plausibly make common cause with young people of very different backgrounds. These changes affect all of us.

But when you're talking about poor and working-class young people like Jerome who don't finish, or even begin, college, too-easy comparisons are worse than useless. A false sense of commonality pervades the American understanding of class. Somehow, we amiably tolerate a level of inequality to rival the plantation societies of Latin America, by simply ignoring it. Rich and poor alike, we play up our similarities and gloss over our differences. We continue to believe, in the face of evidence to the contrary, that the disadvantages of birth count for less than talent or ability. As progressives never tire of decrying, working-class people voted twice in large numbers for a patrician president who slashes taxes on the very rich, at least in part because they believe that one day they, too, will be wealthy.

By pointing out that class is a real barrier in American life, I don't advocate resignation to the status quo. Higher education remains the most important engine of social mobility, and it needs to be available to many more. The real open debate, for me, is how we should think about the futures of those who aren't completing college, and who are falling further behind each year.

Jerome's post–high school drift represents what Marc Tucker, the founder of the National Center on Education and the Economy, calls a faulty school-to-work system. In 1992, Tucker coauthored a book with Ray Marshall called *Thinking for a Living* that made a splash when it was spotted on President Clinton's reading list. "In the book we basically reported that this country has one of the worst school-to-work transition systems in the industrialized world," Tucker told me in an interview. "Since then, the stakes have gotten higher and the situation may have gotten worse."

The school-to-work system encompasses the public and private institutions connecting young people with meaningful training and eventually good jobs in areas of demand. It's hard to even understand this concept in the United States, because unlike the European Union countries or the "Asian Tigers," we have no national coordinated dropout recovery program, little in the way of federally funded vocational training, and no integrated system to link youth with employment.

In the United States, vocational education bears an enduring stigma. Think of Bender, the "criminal" in the '80s teen classic movie *The Breakfast Club;* the only class he's passing is shop. The idea of an inflexible "tracking" system training young people for various desired outputs smacks to some of socialism. Yet gaining the skills for decent jobs can far outweigh the opportunity costs of specializing early, especially when programs are designed flexibly, to give people many chances to improve their credentials and move up.

Once again, Americans have accepted a lack of public support of young people under the guise of more freedom. Just as we have reconceptualized higher education as primarily a private investment, the popular image of the school-to-work transition is a personal quest to "discover your dream," "follow your bliss," "find your passion." The truth obscured by these New Age clichés is that young people often negotiate this passage alone in the dark.

In 1970, remember, high school graduates entered the world of GM and $17.50 an hour. In 2006, they enter the world of Wal-Mart and $8 an hour. If they don't have the money, merit, social connections, perseverance, and luck to get a valuable credential, they are shut out on the wrong side of an ever-wider divide between higher-wage knowledge jobs and lower-wage service jobs.

Thinking *for a Living* argued for an entirely new labor-market policy in the United States, one more like those in Japan and throughout Western Europe. Labor-market policy is, simply, the nation's process of matching the supply of workers with current and future demand for skills. In the systems Tucker recommends, governments enforce high national academic standards and, starting in early high school, offer young people an explicit choice between university-level or vocational education, with each path equally well thought out. Employers are given incentives or required to invest in training new hires, updating skills of longtime employees, and developing higher-quality jobs that draw on the creativity of each individual. Governments offer extensive free job training and operate employment placement centers that are used by everyone, not just the chronically unemployed, as in the United States.

At the Lisbon European Council, a summit held in 2000, the European Union set a strategic goal to make Europe the world's foremost "knowledge economy" by 2010. The EU is putting real time and money behind the words. National governments, employers, and community groups are investing in new training, coaching, lifelong learning, and e-learning programs to engage people at all skill levels and life stages.

Admittedly, Western Europe is not a perfect model. These countries have been plagued for decades with persistently high unemployment rates, and with youth unemployment rates often double those of adults. They also face a contracting labor supply because of a population that is aging even faster than that in the United States. Despite, or maybe because of, these difficulties, Europe has newly recognized that the key to competitiveness and wealth in the information age is human capital.

Meanwhile, the emerging superpowers of China and especially India are each producing more college graduates per year than the United States. As of now, they export thousands of teachers, doctors, scientists, and software engineers here, but as Thomas Friedman pointed out in his 2005 best-seller *The World Is Flat*, their power to compete with us at home, drawing away highly skilled jobs, is growing every year. The irony is painful, and damaging: Even as American kids' education level stagnates, smart kids from around the world continue to come here by the thousands to take advantage of the world's best universities. One-quarter of science and engineering degrees at American universities are awarded to Indian or Chinese nationals. Just as in a Cold War spy flick, knowledge, our most valuable asset, is passing unnoticed into foreign hands.

Every patriotic American has a stake in ensuring that our young people are well trained and well qualified. As Tucker and Marshall argue, if Americans don't follow the "high road" of creating higher-skilled, higher-wage jobs and preparing people to fill them, we have little chance of continuing to improve our standard of living or increasing productivity. In a 2002 American study of training practices in forty-two countries by the American Society for Training and Development, a trade group, the United States ranked the lowest in the percentage of payroll spent on training employees.

The country is missing out on the contributions of millions of young people trapped in low-wage jobs, a sacrifice we can ill afford. Plus, it's just not fair to leave young people to find their own way in a disconnected world.

"My name is Latoya," read the e-mail in my in-box one morning in fall 2004. "I am not sure what you want me to write. I can tell you that I am currently 17 years old about to go into the Air Force (already took oath) because I need a better life. I am working at Chick-fil-A making $6.25/h. I also attend Community College of Philadelphia. I graduated early at the top of my class from a private school. I live in South Philly with just one parent (my mom). If you need more information or I am not qualified please let me know."

Latoya was asking if she was qualified to respond to a posting

I had placed online, seeking to interview young people working for low wages. She might have been asking if I thought she had what it took to get that better life. Compared with others in her neighborhood and even in her family, Latoya has a lot going for her. She is the middle child of three children; her mother works as a certified nursing assistant for about $10 an hour. Her twenty-one-year-old brother "doesn't do nothing," she says. "He just sits around." Maybe with his example in mind, Latoya's mother transferred her out of the local public school and secured her a scholarship to Northeast Preparatory School, a respected alternative school. "At the public school, teachers don't give too much attention, and students don't pay attention," Latoya explained. "I didn't go to class all the time in public school—I was with my friends. And it just didn't work out."

On February 26, 2005, Bill Gates announced a $15 million donation from the Bill & Melinda Gates Foundation to states to make improvements in high schools. With the cash he delivered an intense browbeating. "America's high schools are obsolete" and are "ruining the lives of millions of Americans every year," he told the National Governors Association. "When I compare our high schools with what I see when I'm traveling abroad," he added, "I am terrified for our workforce of tomorrow."

I agree with both Bill and Latoya that public schools are not working out for American kids. Among the thirty Organisation for Economic Co-operation and Development countries, the United States now ranks first in high school completion rates for middle-aged adults, forty-six to sixty-four, but tenth for twenty-five- to thirty-four-year-olds.

Moreover, an American high school diploma isn't much of an achievement anymore. Except in a small number of highly specialized "career education" programs, it prepares you for very few jobs and now makes only a small difference alone in average employment and earnings. What matters most is whether you leave high school prepared to succeed in further education. Today, two-thirds of U.S. high school seniors collect a diploma, but less than half are actually prepared for college-level work, as measured by their scores on entrance exams. Many young people today arrive at college after sliding through substandard high schools and find that they don't have the skills they need to get a valuable credential. To accommodate them, community colleges and state universities offer remedial high-school-level classes; half of all students who enroll in public colleges must take at least one of these courses.

Meanwhile, the underlying causes of the public school crisis are much debated. Is it weak standards? A lack of school choice? Inadequate testing? Not enough computers? Underskilled teachers? What's clear is that even as more traditionally underserved and underperforming students—including immigrants, Latinos, African-Americans, and the learning-disabled—enter the system each year, money and resources are chronically lacking in school districts where they are most needed.

Latoya chose the academic program at Community College of Philadelphia, the only public, broad-access college in the city. But

the classes left her cold. "It's boring," she said. "I'm not used to
the way they teach. The professors are old and they sound like a
tape recorder."

Low high school standards, combined with the economic obstacles discussed in Chapter One, help explain why the college
graduation rate has not improved much in the past thirty years.
Motivation is also crucial. Latoya had funding for college, from
Pell Grants, and she had support from her mother, but they
weren't enough to keep her in school. For whatever reason, she
didn't show the same hunger as her contemporaries at places like
the Indian Institute of Technology in Delhi, young people participating in an entire nation's rise with a good chance to pull their
own families out of poverty.

A smart young woman, Latoya just didn't see a connection
between her dull classes and a good secure job. And she was
right—a nonvocational associate's degree doesn't guarantee much.
It wasn't helping her concentration that Latoya was also putting
in twenty to thirty hours a week behind the cash register at a
Chick-fil-A in a mall, after school and on Saturdays. Less than a
month had gone by in this way before she decided that college
wasn't for her.

Jerome's and Latoya's experiences show that there is more to a
successful school-to-work system than cash. There are formidable
social barriers to overcome. Jerome barely knows anyone who goes
to college. He has little access to the world of Kaplan prep courses
or the Free Application for Federal Student Aid or internships.

Now that he is out of high school, each passing year makes it less likely that he will ever get to college. In the same way, Latoya ended up at a community college, even though her school performance, ambition, and background made her an attractive candidate for aid at colleges all over the country. Community College was the only school she was familiar with that she knew she could afford.

Social networks likewise steered Latoya to the military. Though she barely knew him while she was growing up, Latoya was aware that her father served in the Navy. "The forces have been very good to him," she said. In September 2004, she applied to be an Air Force police officer, leaving Community College of Philadelphia after just one semester. She is uncertain whether she will complete college after her tour of duty or make her career in the military. Right now, the military promises Latoya benefits, like health care and paid vacation. Her father has appeared back in her life and is very proud of her. Most important, it's a way out of her neighborhood. "I think if I don't go I'll be stuck in Philadelphia, and I don't want to do that," she says. "I want to live in a suburban area, somewhere nice to raise children in. Philadelphia has too much traffic." She says she hasn't really thought about whether she will serve in Iraq or Afghanistan.

In the thirty years since the United States ended the draft, the military has become the default option for ambitious working-class kids trying to get training for jobs or GI Bill funding for college. The Army is one of the few institutions in our society with a national marketing and recruiting operation offering the average young person a chance at a better life. The armed forces must recruit 365,000 people each year; every branch except the Air Force has been missing recruitment targets since the war in Iraq began.

President George W. Bush's 2002 No Child Left Behind Act included a new requirement that every public high school release its students' home contact information to military recruiters. Working-class and minority students commonly report that recruiters target them much more heavily. At colleges like Community, recruiters may set up tables three or four days a week, convincing many kids like Latoya to quit school. Incentives like signing bonuses and GI Bill money have increased, even as the risks associated with joining get worse. "McFarlane joined the Army to get money for college. He had hopes of studying computers or designing cars," went a typical story on Minnesota Public Radio on January 11, 2005, after twenty-year-old Dwayne James McFarlane, a Native American from a poverty-stricken reservation, was killed by an improvised bomb outside Baghdad.

A national "counter-recruitment" movement has sprung up in the past few years to make parents and kids aware of the No Child Left Behind provisions and their right to opt out, and to get them thinking about the dangers of service. The activists' key goal is to get more balanced information out to kids about financial aid for education, jobs programs, internships, and training programs, so they know what options they have besides the uniform. "At many schools, college and job recruiters come once a year at career night," says Amy Wagner, an activist with Ya-Ya (Youth Activists–Youth Allies), working with youth on counter-recruitment concerns in New York. "But military recruiters come every week."

.   .   .

In the youth "futures market," the only organizations that spend as much money on PR as the military are for-profit colleges. The University of Phoenix, Capella University, and hundreds of others paper city buses with ads featuring smiling, highly caffeinated, multicultural models. Instead of commuting to a dead-end job, they suggest, you could be on the express to a better future. Local, regional, and national for-profit schools offer short courses of study certifying you as anything from a manicurist to a truck driver, with heavy emphasis on computers, health care, business, and other growing fields.

The economic onus to get a postsecondary credential has fueled the growth of these proprietary schools just as the growing expense of an education steers students to commercial loans. And for-profit schools, just like commercial loans, are more expensive than the public kind. Proprietary schools cost an average of over $10,000 a year in tuition, as compared with around $1,000 for community colleges.

For-profit institutions have grown in the past decade partly by pioneering online and distance education. The University of Phoenix, for example, has over 200,000 students, half online and half at 151 campuses. It's the same size as the University of California system. In the fall of 2001, total enrollment in proprietary schools was 765,701 students, 30 percent more than in 1996.

These schools argue that they are responding to the demand for specialized, flexible, convenient career education. With a customer-service ethic, they are good at attracting nontraditional students; up to 70 percent of their students are the first in their families to go to college. Some proprietary-school programs have strong industry connections and offer extensive job-placement and counseling services to all their students, help that the average grad of a state university might envy.

Not all customers are satisfied, though. Since the Senate regulatory crackdown in 1992, major media reports of misconduct by proprietary schools have continued. In the fall of 2004, for example, the University of Phoenix agreed to pay a $9.8 million settlement to the Department of Education for allegations of violations in its recruiting practices. In 2005, a *60 Minutes* exposé found another career college wildly overreporting its graduation and job-placement rates, which were actually well below 50 percent.

Craig, twenty-eight, grew up in the suburbs of Minneapolis and graduated from a regional state university with a degree in mass communications and $22,000 in student loan debt. Unsure of what to do with his degree, he decided to study graphic design at a proprietary school. "It was called the 'Minnesota School of Computer Imaging.' They tried to make it sound really professional," he remembers. "There was one instructor who really knew his stuff. The rest didn't seem like they wanted to be there. They were just out-of-work people in the industry that we wanted to get into." Disappointed, and out another $5,000 in student loans, Craig left the program after three academic quarters with little to show for it. Today, he lives with his parents and works as a temp.

For-profit education companies did better than any other single industry on Wall Street between 2000 and 2003, according to one analyst quoted in *The New York Times*. Boasting profits in the billions, the large proprietary schools have become major education lobbyists in the past decade, and are winning more favorable consideration in Congress. With the mixed results seen so far, can we afford to have the market assume control of an enterprise as important to our nation's future as higher education? Wouldn't it make more sense to rededicate scarce federal financial aid resources to institutions whose top obligation is to students, not to shareholders?

In the absence of a true American school-to-work system, a patchwork of private organizations is filling in. The Center for Employment Training (CET), with operations in eleven states and D.C., is one of the largest nonprofit job-training organizations in the country. Before the location I visited closed in June 2005, CET was one of the few places in Oakland, California, where you could get certified as a forklift operator/warehouse specialist; other popular courses included Medical Administrative Assistant, preparing billing clerks for America's growing health insurance bureaucracy.

Although a nonprofit, CET charges tuition of $6,500 for a twenty-one-week course, more than the cost of a year at UC Berkeley for in-state students. This amount is only partly covered by Pell Grants to its overwhelmingly poor students, so many must take out loans.

The Oakland location of CET was a drab one-story building in a residential subdivision where castoff metal desks jammed gray-carpeted classrooms. Bulletin boards at the center were papered with flyers offering supplementary job-placement counseling, emergency financial assistance, training for citizenship tests, and a program providing women with secondhand suits for interviews. When I talked to students, it seemed clear that the classes were designed for those with minimal academic skills and relied on workbooks and rote memorization. The students were mostly people who had run out of other options—immigrants, ex-inmates, people coming off welfare, people in recovery from drug and alcohol addiction.

I met Jerman, twenty, on a visit to the Oakland CET in November 2004. He was a shy, pale boy with spiky hair and several piercings. Jerman had grown up in King City, three hours south of San Francisco. His parents, immigrants from Guadalajara, Mexico, had worked in the fields for over twenty years. In the past decade, they had come up in the world as labor contractors and owned several homes and wineries in San Luis Obispo County. Despite the newfound wealth, all had not gone well with Jerman's family. "My brother has five kids by five different girls, and he's twenty-eight," he said. "His paycheck be going all to child support. My sister has four kids at twenty-one; the oldest one has a different father. They live with my parents—brother, sister, boyfriend, four kids. I want to learn from their bad experiences."

Jerman has had bad experiences of his own. He graduated from high school and then took some courses at a community college, but along the way he got involved in King City's drug scene. Jerman told me he lost three friends to violence in less than a year. Drug dealers murdered one of his childhood friends over a bad debt. "I was with him the day that he went missing," he said. "They caught up with him that night. He'll always remain my best friend, no matter what happens." On his eighteenth birthday, Jerman was arrested for reckless driving and possession of methamphetamines, and sentenced to three months in the county jail. Then he went to stay with relatives in Mexico and saw a therapist for several months.

Jerman heard about CET from friends and signed up to become a medical administrative assistant. The next time we spoke was in February 2005, around the time he was supposed to be finishing the program. He had been hospitalized briefly for depression; in the meantime, the Oakland location of CET was closing, and he wasn't sure whether he would have to repeat his six-month course elsewhere—and pay $6,500 again—to get his certification. He had already taken out a commercial loan of $2,500 and didn't want to borrow again; his parents, who were partly supporting him, were unwilling to pay more. He was applying for a job at a rental-car place and thinking about taking a $400 bartending course.

Jerman is comparatively lucky. There are plenty of young people flushed out of the school-to-work system altogether. A rising number of sixteen-to-twenty-four-year-olds in the '00s—a record 5.5 million by 2002—became officially "disconnected," not employed, not in school, not in the military. Some are living off family and friends, or on public assistance. They have dropped out of school, been released from juvenile hall, or aged out of foster care. They are runaways, throwaways, or are simply hanging out, headed nowhere.

Young men of color, in particular, are not merely drifting away. They are arrested and wrenched out of their families and communities and into the world's largest prison system, mostly because of the war on drugs. A nonprofit reported in 2000 that black youths were forty-eight times more likely than whites to serve time in juvenile prisons on drug offenses. In the 1990s, the Justice Department estimated that in the nation's largest cities, a third of the black men aged eighteen to thirty-four were in state prisons, in city jails, on probation, or on parole on any given day.

Whether behind bars or on the streets, disconnected youth are the write-offs of our society. Advocates such as Robert Ivry of MDRC, a nonprofit social policy research organization, say turning around the lives of young people like Jerman demands an intense focus on the whole person—family dynamic, mental health and self-esteem, parenting skills, basic material needs. Community colleges and job-training programs can't do it alone, especially when people hardly know how to get to their doors.

We are all used to blaming the public school system, violent neighborhoods, and fragmented families for the failures of kids like these. Yet the business community also bears responsibility for our faulty school-to-work system. The chains slung across our landscape increasingly look for young workers with low expectations, few skills, and less experience. Workers under twenty-four accept work at lower wages. They don't expect job security and they don't ask for child care or health care. Youth workers are the mainstay of the strip mall economy. Jerman's résumé says it all: cashier at a local restaurant, manager at a Hollywood Video and a Domino's Pizza, supervisor at a Carl's Jr. hamburger joint.

In this country, instead of "school to work," we have "school and work." Even at the most prestigious universities, there is little attempt to connect the bachelor's degree to employment. The diploma itself is supposed to be the qualification. Most young people work while enrolled in both high school and college, yet the vast majority of the jobs they do, even more so than in the past, require minimal training, have little connection to academics, and lead nowhere.

Stuart Tannock, author of the 2001 book *Youth at Work,* conducts research on young workers at the UC Berkeley Labor Center. The center is one of the only academic organizations in the country studying and advocating for young low-wage workers. Tannock says that the new economy has created a new stage in the average work life—that of churning through designated "youth jobs."

"If you go back to the '60s, in the grocery industry for example, three-fourths of the jobs were career, full-time," Tannock says. "About one-fourth were part-time—students, moms, people not fully in the workforce. Now that's completely flip-flopped. The majority of the jobs are part-time, and employers are explicitly thinking of young people as they design these jobs."

Tannock cautions that for the young people he studies, education is not a guaranteed means of improving their lot. "In industry after industry, as unionized high-wage jobs start to disappear, more and more young folks are turning toward higher education as the only way out," he says. "One big problem is that no matter what side of the political spectrum you're on, you have to concede that no more than 30 percent of jobs are going to require a college education. So what we have now is essentially a lottery system. A lot of people are going into debt for college, and the promise is illusory."

Asked where the question of access to higher education fits into the larger struggle for better lives for the majority of youth,

Tannock pauses. "This is a question I'm working on currently—
it's really tricky," he says. "The higher education system is becoming skewed to rich and middle-class kids, and as long as college
remains the only chance for youth to get a decent standard of living, educational access is going to be really important. But there's
a limit to that project. The bigger problem is the deterioration
of the vast majority of jobs in this country. We can't pin all our
hopes on a college education."

Young people by definition have their whole lives ahead of
them. We are inclined to be optimistic and think of current set-
backs as temporary. It makes everyone feel better to think this
way. If a bachelor's degree is really worth a million bucks, the best
solution to poverty among the young ought to be to increase the
numbers of people who have college degrees.

Except for one thing: As Tannock suggests, and a variety of
measures confirm, more education alone simply can't lift everyone's
boat. Even if we doubled the Pell Grant next year and tripled the
numbers of college graduates, without changing anything else in
the economy, we'd only be creating more overeducated baristas
and housecleaners. This is because of a concept called the wage
structure. The prominent economist James K. Galbraith, in his
1998 book *Created Unequal,* documented the increasing polarization of American incomes. To illustrate the wage structure, he used
the metaphor of a skyscraper with a certain number of rooms on
each floor. Right now, the lower floors, representing lower income
levels, have more "rooms" where people can work than the higher

floors. It doesn't matter how many people become qualified to work on the higher floors, they are not guaranteed a space in the current structure. Hence, education as a lottery for elevator tickets.

"Promoters of schooling as a cure for inequality are arguing, in effect, that fixing their initial placement of disadvantaged people or groups will have, by itself, an effect on the equality of pay in the society that results. This is a serious fallacy," Galbraith writes.

Income inequality has only widened since Galbraith's book was published. For the past two decades, the lowest floors in the American wage structure have been expanding, the highest floors are getting higher, and the middle floors are getting smaller. (The revolving doors are also revolving faster, but let's not get carried away with the metaphor.)

Moreover, most economic analysts agree that the jobs of the next decade will require only slightly more educational credentials than today's do. In 2002, according to the Bureau of Labor Statistics (BLS), 26.9 percent of the workforce needed a college degree or more to do their jobs. This share will rise by just one percentage point by 2012, says the progressive nonprofit Economic Policy Institute.

In fact, at the annual meeting of the American Economic Association in early 2005, experts agreed that the return on a college education has leveled off. Bachelor's degree holders currently earn 45 percent more on average than high school graduates. It's a substantial advantage, but one that has not changed much since the late 1990s and even shows some sign of declining. Earnings for workers with four-year degrees fell 5.2 percent—after inflation—

between 2000 and 2004. "There is no rule of law that says demand for educated labor will always rise faster than the supply," Richard Freeman, an economist at Harvard, told *The New York Times*. "It could go the other way."

Every two years since the GIs came back from World War II, the BLS has issued the *Occupational Outlook Handbook*, a publication meant to give the general public an idea of which careers are booming and which are in decline. According to the 2004–2005 *Handbook*, seven of the top ten fastest-growing job areas in 2004 are poorly paid, dead-end, low-skill positions: retail workers, cashiers, customer service representatives, nursing aides, janitors, food preparers, waiters and waitresses. Of these jobs, five skew toward youth. Only one job out of the top twenty—postsecondary teacher—requires more than a college education, and that job itself is becoming more likely to be short-term and part-time, with the rise of adjuncts.

Contrary to popular belief, the entry of technology into almost all aspects of business has failed to improve the quality of most jobs. Richard Florida, in *The Rise of the Creative Class*, points out that the flexible work hours adopted by information-economy businesses have brought forth the twenty-four-hour convenience service economy. For every $75,000-a-year "information architect" burning the midnight oil for an important presentation, there are literally three or four $7.50-an-hour cashiers working the graveyard shift at the drugstore or grocery, whose interaction with technology is limited to the touch-screen register and the debit card reader.

Another antiyouth wrinkle in the transforming economy, as revealed in the *Occupational Outlook Handbook,* is that the low-skill sectors are becoming segregated by age, with older people holding on to more stable and decently paid jobs while the worst new jobs are going to the young. In declining industries—like manufacturing, farming, and fishing—the average age is creeping up. Which makes sense: job creation in those industries is in the hundreds of thousands, compared with the millions of new service jobs. Meanwhile, people between the ages of sixteen and twenty-four represent a third of the growing retail workforce. Food-and-drink establishments, a sector dominated by the large fast-food chains, employ a far higher proportion of sixteen-to-twenty-four-year-olds than any other business—44 percent of their workers were in that age group in 2002. McDonald's alone has provided a McJob for one out of every eight adults in this country at some point in his or her life, overwhelmingly before the age of thirty.

The *Occupational Outlook Handbook* contains the most comprehensive information we have about the job market. As a BLS economist explained to me, however, its projections are based on current demand and assume full employment. Therefore, it can't account for unfilled positions or capture the dynamics of supply and demand. Richard Florida argues that an influx of young college graduates into a metropolitan area stimulates innovation and entrepreneurship, such that the educated newcomers can actually create and attract more new jobs than they themselves can fill. Human capital acts as a catalyst for growth. It makes sense to me that the converse also holds true: Job creation can be stalled by a shortage of qualified people. When young people are trapped in low-wage and dead-end jobs instead of building their futures, it is bound to create a vicious cycle of stagnation.

In the '60s and '70s, when today's student aid system was built, policymakers talked about "college" versus "noncollege" youth. Today, with the decline in the value of a high school diploma, that concept no longer holds. Many more people at least try to pursue some kind of postsecondary studies, knowing that otherwise they'll probably never make a decent living. The economic difficulties these students run into while trying to complete college put them into a third category: "between-college" youth.

This is my term for nearly three out of four young people today—the ones without four-year college degrees. They are from poor or working-class backgrounds, and increasingly, downwardly mobile children of the middle class. They are working full-time or close to it while picking up postsecondary credits whenever and wherever they can. They may stay in this limbo for six or seven years or longer, stuck at the same low level during a time when their income should be climbing. The types of jobs they hold are unlikely to lead to a decent-paying career, and they can't afford an education without working. The sheer length of time young people are spending in this between-college limbo, and their numbers, give them a permanent, unhappy role in the new economy.

Nita, twenty-four, of Chicago, has already spent six years in between-college land, and she's resigned herself to putting in at least five or six more. Nita's mother is Puerto Rican, her father Anglo. She tells her story with intelligence and self-awareness—

"Sound pathetic enough?" she asks me—but her frustration is barely below the surface. "I graduated from Lakeview, a public high school, in 1998," she says. "I enrolled in junior college [Wilbur Wright, a public community college] and I hated it. It was just like high school. On top of that it was really far from my house. I had to pick the school that took me an hour to get there. I dropped out after six months or something." Nita has worked low-wage jobs both part-time and full-time since age sixteen, first at a Jewel grocery store, then at Pier 1, Borders, and Home Depot, where she earned her top wage of $10.25 an hour at eighteen. She hasn't had health insurance since she was excluded from her parents' policy at the age of nineteen.

"I lived at home until I was twenty-two," she told me. "I was working these dumb jobs with the idea of saving money to go to college. But you never truly save enough money. You get a pile of money and just blow it." Nita barely manages the monthly minimum payments on $10,000 of credit card debt, mostly run up in one summer two years ago of "being a tourist in my own city," shopping, eating out, and partying. "They can bother me all they want, but I can't pull $10,000 out of my ass, as much as I try," she says.

In the fall of 2000, while at Borders, Nita and some coworkers got motivated to enroll in school once again. This time, she picked Chicago's Columbia College, a private institution specializing in arts and communications and charging $7,400 a year. "I was going to do sound and radio," she says. Unfortunately, two weeks into the semester, Nita got the news that she had been denied federally subsidized loans. She still doesn't know exactly what happened,

only that "my parents always had crappy credit." Nita is living out
a second generation of deferred educational dreams. Her mother
is unwell and no longer works. Her father completed college and
some graduate study in geology, but as Nita puts it, "I was born,
turn of events, and he had to get a real job." For her entire life, he
has worked for the Chicago Transit Authority.

Nita had invested a part of herself in this dream of going to
college, a "real college," and it hurt to give that up. "I had attended two weeks of classes. Then I got this little slip of paper and
I ran around and dropped every class," she said. "I had rearranged
my work schedule, and I was talking all this crap, 'I'm going to
school, blah blah blah,' and then I had to drop out. I was like,
'Oh. Back to Borders full-time.'"

Through most of America's history, teenagers, and twenty-
somethings of course, worked the same jobs as everyone else.
Some apprenticed to skilled craftsmen. More were schoolteach-
ers, ranchers, farmers, miners, shop clerks, domestic servants,
and factory workers. Teenagers' employment began to decline
with the Great Depression, but it was still possible into the 1970s
for an eighteen-year-old with a high school diploma to find a full-
time job that paid enough to support a family.

The kind of short-term, part-time, low-skilled job that Nita
has spent her "career" in first appeared in a quieter America of
mom-and-pop diners, filling stations, and soda shops. In the
1960s, for example, my father helped out behind the register in his
father's pharmacy and soda fountain in Baltimore after school
and on weekends. Because it was his family business, he shared

indirectly in the profits, and he had the opportunity to learn the trade and follow in his dad's footsteps, although as it turned out, that wasn't in the cards.

Today national franchises have replaced independent businesses. The nature of youth jobs has changed in the past generation, tilting decisively toward the grinding, the impersonal, and the dead-end. Whether the product is a hamburger, a latte, or a hardcover book, young people joining these establishments without a degree or specialized training face a similar situation. They are likely to be working for large corporations with inflexible rules, including random drug testing, uniforms, video surveillance, and write-ups for minor infractions like wearing the wrong color shoes. Their jobs have been standardized for efficiency and involve minimal training, a narrow range of repetitive tasks, unpredictable part-time work schedules, and little opportunity for frontline workers to move up. Not to mention low wages, high turnover, and rare benefits.

A generation ago, Nita could have paid her way through a four-year public university and supported herself by working a job like the one at Borders, perhaps fifteen hours a week and full-time in the summer. No more. Wages at these jobs have sunk too low as the cost of college has shot up. As of this writing, the federal minimum wage of $5.15 an hour has not been raised since 1997, tying for the longest time it has been frozen. It has the second-lowest buying power in fifty years.

As wages stand still throughout the job market, the least experienced workers are naturally being dealt from the bottom of the pack. Young adults are the first to get laid off: In the fall of 2001, for example, the steepest short-term slump of the post–dot-com recession, 95 percent of workers who lost their jobs were between the ages of sixteen and twenty-four.

Nita is very familiar with the paltry options available to people with her background and qualifications. "Obviously, with a high school education, I'm stuck in retail. I don't have any other skills," she says. Nevertheless, she is defiant about her long-term fate. "I absolutely refuse to be working in retail [forever]. It's soul-sucking; it's horrible. There's nothing worse than being a slave to another person," whether boss or customer. When we spoke, Nita had sunk to what she called "the lowest I've ever gone on the bad-bad-job scale." She was working part-time, irregular hours, for the minimum wage at the cash register of a dollar store. Still, she says, the job is still marginally above what she considers the bottom of the barrel: a gas station convenience store or, heaven forbid, McDonald's.

For the moment, it appears self-evident that a job like Nita's will never be the source of the kind of working-class pride that a job on the factory line was for previous generations. But why? Both classes of work can be dirty, sweaty, and exhausting. Retail and services are just as important to the American economy today as manufacturing ever was. We've simply exchanged the hard hat for a hairnet, the tough leather gloves for a polyester smock.

A Bush administration economic report released in early 2004 elicited derision when it suggested reclassifying fast-food workers as manufacturing employees, which would make the job-growth numbers look much better. But maybe they had the right idea—

except instead of just calling them manufacturing jobs, we need to make them into good jobs, with labor protections, benefits, and middle-class wages.

If companies paid these workers enough to live on and raise a family on, they'd have to train them well enough and keep them long enough to justify the investment. Better-trained workers would be able to accept more responsibility and perhaps move more frequently from the front line up to management. This is what Marc Tucker calls the "high-road" method of work organization. All of a sudden, these jobs would no longer be interchangeable or disposable. They'd be recognized as worthy contributions that keep our country and our economy running. The young people filling these positions would no longer be discounted. We wouldn't assume that their positions are temporary, and they wouldn't assume it themselves.

Lest you think this is a left-wing fantasy, you can already see the high-road phenomenon in place with certain prominent and profitable retailers, like Costco, Home Depot, and Whole Foods. I have a few friends, with and without college degrees, who work at Whole Foods and are proud of it, because of the relatively high wages, the benefits, the team-based work organization, and the company's strong sense of mission. It's not the work that's necessarily any better—it's the job.

All of which implies that if we really mean to take seriously the future of Generation Debt, we need to consider young people not just as students or as future members of this or that profession, but as workers in their own right, right now. And to do that, we need to overcome outdated stereotypes.

Almost everyone I know has low-wage memories. It's an American rite of passage to wait tables or bartend, babysit or work construction during your formative years. But generalizing from one's own experience can be deceptive. In fact, the central conservative argument against raising the minimum wage is that those earning it are primarily unskilled teenagers, whose labor is worth little and whose income is nothing more than a supplement to a household. According to the conservative Heritage Foundation, three-fourths of those working minimum-wage jobs are enrolled in high school or postsecondary school.

Students they may be. But they are also workers. Far from being time fillers for middle-class teenagers, most minimum-wage jobs provide income to those who really need it. The Economic Policy Institute has found that if the minimum wage had been raised in 2005, most of the extra earnings would have gone to lower-income families. Nearly half of minimum-wage earners are working full-time.

On paper, at least while she was still living at home, Nita looked like one of those carefree and expendable low-wage workers. This characterization excludes the force of her hopelessness, the way she has been stuck in limbo for six years, left behind on the way to a better life.

Nita hopes to enroll in college a third time, maybe at the Art Institute of Chicago to study printmaking. She has given herself a deadline of age twenty-seven to get her act together. "My current boss has some bs degree, but he's qualified to be my manager just because he attended four years of a university." Nita dreams of a quiet office job, even as a file clerk, unmolested by her boss's constant orders. "Retail doesn't ensure security. With an office job at least I could ensure a false sense of security and a white picket fence. I want to have something to my name, a house, a car."

Unfortunately, there are snags in Nita's dream, modest as it is. Researchers identify students at risk for dropping out by looking at all the ways they differ from the stereotypical college kid. Students are nontraditional if they are over twenty-four, are married, have dependents, are self-supporting, attend school part-time, work full-time, commute, took time off after high school, or don't have a high school diploma. These students are the most likely to be lower-income and racial minorities, and are found in the highest percentages at community colleges.

The more of these characteristics you have, the worse your chances of graduating. Among highly nontraditional students, with four or more of these characteristics, an astonishing 89 percent leave college without getting the bachelor's degree they aimed for.

Students like Nita are caught in a double bind. It's nearly impossible to be fully committed to both a full-time job and a full-time college program. Nevertheless, over half of community college students work full-time, mostly at low-wage jobs. Almost half of them say that work limits their class schedule.

Even if they do manage to slog their way through, the hours spent at work rob these students of the intangible benefits of education. "It is simply not possible today to work enough to cover college expenses without taking a heavy toll on student academic performance," concluded a 2002 congressional report. A lot of the value to be gained from a traditional college education comes from what you do in your free time. I got started in journalism not in a class but as an editor at my college magazine. Getting to know teachers and classmates, spending time in an environment where intellectual debate is encouraged, and exploring activities to find new passions are all part of a true liberal education. A student who must work thirty or more hours a week can't do these things.

In one study by the National Center for Education Statistics, two-thirds of college students over age twenty-four said they were employees who happened to be studying. Just one-third said they were students who happened to be working. These are the priorities we're forcing young people to have. If you're spending over six years to get a bachelor's degree, like a majority of community college students, that's not exactly temporary. If you leave school without getting a degree, that's not exactly leading somewhere better, or anywhere at all.

That the majority of young people in this country are wasting years of their lives in low-wage, low-skill jobs is an economic and moral disaster. Improving their chances demands more than hard work—as we've seen, they are already working day and night. It demands hard choices.

The first order of business is to restore the promise that no young person who wants to and is qualified to attend college should be barred by a lack of money. The shameful gaps in college attendance between rich and poor and black and white must be closed. Equality of opportunity should be the first banner that we pick up from the dust, shake out, and hang up once again.

But the work doesn't end there. It's time to admit freely that a traditional four-year college education is neither available, nor suited, to everybody. The college-for-all ideal doesn't serve young people and it doesn't serve the truth. This is not only a class-based argument. Among the nation's poorest families, earning less than $35,377 a year, only about one in seventeen young people earns a bachelor's degree by age twenty-four. For the nation's wealthiest, those who earn $85,000 or higher, the figure is still not that impressive, just over 50 percent.

Managing people's expectations about the bachelor's degree may seem reactionary, undemocratic, and antithetical to the American Dream. We tend to embrace the consumerist idea that everyone should have infinite choices. Unfortunately, not even nineteen-year-olds have unlimited time, and they deserve some real options.

Post–high school training is a necessity. But it doesn't have to be an expensive hardship that takes the better part of a decade. If education received more public support, and if more young people found their way to well-designed and highly focused vocational programs, we wouldn't be seeing the same delayed economic independence.

Community colleges—with their convenient locations, low prices, and often open admissions—are most young people's best option for career development. Over 1,100 public and private community colleges currently educate students nationwide. These schools enroll 6.6 million students for credit, nearly half of all undergraduates.

The experiences of two graduates of Delgado Community College in New Orleans, Louisiana, show that well-run vocational programs can indeed improve kids' prospects. (I spoke to them nearly a year before Hurricane Katrina.) Recognizing that their choices have been limited by economic realities, academic requirements, and the tracks offered by their school, these young people took no less pride in their accomplishments.

"Raquelle," twenty-two, hails from a close-knit Cajun family in rural Lafitte, Louisiana. She always knew she wouldn't be happy in a traditional academic program. "I said as soon as I got out of high school that I didn't want to go to a big four-year college," she said. "I was scared. I didn't want to be away from my family so long."

Raquelle first wanted to be a second-grade teacher, but she found the Delgado education coursework too hard, especially since she had to balance it with a full-time job. She was ready to quit by the middle of her second year, but her mother talked her out of it. Instead, Raquelle transferred to Delgado's culinary arts program.

Delgado's program functioned as a hiring hall for New Orleans's then thriving restaurant industry, in a relationship that Tucker and Marshall, authors of *Thinking for a Living,* would call an ideal public-private partnership. She was put in a kitchen right from the start, with forty hours of work a week, and written assignments were kept to a minimum.

When we spoke, Raquelle was a few credits away from an associate's degree in culinary arts and had already worked at five restaurants. She was in a kitchen sixty hours a week, full-time as an assistant pastry chef at an upscale bistro, and part-time at a friend's Caribbean restaurant. She earned just under $30,000 a year, lived with her family, and was saving money.

"Compared to my friends from high school, I'd say I'm doing slightly better," she says. "I'm actually in my career. I'm not making the $40,000 that I hope to be making one day, but I'm no longer in school and I'm doing what I want to do with my life. And I just got loans at the precise amount I needed to pay for school. I owe $5,000. I know people who owe $40,000."

Raquelle counted herself lucky to have found a program that let her learn on the job. Otherwise, she knows, it is nearly impossible for working-class students to balance financial demands with college. "I'm not just doing a here-and-there job just to pay bills," she says. "Most of my friends are either not working, 'cause they can't because school is too hard, and living off their parents, or they're working all the time and just fiddling off at school."

Most important, Raquelle loved her work. One day she planned to open her own pastry shop in Florida or Georgia, not too far from home. "I have the career of my life," she says. "It's open. You never stop learning. You have a job almost anywhere in the world that you go. You learn so much. There's not a day that I go into the job that I don't learn something."

James, a twenty-four-year-old African-American, had a slightly less sanguine take on his school-to-work path. His high school was right across the street from Delgado, making it his fallback for continuing his education. "Things didn't go as planned as far as my ACT scores," he says. "I was going to try to get my grades up so I could go to a four-year university, but that never materialized." James had some regrets when he started at Delgado, as some of his classmates headed to Louisiana's historically black colleges, with their proud histories and nationally known football teams. "You see your friends, they're going to Southern and Grambling, and it's like you're not really going to college 'cause it's still at home. It's not so much for the academics but college life—that's what I was looking forward to."

Once at Delgado, James found his interests further restricted by the programs that the public two-year school had to offer. "I'm a sports guy. I actually wanted to be an occupational therapist or a physical therapist, working with athletes. But my counselor felt that with the grades that I had I could handle the radiology program, and so I tried it out and enjoyed it." Like a majority of community college entrants, according to studies, James had little knowledge of the academic requirements of the sports medicine program he wanted, and he was unprepared by his high school education to work up to the required standard.

Nevertheless, compared with many young people in this chapter and even some four-year-college graduates, James was sitting pretty. He is qualified in a field that can pay $25 an hour. He graduated from his two-year program in October 2003 and had a job as an X-ray technician at New Orleans's Memorial Medical Center by the end of the month, which became a full-time position. His job even had a loan-repayment program for his $7,000 in student loans, and since graduating he had managed to pay down $2,000 in credit card debt while living at home to save money.

James, like Raquelle, had concrete ambitions. "At Baptist, we have the contract for the Saints, so I get to see some of those guys," he says of New Orleans's beloved NFL team. "I'm not going to let my dream die as far as sports medicine." His immediate plans were to finish his bachelor's in radiology, which will increase his earning potential, and to marry his girlfriend, another X-ray tech he met in school.

At the same time, James had a sense of something given up. "It's not exactly the route I had in my head," he said of his vocational track, "but I'm happy with it. Delgado was a blessing in disguise. It's not where I wanted to be, but it got me where I wanted to go."

James and Raquelle are best-case scenarios under the current school-to-work system. They overcame their lack of preparation for college work, not to mention a culture that tells them to shoot for the moon, be satisfied with nothing less than the best, and charge it if they can't afford it. They adjusted their expectations to reality, and success followed.

As Stuart Tannock, who has been studying these issues a lot longer than I have, puts it, the question of how to best improve opportunities for young people from all backgrounds is "really tricky." I am trying to thread the needle here in presenting both the need for increased access to education for all and the need to look realistically at the status quo. The ideal American system would be one where the brilliant son of a janitor finds it financially feasible to earn a Ph.D. in literature, and the down-to-earth daughter of a CEO feels equally free to become an auto mechanic. The system we have is one that promises the world to all young people, and delivers very little to very few.

FOUR

Temp Gigs . . .

What do you do with a B.A. in English,
What is my life going to be?
Four years of college and plenty of knowledge,
Have earned me this useless degree.

I can't pay the bills yet,
'Cause I have no skills yet,
The world is a big scary place.

But somehow I can't shake,
The feeling I might make,
A difference,
To the human race. . . .

—"WHAT DO YOU DO WITH A B.A. IN ENGLISH?"

AVENUE Q, 2003

venue Q, a Broadway show featuring people acting
and singing alongside Muppet-like puppets, won
Tonys for 2003's best musical, best book, and best
score. In the show, Princeton, a goggle-eyed twenty-two-year-old
college grad, moves to the only cheap neighborhood in New York

City. His first job offer falls through. With no marketable skills, he runs out of options fast. The kid ends up in substandard, over-priced housing, depressed, behind on his bills, and charging all his expenses on credit cards, including way too much beer. He begins a relationship with a furry monster, but it falls apart when he can't commit—he's still searching for his real purpose in life. Meanwhile, his peers in their twenties and early thirties are unemployed, underemployed, frustrated, or aimless. His girlfriend gets fired, and another friend gets thrown out of his apartment. They all agree that happiness and security are temporary at best.

Avenue Q's young creators, Robert Lopez and Jeff Marx, were open about their personal inspiration. "When we started writing *Avenue Q*, Jeff was an intern and I was a temp," said Lopez, then twenty-eight, in his Tony acceptance speech. "Our lives kinda sucked, so we came up with an idea for a show about people like us whose lives all kinda suck."

Most Broadway theatergoers are over forty. And while they laugh at songs like "What Do You Do with a B.A. in English?" and "It Sucks to Be Me," it probably never occurs to them that these are actually serious problems for millions of people. Just like Princeton, the lovable, fuzzy English major in the show, real-life young grads are suffering from job erosion, temp hell, the intern trap, low pay, no benefits, and the uncertain quest for a fulfilling career.

The problems of America's school-to-work system and job downgrading extend to the college-educated. Stable living-wage jobs are harder to come by for recent grads, and benefits like

health coverage are ever scarcer. The cause is not a temporary recession but structural changes in the economy. In income and
occupational prestige, young adults are behind where their parents were at their age. Unless something changes soon, entry into
middle-class comfort is far from guaranteed for most of us.

Many college kids, like the between-college youth in the last
chapter, also have an expectations problem. We were raised to
dream big. While we face real challenges, our chronic dissatisfaction can itself be a stumbling block. We spend too much time and
borrow too much money shooting for the stars.

When I first met "Sean," a cheerful twenty-three-year-old from
the New York City suburbs, he was, not unlike Princeton, looking
for his first real job. He was standing in the summer heat, résumé
in hand, in a line that wrapped around three sides of a city block
to get into a giant commercial job fair at a Midtown Manhat-
tan hotel. Sean had graduated from the University of Vermont
in 2003 with a degree in psychology, had delivered pizzas and
temped for a year in Burlington, Vermont, until his girlfriend
graduated, and had moved back home in the summer of 2004 to
try his luck in the New York area. At first he thought he wanted
to work in media or entertainment, but he quit after just one day
as a production assistant on a film shoot.

"I just realized it wasn't right for me," he said of the low-paying
job, which mostly involved telling passersby not to disturb the set.
"It wasn't what I wanted to be. It was a tough feeling. You think
you know what you want and it turns on its head."

Sean hopes to make six figures someday, but he has no clue how he's going to get there. He wasn't alone; while a few of his recently graduated friends were headed to Columbia Business School, more were in what he called "career denial," marking the summer as lifeguards or caddies. By mid-September 2004, Sean, who had told me in July how much he would hate to work in sales, had nevertheless settled for a position with a small marketing firm. He was still living at home, because he was making just $10 an hour, with no benefits. "I'm just kind of rolling with the punches," he said.

Sean turned unexpectedly morose when asked about his expectations. "It's absolute darkness, permanent darkness," he said. "The glimmer of hope really is that light that you're searching for. Your patience wears thin waiting for it to happen." Sean said his father, a successful financial adviser, was especially concerned about his job search, and with good reason. Other things being equal, the son's chances of finding and keeping a job with a livable, growing salary are worse than his father's were.

A large amount of recent research has found young people in the '90s and '00s doing worse than previous generations. In 1998, two economists with the Bureau of Labor Statistics published a study comparing government income and spending data for a broad sample of independent, single eighteen-to-twenty-nine-year-olds in 1972–73, 1984–85, and 1994–95. It turns out that reality really did bite in the 1990s. Compared with the earlier groups, it took longer for the 1994–95 cohort to complete their schooling and get out on their own. Only one-third had a college degree, compared with 56 percent for their counterparts in 1972–73. The 1990s singles' average yearly income, $19,891, was $2,522 less in constant

1995 dollars than that of the young adults in 1972–73. The report concluded, "With the possible exception of having a larger array of entertainment and other goods to purchase, members of Generation X appear to be worse off by every measure."

According to the National Center for Education Statistics, young men at all education levels earned less in 2002 than their counterparts a generation earlier. (Women's earnings have increased along with their education and opportunities.) In fact, the value of a college education has grown in the last generation not because college grads make so much more but because high school grads make so much less.

In yet another government study, "Comparing the Labor Market Success of Young Adults from Two Generations," economist Kurt Schrammel concluded that "young adults in 1996 were more likely than were their counterparts in 1979 to be employed in lower-paying occupational groups, and less likely to be employed in higher-paying occupational groups."

In 2001, Annette Bernhardt, an NYU economist and policy analyst, and several coauthors published a major multiyear study on the economic fates of young workers. The research, collected in the book *Divergent Paths,* drew on two U.S. government surveys following thousands of people through their early working lives, from age sixteen through their mid-thirties. The first group began in the late 1960s and the second started out in the early 1980s.

In case you're reading this in a secluded Himalayan monastery, the U.S. economy has transformed radically in the past thirty years. The new reality is postindustrial, nonunion, service-oriented, highly competitive, highly flexible, and technology-dependent. Bernhardt found that in most industries and for most workers, these changes have been bad news. Wages overall have been declining for almost three decades, with lower-wage workers falling far behind and higher-wage workers barely standing still. Bernhardt and her coauthors summarized these trends as "stagnation and polarization."

In the '80s and '90s, most industries saw flat wage growth, and the majority of jobs the economy added were lower-paid and lower-quality. Wage growth picked up for a few years in the late '90s, when the labor market was at its tightest, at the height of the tech boom, but fell again in the early 2000s.

Bernhardt et al. found that a large majority of the later workers saw a loss in lifetime earnings compared with the earlier group. Young men in the '90s had lower earnings, higher job instability, and less upward mobility than their counterparts in the 1970s. Outcomes were more unequal as well. Not only did the rich become much richer and the poor much poorer in the 1990s, people with similar backgrounds and education had more disparate fates. For young men with some college or less, the cumulative loss in wages, over all these trends, came to more than $100,000. Even for college-educated workers, a minority of whom have benefited from the transition to a high-tech economy, the average cumulative wage penalty totaled $40,000. Two-thirds of all college-educated workers have seen their real income growth decline in the past generation. "The majority of young adults in recent years," Bernhardt et al. concluded, "have fallen far behind. . . . The structure of economic mobility in this country has been fundamentally transformed, to the detriment of the majority of the workforce."

Sean's personal "darkness" may be a temporary anxiety. But his generation's worries are not just about dealing with a low salary in an entry-level job, or even being out of work or underemployed for a few years. It's the danger of being stuck in an elevator that doesn't even go to the top floor. It's the inability to make plans— like, say, buying a house or having children—that depend on steadily rising income, because predictable annual raises are a thing of the past. It's entering a world where middle-class guarantees, and middle-class security, are no more.

For previous generations of workers, annual income grew the most and the fastest within their first decade in the workforce. New workers added skills and moved among employers and positions before settling in to a full-time job and small annual raises. Two-thirds of lifetime wage growth, on average, has happened in the first decade of employment. But with the longer transition from school to work, and the highly unequal and unstable job market, that upward slope in the first ten years has taken on a wobble.

Many of the people I've talked with are experiencing this strange combination of stagnation and fluctuation in wages. Some have landed good jobs, only to lose them. Some have changed careers quickly and started over at a lower level. Others have taken a hit in earnings to go back to school, only to face big debt and uncertain returns. Over their first four or five jobs, that crucial first decade in the workforce, their incomes have bobbed up and down without any definite upward arc.

While job changing at the beginning of one's career can be the ticket to moving up faster, too much movement keeps your earnings from growing. The median job tenure of workers aged twenty-five to thirty-four is now just 2.7 years. Compared with people entering the workforce in the 1970s, twenty-somethings today hold jobs for shorter terms, change industries more often, and have more frequent periods of unemployment and underemployment. As Bernhardt's research indicates, all this may very well add up to lower lifetime incomes in constant dollars compared with those of our predecessors.

The raw amount of money isn't the whole story, either. Historically, arriving in the middle class wasn't just about attaining a certain level of consumption. It was about security and stability, the house and the white picket fence, the ability to make plans and keep obligations. As President Franklin Roosevelt described it, the American Dream was about "freedom from fear," as well as "freedom from want." While recent college grads in some jobs, chiefly technology and finance, are pulling down higher pay than their folks did in the 1970s, they have reason to doubt that their job, or the company, or even the industry will still be there next year. And that doubt makes a tangible difference.

Take me, for instance. I don't have a job. I've never had a job, at least not one that combined a salary with benefits. I did not set out to become a part-timer, a freelancer, an occasional dog-sitter.

On the contrary, I had already chosen my future career, journalism, by tenth grade. That's when the trouble started. It turns out that print media is one of those creative industries that these days expect you to earn entry-level experience on your own dime. Among liberal arts graduates of my acquaintance—in fields like media, publishing, advertising, arts and nonprofit administration, and graphic design—everyone always seems to be looking for a job. Some are eking out a living as freelancers, while others labor in low-paid contract positions with no benefits, only vague assurances that they'll be hired for real at some later date.

I became a part-time assistant to a few wonderful writers, who I believe hired me mostly out of kindness. I've done freelance copy editing and fact checking, paid by the hour. Even selling this book creates no expectations of long-term stability.

My marginal status in the work world is more representative of my generation than almost anything else about me. The BLS classifies as "contingent workers" employees who do not expect their jobs to last. In 2005, contingent workers were twice as likely as noncontingent workers to be under age twenty-five. More than half of contingent workers would prefer a permanent job.

In all, about 30 percent of American workers now fall into the various categories of alternative work arrangements, including contingent as well as freelance, part-time, independent contractor, and on-call work. This percentage grew in the 1990s. Just as the swelling number of young people in service jobs reflects an overall shift toward the sector, these tenuous relationships with employment may persist throughout the lives of college-educated young workers.

. . .

The changing labor market is the fundamental reason recent grads have fallen behind. At the end of the twentieth century, businesses in all industries were cutting costs by limiting their full-time staffs. So good jobs have gotten harder to find and harder to keep. To a surprising degree, the jobs haven't disappeared or been sent overseas. They've been downgraded into crap jobs.

"Crap job" isn't the industry term. Businesses call it "internal outsourcing," contingent, freelance, part-time, or contract work. IKEA, the mainstay of new grads' apartments, sells nice-looking furniture, but when you get it home you realize it's put together from cheap laminate, not solid wood. In the same way, employers have cut corners, shifting from solid, full-time, middle-class jobs to cheaper, flimsier models, thus saving money on benefits and wages. Generally, crap jobs pay less than equivalent real jobs, and like Sean's entry-level position, they don't provide benefits.

Manpower, the nation's largest temp agency, has more American workers on its books than Wal-Mart, the nation's largest private employer. Temporary and contingent employment is the second-fastest-growing industry in the country. And just like IKEA couches, crap jobs are disproportionately a young people's thing. Half of all temp workers in the '90s were aged twenty to thirty-four.

One variant of crap job is reserved exclusively for students and new grads. It directly drives down wages and even eliminates entry-level jobs for college graduates, while it also widens social inequality. It's the unpaid internship, an increasingly common hurdle for entry into full-time employment.

In high school and college, I served four internships at publications. Each offered the chance to learn skills and make connections I couldn't have gotten any other way—and each required that my parents support me or that I work another job at the same time. Internships fill a growing desire for practical career education among America's college students, a need that is not being met on campus. The 2004 edition of the Princeton Review's *Internship Bible* lists over 100,000 internships nationwide. According to surveys by Vault, a career-information website, 82 percent of 2005 four-year college graduates completed an internship while enrolled. The figure was up from 60 percent just ten years before. It is estimated that about half of all internships, which can last anywhere from ten weeks to nine months, are unpaid, while many others provide tiny stipends. Glam industries like music, fashion, publishing, television, film, and architecture, plus emotional draws like politics and nonprofit advocacy, are the most likely to use free intern labor. The White House doesn't pay its hundred-plus summer interns. Neither does MTV, which employs student interns in five cities year-round.

For every internship that involves mostly photocopying and surfing the Internet, there's another with potentially important duties. "Looking for a place where you can be creative? Where you can realize your potential?" goes a typical pitch. "MTV Networks is a cutting-edge company that nurtures talent and encourages its interns to succeed!" Almost everywhere, interns are given administrative tasks that would normally be accorded to entry-level assistants, fewer of whom are then hired.

Most students accept internships as the best means to a good job, and they are sacrificing to get them. Yet companies are getting plenty out of the bargain, too. Let's assume that out of 100,000 internships listed, 50,000 unpaid interns are employed nationwide each summer, full-time, for twelve weeks. At the minimum wage, they would each earn $2,472 before taxes. So their unpaid labor represents a $124 million yearly contribution to the welfare of corporate America.

Systematic research on the economic impact of internships, especially the jobs they crowd out, is hard to find. The Bureau of Labor Statistics doesn't study it. A study by the UK's National Union of Journalists in January 2006 found that an influx of unpaid graduates to the industry in that country reduced wages and patched up the gaps left by job cuts. A casual review of the job sites indicates that in highly competitive industries like media, unpaid interns far outnumber entry-level openings each year. The effect of the growth in unpaid internships on economic mobility is easy to figure. Although there are stipends and scholarships, they are hardly enough to provide opportunities to all of the young people who must work full-time to put themselves through school.

If those young people do manage to graduate, they often sign up with a temp agency while looking for full-time work. On any given day, about 2.6 million Americans get up, put on a tie or a skirt, and go to an office. They sit at a desk, file, and answer phones. Despite appearances, they don't have jobs. They're temps.

At thirty-two, Angus has been drifting in the crap-job market for ten years. It all started in 1994, when he flunked out of a Ph.D. program in linguistics at the University of Chicago, with $19,000 in student loans, and moved to New York City to live with his father. Since then, Angus has mostly temped, working in data entry for $8.50 an hour, at a Calvin Klein store for $10 an hour, doing custom word processing for $16 an hour, and as a computer support specialist for large financial firms for $20 to $30 an hour. His résumé is rounded out by stints as a self-employed computer consultant—essentially another form of temping, he says—and short tenures at a dot-com and a nonprofit, his last "real job," from which he was laid off after a year.

Angus's long haul is pretty unusual. Less than 15 percent of temp workers stick with it longer than two years. "I've had difficulty focusing," Angus admits with a sheepish smile. He says his wife, a tenure-track professor at a community college, initially saw his serial temping as "evidence of a lack of commitment." And in a way, he says, that's true. He is bothered by the "profit motive" in big corporations, the fact that his labor is enriching fat-cat CEOs. "Temping allowed me to distance myself," he said, "to say, Okay, this isn't me." The other side of that same distance, of course, allows corporations to treat temp labor worse than their own employees.

In 1998, Angus set up a website where New York–area temps can rant. They complain most often about wage lowballing. According to a 1999 report, temp agency workers under thirty-five earn on average 16.5 percent less than they would if they worked directly for the client company. Temp workers' average wages actually declined in the 1990s as the industry grew. An agency may pay a worker $10 an hour for a secretarial job for which the agency is getting $20 or $25. Or they will invite the temp to submit a lower bid than what is offered.

"I've heard of shocking treatment, as well as good things," says Angus. "The disrespectful attitude bothers me as much as the substantive abuses." He voices a common feeling among people who hold crap jobs of all kinds. What really stings, along with the actual conditions of employment, is the feeling of being jerked around and sometimes even lied to, and of having zero power to change your situation.

Once justified as a stopgap tied to market cycles, crap jobs are now a long-term strategy for cutting costs. The oxymoron "long-term temporary" is now want-ad shorthand for a job with lower pay and no benefits to offer.

Crap jobs are multiplying because they benefit companies in myriad ways. Employers can pay less into pension funds and health plans, two of their fastest-growing expenditures. Temps, contractors, and freelancers don't get bonuses or employee discounts or paid vacations. They can have their contracts terminated at any time for any reason, with a single phone call; companies don't have to go through the stress or bad publicity of mass firings. These workers may not even get invited to the office Christmas party.

Crap jobs, and the threat that companies will create even more of them, are setting the tone for the entire job market. Not only do crap jobs pay poorly, they are actually designed to stiff workers on their rights. "The very category of work is designed to get around the Fair Labor Standards Act and collective-bargaining agreements," says Suren Moodliar, of the North American Alliance for Fair Employment, a workers' rights nonprofit in

Boston. Contingent workers often lack either the means or the established right to organize, collect unemployment benefits, fight against discrimination, or take family and medical leave.

Employment agencies share liability with employers for training, enforcing safety standards, payroll, and hiring and firing crapjobbers. This means that when legal issues, like harassment or unsafe working conditions, come up, both parties can point fingers and pass the buck. The rise of contingent work opens up a big hole in the old social safety net, which depended on the cooperation of the government, organized labor, and private employers. The threat of being replaced with temps coerces all workers, even those in unions, to accept lower wages and reductions in benefits.

Temp and contract arrangements are found in every workplace, from hospitals to universities, suburban call centers to high-rise corporate offices. Practices once common to sweatshops and farm fields have crept out of the shadows and into fluorescent-lit hallways.

Crap jobs have an even more insidious permutation: permatemping. This is the practice of reclassifying full-time employees as temps. A professional employment organization, or PEO, serves as the nominal employer, allowing companies to subcontract their labor needs without physically outsourcing them. Permatemping can be ruled illegal if a court finds that a company is deliberately misclassifying people in order to avoid paying benefits.

Typically, a company will downsize on paper by "payrolling" its workers. Entire departments of full-time workers—such as computer support workers or clerical workers in hospitals—are fired. Then they are rehired, but on the payroll of the PEO, or "employee leasing firm."

Alternatively, workers like janitors or nurses may be misclassified as independent contractors when in fact their work is independent only in name; they are subject to supervision just as they would be in a conventional job, and they don't set their own pay rates. Large companies like Microsoft and Time Warner thus avoid paying these "contractors" at rates equal to what they pay their other employees, or offering benefits.

The practice of permatemping first drew national attention in the early '90s, when thousands of so-called independent contractors and temps filed a class-action suit against Microsoft. The engineers, graphic designers, and other highly skilled employees represented in the suit worked for years, full-time, at a lower pay scale and without benefits. Just like characters in a story by Dr. Seuss, the permatemps wore orange ID badges, while real, "headcount" employees got blue ones. The Orange Badges weren't invited to office parties and couldn't shop at the company software store. Most galling of all, they were barred from participating in the employee stock-purchasing plan that was making many of their coworkers rich. The Microsoft class-action suit was originally filed in 1992, and in December 2000, a judge found that the permatemps were in fact "common-law" full-time employees of Microsoft, which owed them back pay and money based on their lost stock options. The group of up to 12,000 Orange Badges was awarded over $97 million.

The law says companies must offer retirement benefits equally to all full-time employees. Companies have more legal leeway when it comes to "fringe benefits" like health care and paid vacation, yet older companies extended these benefits to all full-time employees as a matter of courtesy. Permatemping concocts a way around both law and tradition. According to one internal industry report by a PEO consulting firm, made public by Seattle's Center for a Changing Workforce, two-thirds of employees of PEOs receive no benefits.

The PEO industry's profits grew 520 percent in the 1990s. PEOs are growing even faster than temp agencies, 25 percent a year, with annual revenues of $43 billion in 2005. Advocates estimate that there are nearly 2 million permatemps nationwide.

As the Microsoft suit suggests, the rise of crap jobs is intimately related to the new economy. High-tech companies founded in the 1990s pioneered permatemping among a host of new practices designed to cut start-up costs and shift more of the risks of doing business onto employees—compensation with stock options is another example. While the dot-coms doled out much-publicized new perks to the whiz kids with irreplaceable skills, the less fortunate, and less unique, got the shaft. To add insult to injury, many high-tech permatemps have seen their jobs outsourced to other countries in the past five years.

In the mid-'90s, up to 40 percent of workers in Silicon Valley, the cradle of the new economy, were considered contingent. The field is still disproportionately young, since recent college grads are more likely to possess the most up-to-date skills. For Generation Debt, the dot-com boom bears a grim legacy, worse than any temporary market downturn. It established a model of business success where a company grows fast while offering benefits to only its core workers and spreads the risk around by paying people in stock options of unknown value. All those dot-commers were so psyched about wearing jeans to the office and playing with Nerf balls, they happily bade farewell to job security, benefits, and permanence. Now young workers are paying the price: this treatment has become the norm in all kinds of jobs.

Nor have good opportunities been easy to come by even in traditional industries. Christopher, thirty-one, is a serious, methodical, pragmatic person. Ever since his parents divorced, when he was thirteen, he and his mother have had to be very careful with money. A watershed event for him as a kid was when, "a couple of years after Dad left, Mom was able to purchase a dehumidifier for our basement as well as a VCR," he says without cracking a smile. Christopher worked and saved his way through school—no credit card debt for him. He graduated from St. John's University in Minnesota, a small Catholic school then charging over $20,000 a year in tuition, with just $8,000 in student loan debt. Then he paid it down, and paid off a car loan, while working at a small printing press, first as a shipping-and-receiving clerk and then as a proofreader.

Christopher has high standards for his career, like me and just about everyone I've talked with. "It's necessary for me to believe in and be motivated by what I'm doing," he says simply. While marking time at the press, he considered his options carefully. The desire to be a professional, make a good living, and use his

academic skills led him to enter a graduate program in information science at the University of Minnesota in Minneapolis, his
hometown. He borrowed its entire cost, $20,000.

When Christopher first enrolled in library school, he antici-
pated a run of retirements and therefore new openings in Minnesota's library system. Instead, state budget cutbacks, here as
around the country, meant that full-time professional openings,
which can pay starting salaries over $40,000, were scarce. "Qual-
ified and experienced people are back out on the market. I'm
competing against people who have already worked in the field,"
he says. For the past two years, Christopher has been at the Minnesota Historical Society, earning just $23,000 a year plus bene-
fits. While he doesn't regret getting his master's, it has not yet
proven to be worth the debt.

The specter of Christopher hanging around, waiting for some of
Minnesota's elderly librarians to pack it in, raises a sore subject.
The college-grad job market is dominated, at least symbolically,
by the type of absorbing, cerebral jobs that people hold on to well
past traditional retirement age. Could the prospects of people
coming after the Boomers be distorted by the impact of having
America's largest generation stay at their posts?

The AARP reports that 69 percent of employees now over forty-
five plan to work past sixty-five, partly to cover the rising cost of
health care. By 2010, more than half the workforce is projected to
be forty or older, one-third more than in 1980. Young hopefuls, especially in areas like education and the arts, can expect to compete
with many more older, experienced workers than in times past.

Yet another kind of job instability young people are experiencing is geographical. These days, people are expected to move across the country to find their first, second, or third job. Opportunities for educated workers are as concentrated in major metropolitan areas as they have ever been.

Christopher faces a lack of library openings partly because he's unwilling to move out of Minnesota. Many more young people are leaving the cities where they grew up or went to college. Richard Florida, in *The Rise of the Creative Class,* argues that with employer-employee attachment weakening, it is increasingly important for both workers and companies to cluster in areas with highly educated labor pools and lots of opportunities. Rather than move for one job, people move to a place with lots of jobs.

This mobility, however, is an expensive privilege. Young professionals concentrating in certain areas drive rents up out of reach. The Los Angeles and New York areas, perennial creative-class meccas, have the highest percentages of people who are officially burdened by housing costs, meaning they are paying more than 30 percent of their gross income. If you have a messy financial life, with multiple student loans and credit card bills, moving out of contact with your creditors can lead to late payments and even defaulting. Moving far away from family deprives young people of both material and emotional support.

Transportation is yet another pricey necessity of the mobile life. Employment in most of our country's growing population centers requires a car. Commutes are getting longer as real estate goes up. Car payments and unexpected repairs are a common cause of credit card debt among young people.

. . .

Despite all this, crap jobs, the wave of the future, aren't all bad. As many new-economy gurus have noted, temps can rack up much more varied experience than was common in previous generations, and pick up valuable skills along the way. Creative workers like graphic designers, interior decorators, public relations specialists, and event producers have followed the lead of actors, musicians, and writers, accepting freelancing as a way of life. According to the Bureau of Labor Statistics, true independent contractors, 6.4 percent of the working population, actually earn more than people with equivalent qualifications and full-time jobs. Real self-employment means setting your own work rates and dictating how much and when you work. Unlike other nontraditional workers, the self-employed report preferring their arrangements to full-time employment.

There are a couple of not-so-intangible benefits missing from this rosy picture, though. Respect is one. A reliable income is another. A built-in work community, with easy access to colleagues and mentors, and a clear path to advancement are two more. The difference between my occupation as an editorial freelancer and having an actual job became glaring during two short stints, one of five weeks and one of three months, as a contract worker doing research at start-up magazines. Both times, I jumped at the chance for a paycheck as a break from the unpredictability of freelancing. Both assignments had all the hardest elements of full-time jobs. I put in sixteen-, eighteen-, even twenty-four-hour days, leapt to answer my bosses' queries nights and weekends, learned to perform tasks far outside my original job description, and generally acted like a loyal, go-getting employee who hopes to move up in the company.

Only there was no company. These gigs weren't real jobs. There were no benefits and certainly no guarantees. Each stint, in fact, ended abruptly when the projects lost financing and folded. My former colleagues were scattered to the four winds, hard to reach for a reference or a networking opportunity.

After the second contract ended, my perspective had changed. Most of the dozen or so publications I have worked for as a writer, fact checker, and copy editor could not get by without the contributions of hungry young freelancers. I know that I have been very, very lucky in this game. I know it is natural for those of us starting out to have to hustle and struggle. Of course I am grateful for the chance to do what I love. I have even been fortunate to find amazing mentors within the casual editor-freelancer relationship.

But if I weren't so lucky, I would really be in trouble. In the past three years, I've earned as little as $10 an hour or 10 cents a word. (The National Writers Union reported in 2002 that freelance writers' per-word rates have declined 50 percent in real dollars since the mid-1960s.) I sometimes have to submit multiple invoices and wait months to get paid. The entire journalism industry—with its expressed values of truth, justice, and the public interest—operates on the backs of people like me who have to cobble together jobs to make ends meet. What am I really building this way, when my name is only as good as my last assignment?

Freedom and flexibility are the inarguable advantages of working for no one but yourself. Yet there are always trade-offs. To take just one example, I hope to have a child in the next seven years or so. I can't realistically expect paid maternity leave or unemployment benefits. More subtly, because unlike my partner I have no fixed income and no post to return to, the pressure will be on me to stay home with the baby even if I'd rather return to work. I am missing both the benefits and the status that come with traditional employment.

Amelia, twenty-nine, has worked several jobs that could squarely be put in the crap category. The instability has hurt her more than the low pay or lack of benefits. Fresh out of the University of Tennessee, Knoxville, she took a part-time job as a theatrical costumer in Atlanta, making ends meet by selling jewelry and doing other odd jobs. Then she became a travel agent and transferred to Chicago. The gig had glamorous perks but few benefits. "It was supposed to be a commission job, but very few people ever met the minimum" required to earn a commission, she said. "So basically I was making $19,000 a year." Amelia left the travel agency in June 2001 and found a $26,000 job at a company that imported French bath products. She was downsized shortly after September 11.

Amelia is far from alone. The phrase "jobless recovery" popped up in the economic lexicon sometime in the early 1990s. What it means is that, breaking historical patterns, the U.S. economy has come back from the last two recessions, at the beginning of the '90s and the beginning of the century, without adding many new jobs. *"The decline in the overall number of jobs this far into the recovery is unprecedented in the post–World War II era"* (emphasis in original), concluded the progressive Center on Budget and Policy Priorities in a 2003 report.

As of August 2004, the U.S. economy had seen eleven straight quarters of growth, yet there were still almost a million fewer jobs than at the beginning of 2001, just before the recession began. Intensifying the pain, Congress has cut unemployment benefits several times, from over fifteen months of federal benefits in the 1970s to just six months today (some states provide thirteen more emergency weeks). Because of new rules and the rise of contingent work, the majority of workers have trouble collecting any benefits at all.

"At first it was like a party," Amelia said of her downsizing at age twenty-six. "I got the severance check and went out. Everyone I knew was losing their jobs, going out late and drinking." Then the party ended; she was out of work for over nine months. "It was just blindingly apparent that I was never going to get a job in Chicago. Everyone I knew was looking for work. I couldn't even get a retail job, because people were applying with years of experience."

Amelia went from zero to $5,000 in credit card debt and had an emotional breakdown. She returned home to the small town of Norris, Tennessee, and looked for work for three more months, finally taking a job selling classified ads for a local supermarket circular. With her parents' support and the help of $10 weekly sessions with a student therapist, she got her personal and financial life under control. She now lives in Los Angeles and works for a small publishing company, making slightly more than before she was downsized. She has started selling clothes on eBay on the side, as a kind of insurance against being fired again. Amelia's own "jobless recovery" was just as hard psychologically as economically. "I turned twenty-seven while I was home and I was freaking out that I was going nowhere with my life," she remembers.

. . .

The odds are certainly against college grads' finding a happy, stable, and well-paying career and planning for a secure future. Yet as each subject I interviewed has readily admitted, our generation's economic failure to thrive also has roots in our own choices. For example, recall that BLS study: the sole dimension in which young people of the '90s were doing better than young people of the '70s was in "having a larger array of entertainment and other goods to purchase."

Well, goods are not always so great. Today what's considered a basic standard of living is creeping upward. Sixty bucks a month for cell phones with text messaging, $700 personal computers, and $45 a month for high-speed Internet access are deemed essential by eighteen- and nineteen-year-olds in college, to say nothing of those in the working world. In the course of my research I interviewed several people who were under twenty-four, unemployed or underemployed, and heavily in debt, living with their parents, or even collecting public assistance, but who still had their own personal cell phones. Add to these high-tech tools a little entertainment, like $90 a month for cable TV, a $250 Xbox, and a $299 MP3 player (storing 10,000 songs at 99 cents each).

Spending like this leads to credit card hangovers, an average of $4,088 for indebted twenty-five-to-thirty-four-year-olds in 2001. The bankruptcy rate among those aged twenty-five to thirty-four rose in the 1990s; we became the second most likely group to declare bankruptcy, just behind thirty-five-to-forty-four-year-olds.

Anittah, twenty-eight, has worked for the past three years in online credit card marketing, "increasing the national consumer debt one person at a time," she jokes. She says that avoiding the problems connected to easy credit requires both foreknowledge and self-control. "People are not reading the fine print. They're not making smart choices, not paying attention." Anittah knows whereof she speaks. She ran up $12,000 in credit card debt starting in college, and took three years to pay it off despite making a consistently good salary. "I would see a cool pair of shoes in a magazine and just pop online and buy them. It was too easy." Today, using the same organizational talents she displays on the job, she delays gratification. When she sees something she likes, she'll tear out the page and put it in a binder that she goes through once a month.

We twenty-somethings have grown up marinated in the most aggressive advertising and marketing environment ever known. Harvard professor Juliet Schor's 2004 book *Born to Buy: The Commercialized Child and the New Consumer Culture*, details how marketers in the past two decades charted the path to parents' pockets by burning brand awareness into ever younger and more impressionable minds. Research she cites suggests that the more television ads a child sees, the more insecure, anxious, and depressed she becomes.

A channel-surfing restlessness fuels the consumerism of those like Nita, the dollar-store worker, who blew ten grand she didn't have on restaurant meals and new CDs in one summer. We want it all, we are told we can have it all, and we are handed the means to get it all, even if we have to pay it all back with compound interest. Financial independence requires bucking the crowd, and maybe even our parents' advice, and mastering the anxieties we sucked in from the boob tube.

Compulsive shopping is only one symptom of an underlying imbalance between what young people have and what they dream about. Finding and keeping the right job today is harder partly because our definition of the right job has gotten bigger. Personally, I would be miserable doing work that wasn't suited to my talents and that I didn't absolutely love, and most of my interviewees feel the same way. A major source of career dissatisfaction for college grads is not the low salaries or the long hours but the contrast between our bright and shiny expectations and reality. "My generation, we just want more," as Terry, twenty-two, told me.

This idealism starts early. In national surveys, up to 80 percent of teenagers say they would like to be professionals, far more than will actually attain that rank. In a 2001 nationwide survey of high school juniors and seniors, 72 percent said they'd already chosen a career. The majority chose prestigious or creative fields like medicine and the arts. Just as in that 1980s antidrug public service announcement, "Nobody says, I wanna be a junkie when I grow up," nobody picked retail or fast food.

Although the highest-growth industries—like health care, education, and technology—were the most popular, teens gave overwhelmingly personal reasons for choosing them. Three-fourths answered that the job was something they liked, or that they've "always been interested in," or a similar personal reason. Only

8 percent said they chose a job because it paid well or was in a growing field.

These kids, along with most of those I talk to, are taking to heart the maxim "Do what you love, the money will follow." A best-selling advice book of the same title, published in 1987, popularized the phrase. Marsha Sinetar, an organizational psychologist, drew on the Buddhist concept of "right livelihood" for her inspirational tome, but added that key American ingredient: the money.

If my generation holds one piece of conventional wisdom in common, this is it. Having a true calling, and making bank at the same time, is one of our culture's highest values, just as in the Sprite slogan "Obey Your Thirst." The source is important: all too often, marketers deliberately equate independence and self-expression with consumption. In response to this confusion of values, we tend to dismiss as a chump anyone who toils at an unfulfilling job merely to make money, but on the other hand, money is considered a righteous mark of true success. The idea harks back to what Max Weber called the Protestant ethic of godliness through hard work.

In that same survey of high school seniors, they overwhelmingly said that their parents—not teachers, guidance counselors, or even the media—had been the biggest source of career information. If we want to do what we love, that could be because our parents told us that was the right thing to want.

Our parents prospered like no generation before them on the ethic of self-expression. Then they lovingly passed that wisdom down to us, with a new culture of parenting that emphasized individuality, self-esteem, and "quality time." But this intensive attention sometimes had an edge to it. Parents had fewer children than in the past and were far more invested in the success of each one. The message "Be the best!" sometimes drowned out "Be who you are."

The children of the educated were often hyperscheduled and pushed to achieve from preschool on. This perfectionism and pressure came with a steady diet of luxuries unheard of in previous times. Some of us learned to depend on external rewards for motivation, rather than insight into ourselves.

Now we are smacking into the awareness that not only can't we afford all the stuff we were raised with, we may never be the stars we were told we were, or achieve what our parents had. It would be hard for any American generation to accept, but it's especially hard for this one.

"Daphne," the twenty-nine-year-old daughter of Filipino immigrants, recently left a Ph.D. program in medical anthropology at Case Western Reserve University in Cleveland, in order to work full-time in a research lab and pay down $20,000 in student loan debt.

Daphne made an emotional decision to go to grad school after a few years in the working world in order to study something she loved, but since then she has faced some tough realities. "Before, I thought as long as I work hard and study hard there'll be a job for me. In college that's how it works. You study hard and get a

good grade. Recently I realized you have to take into consideration the job situation. You can't necessarily just do what makes
you happy. You also have to be realistic about it."

In today's precarious economic climate, following your heart
can lead to low income, unemployment, and a lifetime of debt.
For too many, received ideas about achievement and the connection between effort and reward lead to real disappointment.

This dissatisfaction is in some ways a luxurious complaint. It's
important to maintain a distinction between the real obstacles
too many kids face, like poor academic preparation, a violent
neighborhood, or a lack of role models, and the problems created
by privileged young adults in our own minds. That doesn't mean
that young Princeton's lament—he wants to "make a difference to
the human race"—is wholly without merit.

Megan, twenty-eight, grew up in Minneapolis and majored in
art history at the University of Minnesota. In the six years since
graduating from college, she has held eight jobs, most of which
she left voluntarily. "My first job was at a children's museum," she
explains. "I hated it. I disagreed with the museum's priorities,
how they spent money and time. I was really idealistic." Looking
back, she sees "it was a fine job."

Quitting after nine months, Megan started searching for her
bliss. She had loved a bookbinding class in college, so she took a
job at a bindery that was "basically a factory job." That lasted
two months. She had been a teaching assistant in women's studies, so she got a job working at a center for substance-addicted
young women, which ended over personality conflicts. This was

followed by another, similar job, which lasted over a year, until she quit to work at a small nonprofit arts organization. Megan loved it, but she had taken a big pay cut and had to work part-time at a thrift store to cover her rent. Then she fell in love and impulsively moved to Los Angeles. When I first spoke with her, she was working as an assistant to a self-employed event planner and earning between $2,400 and $3,000 a month before taxes, less than she had at her first job. When I checked in with her six months later, she had just been fired and was looking for steady work with benefits, never mind her ideal career.

"Why was I so restless?" Megan says. "I still ask myself that today. I was never anywhere long enough to really feel like I was progressing financially."

The life-as-quest approach can have costly consequences when it involves student loan debt. "Brandon," twenty-six, has followed the new typical path to adulthood. As with many of the people I interviewed, recounting his life in just the four years since college takes a half-hour phone conversation. After high school, he studied saxophone, before deciding that a life of endless practicing wasn't for him. He graduated with a degree in sociology. Brandon's parents are divorced; his mother is a teacher and his father is a school psychologist. They encouraged him and his sister to pursue their dreams. "It wasn't a question of *if* I would go to college but *where*."

After college, Brandon taught public school for two years in Houston with the federal program Americorps, which paid for his master's in education. With a blooming interest in social justice, he then moved to Philadelphia and worked at a reproductive-rights nonprofit, presenting sex education programs in schools. He was searching for a career that would unite his values and his skills.

Brandon was laid off from the sex ed job because of federal budget cuts, and while collecting unemployment he decided it was time to go back to grad school. He borrowed the full cost of a second master's in statistics. "My rationale [for borrowing] at the time was that the master's would make me a really good candidate for a Ph.D. program, so my next seven years would be paid for," Brandon said.

Indeed, he received a fellowship to a Ph.D. program in sociology in southern California. But the program, and especially the conservative Orange County surroundings, didn't suit him. We first spoke in November 2004; Brandon had worked hard campaigning for the Democrats and he longed to be out of school, doing activism full-time. The next time I talked with him, only two months later, he had quit school after three semesters for a post teaching and developing curricula at a charter school back in Philadelphia. His $60,000 in student loans would soon come into repayment. Like most of the people I've talked with, Brandon has little to his name besides a car. "People told me to go to a [cheaper] state school for college and I wish I'd listened," he says. "I didn't know my trajectory in life." It's unclear whether he does even now.

Working-class and especially immigrant families may be less likely to support their educated children's quest for a soul-fulfilling career over something more practical. Usman, twenty-eight, immigrated with his parents from Pakistan when he was a child. He has done everything he could up to now to maximize the economic returns on his education. Though he was his high school valedictorian, he chose to attend a community college on scholarship and live at home for two years. When he transferred to the University of Illinois at Chicago to complete his B.A., he had to take out loans for the first time. "At that moment I began to feel a sense of urgency that I had to choose a major that had a payoff," he remembers. "It was the late 1990s computer craze. At the time it seemed flexible, exciting, cutting-edge, a challenge."

After graduating with a B.A. in computer science and spending two years as a programmer, Usman found that just the opposite was true. "I had grown tired of working for corporate America. I was stuck in a job that was not challenging or meaningful." Many of his colleagues, also immigrants or first-generation Americans, had chosen the tech industry for pragmatic reasons like his own. Now they found themselves simultaneously sick of their jobs and worried about keeping them. "Anytime the organization announced restructuring or downsizing, you saw fear in their eyes," he said of his coworkers, mostly settled down with families, kids, and mortgages. "That's an awful thing, to go through your life doing something you don't want to do and fearing losing it."

Usman decided to quit before he got tied down. He dreams of an exciting, altruistic career coordinating aid programs in developing countries like his native Pakistan. When we first talked, he was facing a roadblock. Good jobs in his desired field require an MBA, but his only option for financing it was taking out $25,000 to $40,000 in loans. With that kind of debt, he felt, he would be obligated to return to his previous job for a few years after getting his degree just to pay off his debt. That would leave him in his mid-thirties, no closer to his goal. "I find it, if not disheartening, at least ironic," he said. "If your only option is taking out loans, it sucks you right back into the system."

His parents took a traditional view: he should work at his chosen career, move up the corporate ladder, and get married. His common sense tells him not to get in over his head in debt. The prevailing culture, and his heart, tell him that he should find a way to do what he loves, no matter the cost or the time it takes.

Look at Brandon's, Megan's, and Usman's stories one way and you see idealistic young adults working to help others and fulfill their own potential, while contending with an uncertain job market and outsized educational costs. Look at them another way and you see irresponsible dilettantes who have been spoiled until they expect everything to go perfectly. Both readings hold a truth, and the one you choose may depend on what generation you belong to, not to mention your own path in life.

It might make us anxious college kids feel better to realize that Ralph Waldo Emerson nailed our problem in 1841, in his essay "Self-Reliance."

If our young men miscarry in their first enterprises, they lose all heart. . . . If the finest genius studies at one of our colleges, and is not installed in an office within one year afterwards in the cities

or suburbs of Boston or New York, it seems to his friends and to
himself that he is right in being disheartened, and in complaining
the rest of his life.

Emerson compares the easy discouragement of these upper-
class hothouse flowers to the strength of a working-class son who
pursues the historical version of self-employment: "[He] *teams it,
farms it, peddles,* keeps a school, preaches, edits a newspaper, goes
to Congress, buys a township, and so forth." In self-directed action,
Emerson writes, lies satisfaction: "He does not postpone his life,
but lives already. He has not one chance, but a hundred chances."

In the great American philosopher's generous vision, no youthful effort need go to waste, as long as one remembers that nothing
is merely preparation. Everything is experience.

Young people have always been expected to work hard and pay
their dues, and that's as it should be. Part of becoming an adult is
finding meaningful work that allows you to contribute to society.
Now that the nature of work and the employer-employee relationship is fundamentally changing, this generation is finding
that task harder than ever.

Most college-educated young people allow themselves to be
discouraged just as Emerson describes: Did I choose the right job?
Why can't I find a job? Why did I lose my job? We berate ourselves with these questions, when the time might be better spent
listening to our inner voice, wherever it takes us. Meanwhile, the
question that few of us are asking is the one that might bring us
all together: Why aren't there more good jobs?

FIVE

. . . Without Benefits

"Uh-oh. It's never good when we get mail from the benefits department."

RETIRE NOW OR WE'LL INVEST YOUR PENSION IN HAITIAN PENNY STOCKS.

"Have you noticed a change in tone lately?"

—*DILBERT* COMIC STRIP,
JULY 6, 1994

The original brief of this book was to talk about today's bum deals—the student loan payment, the credit card bill, the low-wage job. I'm a journalist, concerned with the texture of everyday experience. I certainly have no business making economic predictions, or any other kind.

Yet as I explored further what it really meant to be part of Generation Debt, I found I had no choice but to peer into the future. We live in an age of what political scientist Jacob Hacker calls "the Great Risk Shift," in which individuals are compelled to take more responsibility for their own fate. Guarantees that over the past century were provided by employers and the government are being withdrawn. The only way for us to manage this raft of new risks is to plan better than anyone has ever planned before.

Yet as Bruce Ackerman and Anne Alstott write in their 1999 book *The Stakeholder Society,* "Just at the moment we expect young adults to make responsible life-shaping decisions, we do not afford them the resources that they need to take a responsible long-term perspective. Forced to put bread on the table and pay the rent, almost all young adults are squeezed into short-term thinking as they confront an open-ended future."

The stars aligned twice in the twentieth century for legislated social protections in this country: the New Deal and the War on Poverty. In general, Americans have never felt comfortable with the idea of a full social welfare state. Over many generations and through much struggle, organized labor persuaded private companies to fill in the gaps with family health care coverage, pensions, sick leave, family leave, and paid vacations.

In the past two decades, however, both the labor movement and the system it helped build have gone threadbare. Young people are feeling the chill now and will even more later on, as we cope with aging parents and eventually our own retirement security.

By the early 1960s, a solid majority of Americans claimed health care coverage through employers. The Medicare and Medicaid amendments to the Social Security Act, in 1965, took care of the elderly and the poor, who were then the most likely to be uninsured.

In the past few decades, medical costs have soared. The causes include new drugs, new procedures, new technologies, and longer life spans, not to mention the rise of chronic conditions like obesity, diabetes, and heart disease. An increasingly for-profit industry spends more on marketing, too. Health care, particularly the enormous bills for Medicare and Medicaid, is busting state and federal budgets.

Health insurance outpaces most other business expenses in growth. In 2004, for the first time, health care became the single most expensive employee benefit, accounting for 33 percent of the total value of all benefits.

Businesses, especially small businesses, are shifting rising health care costs onto employees through higher deductibles, premiums, and co-payments. Employers also save by scaling back coverage, excluding new hires, part-time workers, and temps. The upshot is that the percentage of people whose health care is covered through their jobs dropped off in the past two decades. The proportion of Americans under sixty-five with employment-based health insurance peaked at around 70 percent in 1987. In 2004, it was sixty-one percent. An estimated 3.4 million *employed* people lost their health insurance just between 2000 and 2003, and the number of uninsured Americans stood at 45.8 million in 2004, up from 45 million in 2003.

Although it's not often framed this way, lack of insurance is a youth issue. About 30 percent of Americans aged nineteen to twenty-nine consistently have no health insurance, double the percentage of the population at large, and more than any other age group.

"Jennie," twenty-four, grew up working-class in a small Oregon town and now lives in Portland. Since earning her GED in 1998, she has held several low-wage jobs, including three posts as a day camp counselor on overseas military bases. She takes community college classes when she can fit them in around her jobs.

For most of the six years since she left home, Jennie has not had health insurance. State medical plans for the low-income are least likely to cover working, childless adults like her. "I was on the Oregon Health Plan for two months and then I missed one $12 premium and they kicked me off," she explains. "I was only able to get on it before because I made hardly any money as a nanny, like $600 to $700 a month. Now I make too much"— $1,000 a month as a day care worker.

In any case, the state program, like many around the country, has recently cut the "extras" Jennie needs most—dental care and mental health services. Jennie says she has had problems with depression and alcohol in the past and recovered with the help of a therapist, a source of support she misses. "I'm doing okay now, but it would be nice to talk to somebody," she says.

Her more immediate problem is her teeth. "I just have a lot of cavities," Jennie explains. "I had a root canal and I didn't get a cap put on it. I can chew but the tooth is pretty much gone." She has looked into getting cheaper care at a dental school or possibly traveling out of state, or even to Canada, for services she can afford out of pocket. "It just sucks to look in the mirror and I have a whole bunch of metal, I have a big space in the back, and in one of my two front teeth there's a big black cavity that needs to be attacked. You can see it when I smile. I'm afraid that it's all going to crumble to pieces." If she doesn't get help soon, Jennie's teeth will mark her as poor all her life. In the short term, they dim the possibility of her getting a higher-paying job.

. . .

Why are young and healthy people so likely to be uninsured? It's not irresponsibility or delusions of immortality. Only 3 percent of young people say they are uninsured because they voluntarily declined coverage. Just as many young people as older adults say in surveys that health insurance is important to them in choosing a job. And most young people sign up for employer-based health care when it's both offered and affordable.

The sheer number of uninsured young people suggests that all of them are not "between-college" youth. They are kids just trying to make it in the new economy. They graduated, took time off, got laid off, moved cross-country, temped, freelanced, worked part-time—the more changes, the more likely they were to lose their coverage. Your nineteenth birthday is the cutoff for coverage as a dependent under most employer-based health plans. Only full-time college students can usually continue to be covered under their parents' plans after that age, and they almost always age out after twenty-three. From what we've already seen of the employment situation for young people, it's easy to understand how school-to-work transitions can include disruption in health coverage.

Does it really matter if young, healthy people can't see a doctor? True, we are less likely to suffer from chronic conditions, but we are much more likely than any other age group to visit the emergency room, whether because of car accidents, sports injuries, or even violence. There are 3.5 million pregnancies each year among the 21 million women aged nineteen to twenty-nine. Just the hospital delivery, let alone prenatal care, can cost over $10,000. One-third of all HIV diagnoses are made in people aged nineteen to twenty-nine. The nonpartisan Institute of Medicine estimates that 1,930 uninsured adults ages twenty-five to thirty-four die prematurely each year because they didn't get proper medical care.

The United States spent 15.3 percent of its gross domestic product—15.3 percent of its total economic output—on health care in 2003. That's proportionately more than any other rich, industrialized country. Yet we are the only rich, industrialized country that doesn't have universal health care. Some underinsured Americans have special federal and state programs. The elderly have Medicare; children have State Children's Health Insurance Programs, created in the 1990s. But young working people have been muddling through without any kind of assistance.

In effect, taxpayers subsidize the business plans of crap-job companies by providing emergency-room-based "health care" to their employees. Wal-Mart has come under attack in recent years for just this practice, as state governments started to add up how many Wal-Mart employees and their children depend on Medicaid and other state programs for care. Some localities accused Wal-Mart of encouraging its employees to sign up for government programs for low-income people. The company refuses to disclose how many of their employees they actually cover, nor can they explain how people are supposed to afford $133 to $264 in monthly premiums on a cashier's wages of $1,200 a month.

It's not just less educated, low-wage workers getting by without insurance. Katy, a thirty-year-old violinist in New York, graduated from Lamont School of Music in Colorado. She works giving music lessons and performs with bluegrass, punk, and gypsy-style bands. Katy had had no health insurance for three years when she had an abnormal Pap smear in October 2004. Although the result turned out to be benign, the bill for lab tests and an outpatient procedure came to $3,500.

According to the 2004 book *Critical Condition,* by Donald L. Bartlett and James B. Steele, uninsured people are routinely billed three, four, even ten times more than an insurance company whose policyholder has exactly the same treatment. Big insurance companies can negotiate for group discounts. In the case of Medicare, the government tells hospitals how much they are going to reimburse, not vice versa. Hospitals, which are increasingly for-profit and owned by large corporations, make up the difference, and absorb the costs of the many who don't pay at all with higher prices on the uninsured.

When Katy got her bill, she had to ask her mother, a retired civil servant, for a loan. Several musician friends later threw her a "Katy's Cervix Benefit and 30th Birthday Party" to help her pay her mother back. "It's so weird to ask for help from your friends," she told me. "It's hard to believe I'm not in a position to take care of myself even though I work pretty hard."

About half of young people with gaps in their health coverage say they have gone without needed medical care. Surveys show that uninsured people skimp on primary and preventive care, missing the chance to catch problems early. Overall, people without insurance receive about half as much medical care as those with insurance. Two-thirds of those with a gap in their health coverage said they had skipped a checkup, had problems paying a bill, missed a prescription, or avoided tests or seeing a specialist because of cost. They are four times more likely to use the emergency room as their main source of medical care, although an emergency room visit can cost $1,000, compared with a $10 co-pay for an insured person to visit the doctor. Some young women are getting by without optimal reproductive health care or reliable birth control.

Ironically, young adults have the lowest health care costs of any age group—around $1,800 per capita in 2004, compared with $5,000 for fifty-to-sixty-four-year-olds. Sara Collins, a researcher with the nonprofit Commonwealth Fund, who has authored many reports on young adults and health care, says, "If you were to require that employers include young adults in their plans, the overall costs of those plans could drop just because you're adding a healthier, younger group of people to the risk pool."

Instead, the economics of private insurance discourage the young from buying into the system. Katy has learned her lesson the hard way, but she still doesn't see how she's going to be able to afford insurance. "For somebody like me who's just hustling up every little freaking thing I can, and having to pay all my own taxes, it seems a little bit excessive." The cheapest basic coverage option for uninsured people in New York City is Healthy NY, a state program for low-income employed adults. It costs $164 a month without prescriptions, and you must make less than $23,800 before taxes to be eligible, which is a tough sum to live on in the city. On the private market, premiums are higher and coverage is skimpier. In 2004, annual private premiums averaged $9,950 for families and $3,695 for singles.

. . .

Even for people with good overall health, getting by without insurance often means acquiring debt. Over one-quarter of families where someone was uninsured reported in a 2003 survey that they had to "change their way of life significantly" to pay medical bills. If you are young and uninsured and the unthinkable happens, you could drag down your entire family with you into debt.

Before a law passed in 2005 made it much harder for middle-class people to discharge their debts in Chapter 7 bankruptcy, doctors' bills were the leading cause of personal bankruptcy. Amber had grown up in a middle-class African-American family. In 1995, she was twenty-four and was getting her teaching credential at Hayward State University in the Bay Area when she developed blood clots and a growth in her brain. She went temporarily blind, had several operations, and had a shunt put in the base of her spine. She had been working full-time to put herself through school yet had no health insurance. "When the bills came, I wrote letters to each doctor asking them to reduce the bill," she says. "I think it went from $80,000 to $72,000. So I declared bankruptcy."

Despite the seriousness of her ordeal, Amber, who now works as a community organizer and is getting her doctorate in education, has been uninsured for three of the past ten years. "I looked into COBRA after my last job, but it was $260 a month," she says. "Since I have a preexisting condition, it cost more." (COBRA is a federal program providing interim health coverage at group rates for those who have lost employer-based care.) Facing nearly $100,000 in debt for her education, including two master's degrees as well as the doctorate, and $9,000 in credit card debt, Amber can't afford her health.

Young people with serious medical histories face complex economic challenges. In 1999, at the age of twenty-one, in the middle of her senior year at Brandeis, Samantha Eisenstein was diagnosed with a rare form of bone cancer seen most often in children and young adults, Ewing's sarcoma. She withdrew from school and moved back to New York City to be treated at Memorial Sloan-Kettering hospital. She returned to finish up her final semester in January 2001, only to be diagnosed with cancer again, this time a precursor to leukemia induced by her previous chemotherapy. She went through a second grueling course of chemo and a bone marrow transplant. Now three years in remission, she tells her story briskly.

"When I was finished with all that, I was twenty-four and went up to grad school at Middlebury," she said. "I was still on my mom's insurance, but I was about to be too old for that, and someone with my history can't go a week without it." In the nick of time, Samantha found a job with a nonprofit public health organization that included full health coverage. Samantha saw other young adult survivors of cancer going through serious financial obstacles to claiming their independence, on top of the intense emotions that come from beating a life-threatening disease.

"Anybody graduating from college knows it's hard to find a job and pay rent," Samantha says. "For young adult survivors, you may have to explain to somebody a three-year gap on your résumé. Everything catches up with you—my student loans came out of deferment. Medically, although the immediate life-and-death stuff is over, there is a still a risk for things to happen. Residual medical bills still linger and you start accruing new ones."

As the prognosis for many types of childhood cancer improves, a whole new group of former patients is entering adulthood, while most resources for cancer survivors are still geared to people in midlife. One in 900 young adults is a survivor of childhood cancer. One of the few large-scale studies of this population, published in 2004, found that 16 percent were without health coverage. The uninsured were less likely than those with coverage to visit a cancer specialist or even get a general checkup. This is true even though they face long-term, significant risks to their health for ten to twenty years after entering remission.

In 2003, Samantha cofounded Surviving And Moving Forward: The SAMFund for Young Adult Survivors of Cancer. Their mission is to give out grants and scholarships for student loan bills, education and professional training, rent, car payments, residual medical bills, and even groceries. "We want to help people go on and pursue their goals and become as productive as they can," she says.

Cancer isn't the only serious health concern young people face. More than 20,000 people with congenital heart disease turn nineteen each year. Thousands more people in their twenties suffer from diabetes, asthma, mental illness, and other conditions that may cause them to be barred from private insurance programs. One in five disabled young adults lacks coverage.

. . .

Although inadequate health coverage disproportionately affects the young, it doesn't require a solution that targets them specifically. A national health care plan with universal coverage would take care of the problem for students, temps, and low-wage workers alike.

The good news is that national health care would probably be cheaper than what we have now. Marketing and administrative costs would be reduced, and the government could negotiate for cost control, as the Medicare program already does. Britain and Canada, both of which have widely recognized universal systems with high standards of care, spend less than we do while maintaining higher life expectancies and lower infant mortality rates. Canada's national insurance system spends 9.9 percent of GDP on health care, while Britain's nationally owned system of hospitals and clinics costs just 7.7 percent.

The bad news: A national plan lies far from the political horizon. A national health care program has been seriously attempted and defeated six times in the past century, beginning during the First World War. Today, insurance companies, pharmaceutical companies, for-profit hospitals, and investors holding stock in biotech companies all have economic stakes in the current, cash-hemorrhaging system. These powerful lobbies spectacularly defeated the Clinton health care plan back in 1993. If we are waiting for a centralized, rational solution to the health care crisis, we might be waiting a long time.

Health care is only the most immediate worry for those of us stuck in the crap-job market. Employer spending on benefits of all kinds has dropped over the past two decades. The rise in health care costs led employers to cut other kinds of benefits, and target number one has been the private pension.

The math involved in retirement planning could give anyone a headache. The basic principle to keep in mind here is that the point of retirement planning is to cushion you in your old age against uncertainty. When it comes to retirement investments, investing with too much risk is like not planning at all. With this in mind, the safest retirement plan is probably a stack of gold bars. Social Security, until recently, was a close second; the government has made good on its promise of a regular, certain, monthly payment to seniors for sixty-eight years. But the Social Security Administration makes clear that retirement planning should be a "three-legged stool," with support provided by the government, private pensions, and personal savings. This stool is starting to look a little wobbly.

In the world of retirement planning, individuals have begun absorbing far more risk than was common in our mother's or grandmothers' day. There are two types of private pensions, and they differ greatly in the amount of security they provide. The more generous kind, known as defined-benefit (DB), and traditionally offered by large employers, guarantees you a certain percentage of your salary at retirement for life. This means an indefinite financial pledge from your employer. These days, DB pensions seem to be known only to executives and public employees.

The other kind of pension is defined-contribution (DC). In these plans, you receive a single payment at retirement, equaling what you saved while employed, plus matching contributions by the employer, plus the returns, if any, from investing those savings. When you get this lump sum, it is up to you to figure out how to make it last for however long you may live. The only completely safe way to do this is to purchase a tax-deferred annuity, a contract with a private insurance company that imitates Social Security by paying out a certain percentage each year until you turn one hundred, or die.

DC plans are a lot riskier for the employee and cheaper for the employer. Many so-called DC plans have low contributions from employers and are little more than employer-sponsored savings accounts. The shift from DB to DC plans looks a lot like the shift from financial aid grants to student loans, and it happened for similar risk-shift reasons. In 1979, according to the Economic Policy Institute, 30 million workers were covered by defined-benefit plans, 14 million by defined-contribution; in 1998, 45 million had defined-contribution, only 25 million defined-benefit. The pension system has also become less equitable, as people getting the big bucks are more likely to have fat pension packages, too. While half of workers overall had some kind of pension in 2000, that figure was only 18 percent for the poorest workers, versus 73 percent for the richest. At least a third of workers never hold a job that boasts a pension.

As the traditional pension declined, the government introduced different types of tax-deferred savings accounts. The employer-sponsored 401(k) and the individual retirement account, or IRA, shift responsibility for retirement security from businesses back to private citizens. The 401(k) and IRA were introduced only in the 1980s, so we don't have good long-term statistics on how much security they can provide for workers through retirement. But economic projections, behavioral studies, and back-of-the-envelope calculations provide some food for thought.

In the case of 401(k)s or IRAs, individuals must decide whether to participate, how much to contribute, how to invest, and how to withdraw the money. Here ordinary shortsightedness can be expensive. For example, if you stop putting money in a 401(k) for a few years, your projected earnings drop dramatically—you could come out in the end with only half of what you would have had if you saved continuously. That's tough to handle if you are planning to take some time to raise your children, or if you merely switch employers an average number of times in the new economy.

The list of mistakes people make when given the responsibility for their own retirement savings is long. A 401(k) plan is available to a majority of workers, but one in four of those eligible do not participate, and of those who do, less than 10 percent put in the maximum. Only 5 percent of all eligible people give the maximum annually to their IRAs.

People buy too much stock in the company they work for—at large companies, an average 40 percent of 401(k) assets are invested in company stock. Despite warnings, they are likely to cash out their 401(k) when changing jobs without rolling it over into an IRA, even though taking out the money negates the benefits of saving over a long period of time and costs them a hefty tax bill for that year. They make many other mistakes in managing their portfolio compared with what a professional money manager would do.

. . .

It's too soon to feel the effects of lack of pensions or private retirement savings for current members of Generation Debt. It's easy
to see what our attitude is toward saving, though: we don't do it.

The Employee Benefit Research Institute (EBRI) publishes
comprehensive nonpartisan research on the economic security of
American workers. In surveys over the '90s and '00s, they have
found that the collapse of the dot-com bubble, the terrorist attacks,
the rise in health care costs, and the assailing of Social Security
have done nothing to change Americans' terrible savings habits.
In the summer of 2005, the national savings rate dropped to zero.

Americans didn't always save so poorly. We used to be more like
Europeans, who still save around 10 percent of household income
each year—in Italy, 16 percent. Beginning in the 1980s, savings
rates here in the United States dropped like a rock. The pits we've
now reached are like nothing seen since the Great Depression.

In my opinion, of the various explanations that have been offered for our dramatic change in habits, the only one that fits all
the facts is the rise of easy credit. Credit card usage is far higher
in the United States than in continental Europe, and we are far
more likely to carry revolving balances. Cheap plastic affects saving in two ways: People at all income levels go into debt for all
kinds of purchases they used to save up for, like, for example, college. Then the rapidly mounting payments eat away the discretionary income that once went into the piggy bank.

In a tango of cognitive dissonance, Americans combine unreasonable confidence in their own resources with unreasonable expectations about retirement. According to EBRI, only 40 percent

of workers in 2004 had even estimated what their needs might be in retirement, which the group considers the most effective way to kick you in the pants and start you saving. Yet 68 percent of all workers are either very or somewhat confident of having enough cash to keep them in golf shoes.

Not surprisingly, workers aged twenty-five to thirty-four always report saving the least in EBRI's surveys. Among workers under forty-four, three-fourths said they had given little or no thought to how to manage their money in retirement. I know I hadn't before I started researching this chapter.

With so many of us heading into our thirties with five figures of debt, saving for a far-off retirement sounds like a joke. Even breaking even seems like a remote possibility. This feeling of powerlessness can breed a careless attitude toward saving. The philosophy for too many of us in Generation Debt is enjoy today and try to make your minimum payments tomorrow. This means that while we are young and unattached, we're forming bad financial habits that may last even longer than our bad credit.

Daphne, twenty-nine, the Ph.D. dropout, is a rare exception to the rule. "I do think not enough young people take advantage of their retirement plans at work and their IRAs—I myself am kicking myself for not starting my 401(k) right when I started working." Daphne says that living through the dot-com boom and bust, and incurring $20,000 in student loan debt, has made her more prudent. To this end, she is heroically saving. She and her boyfriend have recently purchased, and are renovating, a home, which they hope will be a good investment. On top of her mortgage and loan payments, she now puts 20 percent of her salary in a 401(k) and the annual max into her IRA. She also says she's planning to work for at least the next fifty years, having given up her hope of a tenured position at a university.

Despite her newfound saving success, Daphne says, the temptation to spend is everywhere. "I have to say, it's really hard saving for retirement and thinking about long-range plans where there's so much pressure to buy things for now: clothes, vacations, nights out, even little things like lattes. I like to think I can resist the advertising and such, but the consumer culture bears down really hard."

Dallas Salisbury says Daphne's spending distractions are all too common. Salisbury is a professional finger-wagger, warning people to save more. He is president and CEO of EBRI, as well as the founder and CEO of the American Savings Education Council, whose mission is to raise the profile of saving. According to him, telling Americans to set something aside, in a world of constant advertising and free-flowing credit, succeeds just as well as advising them to eat a low-fat diet in the world of Dunkin' Donuts.

"The key is, does the individual save, and does the individual save enough? Do people discipline themselves to reduce their spending today? And in America the answer is too often no," Salisbury says. "Most won't do it. Because they don't save and they don't plan."

Though it may not sound that way, Salisbury's message holds the most hope for people who are just starting their careers. "The first thing to keep in mind is to start very early," he says. The Savings Council, says Salisbury, recommends opening an IRA when you start your first part-time job at the age of fourteen. The sooner you start saving, the greater your chance of having a reasonable cushion for retirement. Saving should theoretically be easier for people who don't yet have obligations like raising a child, caring for an elderly parent, or saving for their own children's college educations.

Salisbury's advice doesn't really compute for low earners or those of us in crap jobs, though. "If individuals would consistently save 20 percent of what they're earning, then that would provide them enough for a rainy day," he says. That number would mean that Christopher, the librarian now earning $23,000 a year, should put away $4,600 and live on $18,400. Take out his student loan payments, and his annual cash flow goes down to $16,360 before taxes. And at his age, thirty-one, 20 percent is almost too little to save anyway. "Most people don't save or start thinking about it until they're in their thirties or forties," Salisbury says. "And by then the percentage you need to save goes up dramatically." When earnings are low or unpredictable, consistent saving is that much tougher.

Money experts say even those with student loans, like Daphne, should put away money for retirement right away, to reap the returns of growth over time. Yet whether you have relatively low-interest federal student loans, private loans, or credit card debt, high monthly payments and low income can easily make saving impractical or impossible. If the interest rate you're paying—for example, on a credit card—equals or exceeds what

your savings can earn, paying off that debt counts as a first priority. And establishing good savings habits is that much harder
when for years and years you have little to set aside.

The other factor working against this generation's long-term
security is uneven and unequal wage growth. Healthy savings
habits require a reasonable forecast of your income from year to
year, which, as we have seen, is harder than ever. You might think
you have enough socked away, but if you divorce, never marry, or
simply end up underemployed for a few years, that nest egg will
be completely inadequate.

Seth, twenty-five, is a seriously quirky guy who worries a lot
about his generation's materialism, including his own. His stepmother asked him to move out of his father's house when he was
eighteen. Influenced by the movie *Fight Club,* with its anti-
consumerist themes, Seth gave his new 4Runner SUV back to his
dad and squatted for a while in an abandoned house on the resort
island of Sanibel, Florida, living on almost nothing. Now he lives
in San Francisco, does modern dance, and attends community college. He gets by as a freelance handyman, restoring Victorian
houses for about $15 an hour.

Seth's affluent upbringing and his current job refinishing the
floors of historic residences have given him expensive tastes that
don't jibe well with his actual income. "I have what I call the G
lifestyle—I spend less than $1,000 a month," he says. "What I
think personally is causing the problem with credit card debt is
kids who say they're struggling but have an iPod. Our generation
has more pressure to buy the granite-and-stainless-steel kitchen

when you're twenty." Torn between his love of Marxist theory and his love of modernist design, Seth himself has an iPod, along with $5,000 in credit card debt. "It's a huge struggle. Do I become a Buddhist monk? I envision myself living in a multimillion-dollar modern home on a sea cliff."

Dozens of the people I have talked with, including Seth, have mentioned owning a home as a goal. Like other bulwarks of financial security, this one is changing unsettlingly fast.

The real estate boom, now slowing, has outlasted the '90s stock market crash and subsequent recession. Boomers and retirees who bought in the '70s, '80s, even early '90s, have seen their home equity go up and up, and have taken out increasingly popular home equity loans that have helped finance the spiraling growth in consumer spending. Many Boomers, including my own parents, are relying partly on their real estate holdings to keep them flush in their imminent retirement.

As the market heated up and interest rates stayed low year after year, it became easier to buy a home with less cash. Surprising numbers of Generation Debt did just that. Between 1995 and 2004, according to the U.S. Census, the percentage of people under age twenty-five who owned homes leapt 59 percent, while the percentage among those twenty-five to twenty-nine rose 17 percent. Meanwhile, the overall percentage of homebuyers grew seven points, to an all-time high of 69 percent. Still, under-thirty-year-olds remain far less likely to own a home than the population at large.

Yes, there's a catch. The very reason that young people are able to make it into this sky-high market is that home ownership is no

longer the safe bet it once was. Traditionally, buyers could qualify
for mortgages if they devoted 28 percent or less of their income to
a monthly payment. Now buyers can spend up to 40 percent,
which qualifies as a "high" housing burden under federal guide-
lines. Moreover, in the past few years, the traditional 10 or 20 percent down payments have given way to deals with 5 percent,
3 percent, or even zero down. Some buyers are even turning to
"interest-only loans," in which you don't begin to pay off the
principal for five to seven years. Get into deals like these and
you're basically renting from the bank, betting that the value of
the house will go up enough to cover your risk.

"There are plenty of dangers for young people and for low-
income people" in this market, says Elaine Toribio, senior policy
analyst for the nonprofit Citizens Housing and Planning Council
in New York City. Foremost among them is that values can't keep
rising forever. Home equity used to be the cornerstone of middle-
class America's net worth, and now it's a matter of frothy specu-
lation. As this book was going to press, interest rates had already
started rising, and headlines about the bursting bubble were ap-
pearing.

The decline in retirement benefits could mean more to Generation
Debt in real dollars of lost income than any other economic change
detailed in this book. And yet our own retirement is literally the last
thing we have to worry about. Our parents, members of the largest,
longest-lived generation ever, have already begun to downshift,
taking early retirement and perhaps a part-time job on the side.
By 2020, there will be fewer workers to support more retirees than

ever before. The Boomers' en masse retirement will permanently change this country's demographics. It will also affect the finances of countless young families. If we're really going to do worse than our parents, how on earth are we going to take care of them?

"Jacob," twenty-four, is facing these questions a little early. "My parents have not been out of heavy debt for most of my life," he says. "I feel an immediate need to make money now. I don't want to be in a position where I can't help them." Jacob graduated from a prestigious university, where he studied engineering and neuroscience. With scholarships, he managed to keep his own student loan debt down to just $6,000. The prospect of his parents' suddenly running out of money to contribute to his schooling kept him up at night.

"The summer after my junior year, I got an internship on Wall Street that paid $12,000 for the summer. It made me so happy. Before there was this huge uncertainty: what happens if there's no check and I have to drop out of school? Since that summer, I've been financially independent." Jacob gave his parents each $6,000 toward the end of college, although he has not been tempted to give them money since. "It's a black hole. I could pay off my father's credit card debt, but he'd probably have it again in two years."

Instead of exploring either of his passions—neuroscience and art—Jacob moved from the West Coast across the country after college to take a job in finance that paid over $100,000 a year. "There's a lot of things that I would probably be doing instead of working in New York on Wall Street if I didn't feel the imminence of a large financial crisis in my family in the near future," he says.

Jacob has used spreadsheets to try to convince his parents of the dangers of excessive debt. Today they are sixty-five and sixty-two. They once owned a successful business together, but it fell on hard times, and they divorced and dissolved the company ten years ago. Since then, he says, his father has become "like a gambler," speculating in real estate, and is $150,000 in credit card debt. His mother is also tens of thousands of dollars in debt. A few weeks after we first spoke, she called Jacob in a panic because she could not make the mortgage payment on her house. She asked him to help come up with the money to renovate it so she could either repair it or sell it.

The situation Jacob faces is an intensified, compressed version of what many people in our generation will come up against sooner or later. Unless you were raised by wolves, you are probably the child of Boomers who need more money than they have saved in order to live comfortably and healthily through retirement. Hundreds of thousands more.

True, our parents' generation has prospered. Yet their working lives have also seen record-high divorce rates, the downsizing epidemic, yawning inequality, spiraling bankruptcy rates, and the leaping up of consumer debt. According to the Federal Reserve, which does a national survey every three years, 53 percent of workers aged fifty-five to sixty-four have no retirement savings account. None. *Nada.* Of the 47 percent that do have one, their median balance (half are larger, half smaller) is $25,000. That's about one-tenth of what you need to retire in anything approaching comfort.

One nationally representative sample of retirement-aged people found that close to a third of them had no assets saved. These were sixty-five-year-olds heading into fifteen, twenty, or thirty more years with nothing to depend on. More than two-thirds of retirees now, who come from a generation where private pensions were more prevalent and household savings rates higher, still rely on Social Security for half or more of their living expenses.

According to the Employee Benefit Research Institute, the total annual national retirement income shortfall will grow to as much as $57 billion by 2030, almost double what it is now. This is the gap between the money retirees need to fulfill their basic needs each year and the personal assets they actually have, including Social Security benefits. Most of the shortfall is due to the rising cost of health care, including multiple prescriptions, new heart valves, and hip replacements, as well as an increasing need for long-term care. We're talking about millions of people outliving their assets, and the bill going to grown sons and daughters as well as all taxpayers.

It's not easy, but all of us who are starting out need to think about current economic realities in terms of our own parents and their chances of retiring securely. Is your mom single? The odds are against her saving enough to be comfortable in retirement. Do your parents own a home they can sell, or is it already mortgaged up to the hilt? Home equity is one of the most important assets people can leverage to retire. Do they have private pensions? It's better to swallow hard and have these conversations now. So many of the people I've talked with were unpleasantly surprised to get to college and find out there were no funds waiting to pay their way. How much worse will it be when your parents need money to stay healthy and safe and you have too little to give them?

As I was working on this chapter, my father was dealing with his own father's final health crisis. Grandpa sold his pharmacy in the early '80s and retired to a seaside condo in west Florida with his second wife, leaving behind four of his children and an extended family in Baltimore. By all accounts, my grandfather and his wife enjoyed retirement, swimming and walking every day, volunteering at their local synagogue, traveling north for weddings, bar mitzvahs, and funerals. Safta, my stepgrandmother, vowed when she married Grandpa that she would never cook again, and so they ate out almost every night.

Talking to my grandfather on the phone, while he lay in the hospital, I was launched into a slipstream of time. At some moment in the decades to come I will doubtless be in my father's position. Will my burden be purely emotional, as my father's and his siblings' are? Or will it be financial, too? And one day after that, I will be facing retirement. Will I have a home of my own? A loving partner to share it with? Two decades of relatively healthy leisure to enjoy the fruits of my life's labor?

These questions are universal, and deep. All we have to answer them are numbers. Assessing the power of personal savings and investments to shore up financial security for you and your family requires a mastery of percentages and probabilities that the average person lacks. I know I do. Yet that is exactly the task the great risk shift puts before us.

SIX

Federal Rip-offs:
Deficits, Social Security,
Medicare

What is really happening: A massive redistribution from
young and future Americans to currently living adults. Our
de facto generational policy has been to indulge the present
at the expense of children living and unborn. This gives
new meaning to "no taxation without representation."

—LAURENCE KOTLIKOFF AND SCOTT BURNS,
THE COMING GENERATIONAL STORM, 2004

The erosion of employment benefits hurts those of us starting out in our careers, or limping along without much of a career. But the damage done to young people's fortunes in the private sector is nothing compared with the grand slam of government policies. Promised federal payments to the elderly threaten our nation's fiscal equilibrium. Yearly budget deficits and the growing national debt are going to mean staggering tax increases on young people and later generations. Simply put, the federal government is paying off current obligations by going deeply in hock to the future.

If you're a Reagan baby, like me, the national debt has been ticking up for most of your life. When the federal government was smaller, throughout the eighteenth and nineteenth centuries, it ran temporary deficits only in times of war or prolonged recession. These were later made up with years of surpluses. But the Great Depression and World War II blew up domestic and military spending for good. Since 1946, the federal government has been in the black only twelve years. The total national debt—the sum of all the years' net deficits, plus interest—has accumulated apace. In 2005, it was three times as large as the entire federal budget— more than $8 trillion.

Bill Clinton's second term in office saw a few years of surpluses caused by a rapid expansion of the economy, which brought a rise in tax revenues. By 2002, though, the budget was back in the red. As of late 2004, deficits had risen for four consecutive years, the first time this had happened since World War II. George W. Bush's 2005 budget projected a deficit of $521 billion, or about 4.5 percent of the nation's gross domestic product.

As analysts at the progressive Center on Budget and Policy Priorities have argued, Bush's massive tax cuts are the main cause of the current deficits. Tax revenues are at their lowest level, as a proportion of total economic output, since 1950. Meanwhile, government spending is just below the average of the past forty years. The government's own budget data show that a decline in revenues, not an increase in spending, accounts for three-fourths of the dip from black into red during the 2000s. Most of Bush's tax cuts were directed at corporations and the richest Americans, who also happen to be middle-aged and older Americans.

What does the national debt have to do with you and me? Snore, right? Well, the current budget deficits amount to skimming the wages of young people to fatten the wallets of today's moguls. As low earners, with the lowest net worth of any age group, we gain little from tax cuts or tax breaks on investment. We will, however, be paying down the national debt with higher taxes throughout our working lives. And with most of our careers ahead of us, we will suffer more than any other living Americans from the likely consequences of deficit spending.

In their acclaimed 2004 book *The Coming Generational Storm*, Laurence Kotlikoff, professor of economics at Boston University, and Scott Burns, a finance writer, laid out in no uncertain terms how the current budget projections pose a danger to young people's financial health. "Young workers are about to get rolled over by greedy middle-aged and older people who have been expropriating their earnings for decades," Dr. Kotlikoff told me in an interview.

Using both official government tallies and independent research, Kotlikoff and Burns paint an ugly macroeconomic picture. As the Boomers approach retirement, they will probably start selling off their assets and liquidating their savings. Rather than invest their money in new enterprises or binge on consumer goods, they'll hold on to the cash, starving the economy of both capital and consumer demand. Meanwhile, the labor supply will contract. Quite possibly, all this will wreak havoc with our economy and with international markets. The rest of the world, from

China to Europe to Mexico, is aging as fast as or even faster than we are—meaning that we cannot rely on borrowing, immigration, or foreign investment to restore balance. *"The nation's aging is going to hurt, not help, the economy and inflict a double whammy on our kids,"* Kotlikoff and Burns emphasize. "They'll face not only sky-high taxes but also lower real wages." According to their models, young workers will take a 40 percent hit in total earnings compared with those of the previous generation, because of the impact of global aging.

Kotlikoff's economic theory, which he has developed over the past two decades, is called "generational accounting." Basically, he takes the principle that there is no free lunch and projects it out over time. Most analysts assessing the fiscal health of the government look at current budget deficits, income, and spending. The generational-accounting approach compares total government spending, including long-term obligations like Social Security, with the total tax revenues expected from living generations over their lifetimes. In the long run, every discrepancy between the two must be made up, with interest, by unborn generations through higher taxes and higher debt payments. Lunch may be free today, but someone, sometime, is settling the tab.

As Kotlikoff's calculations make clear, Social Security, Medicare, and Medicaid are unique among federal programs. They are called "entitlements" because they are budget items that increase automatically every year, and because people feel entitled to receive them; they constitute promises to pay millions of living Americans billions and billions of dollars far into the future. Using traditional accounting, we see $5 trillion added to the debt in the next decade. Generational accounting reveals "unfunded liabilities"— promises to pay entitlement benefits to living generations. The sum of these IOUs is seven times bigger than the official federal debt, at $53 trillion, according to a late-2004 analysis by *USA Today* using government figures. This amount, which the *USA Today* reporters compared to an unpaid mortgage balance, includes $12.7 trillion in unpaid but promised Social Security benefits, and $30 trillion in projected Medicare payments.

Currently, according to Kotlikoff's calculations, the net tax burden, in constant dollars, on *future generations* (born after 2002), created by the government's debt and unfunded liabilities will be double the taxes paid by current generations. Today's young people will also experience much higher taxes than older generations. That's what Kotlikoff says is the consequence of "four decades of mortgaging the future at the expense of the present."

On the other hand, many people worry that these promises will never be fulfilled, because the federal social insurance system, and perhaps the entire federal budget, will simply collapse under the strain of 70 million Boomers. When and if those beams buckle, today's young workers and their children are going to feel the weight.

Entitlement reform means a lot to the generation featured in this book, even though our own retirement is several decades away. On the one hand, we have our parents' security to worry about. On the other hand, we have our own. It may inspire some generational rage to realize that we'll be paying for choices we didn't make and benefits we may not enjoy.

. . .

When I began writing for *The Village Voice* about "Generation Debt" in the spring of 2004, none of these issues was really on the political radar. Higher education financing, youth credit card debt, the rise of contingent work, and the health care crisis did not get a lot of airtime in the last presidential election. In fact, one of the reasons my editors and I were interested in these issues was that they were not being experienced as political. Most members of Generation Debt were muddling along, hardly thinking of their bank balances as a national issue.

In general, young people have had a low profile politically during my lifetime. Every four years, there's some noise made about recapturing the youth vote, which has trended down since eighteen-year-olds got the franchise in 1972. No one seems to take the talk very seriously. In November 2004, youth turnout did spike, but the proportion of all voters who were young did not change, so that the impact of Rock the Vote and other efforts was inconclusive. Voters under thirty were the only age group to prefer John Kerry, 54 to 45 percent, so it's hard to argue that our voice was really heard this time.

But no sooner had President George W. Bush been sworn into office for a second term than he started mentioning young people's financial concerns in every other speech. The issue was Social Security reform. And almost against my will, I found myself agreeing with his rhetoric, if not with the solutions the Republicans were floating.

Bush's argument is simple, and is backed up by a variety of congressional and independent reports. Social Security, he says, will not, under current conditions, have enough money to pay younger workers the full benefits they are promised. "Our duty to save Social Security begins with making the system permanently solvent, but our duty does not end there," he said in an April 2005 press conference. "We also have a responsibility to improve Social Security, by directing extra help to those most in need and by making it a better deal for younger workers."

Hearing this kind of talk from our nation's leader put me in a difficult position. I was glad to hear young people's issues being raised, yet, frankly, wary of the source.

I will turn sixty-seven in 2047, right around the time Social Security is scheduled to need major adjustments to keep it solvent. I agree with President Bush that people my age have the most cause to worry about the future of the program. The Social Security "trust fund" has enough cash to see the Boomers into old age, even if no changes are made. And the Boomers, by the sheer size of their cohort, will probably preserve the political clout to protect the benefits promised during their working lives, no matter what it does to their children's retirement security.

Like many of my interviewees, I worry about the financial integrity of our nation's large entitlement programs. I don't know if I'll be able to save enough to shore up my own retirement without access to a private pension or a 401(k) employer match. And I'm angry at the prospect of paying far more than our fair share because irresponsible politicians have been running up deficits and making promises they can't keep. I'm also nervous about our nation's economic stability.

At the same time, focusing on the welfare of young workers

puts me in a strange position with respect to my fellow progressives. I think some cuts to Social Security and Medicare are inevitable, and I think they should start right away.

We young people have legitimate cause for complaint about the
relative generosity shown to Grandpop and Grandma, a position
that is not highly favored by either party. Instead, I find myself
aligned with mavericks like Peter G. Peterson, a conservative
deficit hawk and himself a member of the Greatest Generation,
who has spent his career in a quixotic quest to get Republicans to
stop cutting taxes and Democrats to stop spending so much, all
for the sake of the future. He points out in his 2004 best-seller
Running on Empty that the total amount of spending on Social
Security and Medicare is equal to seven times what the federal
government spends on kids, including all education spending.

Income and wealth, too, have shifted dramatically toward the
elderly. In the early 1960s, when Medicare was being debated, the
average thirty-year-old had 40 percent more spending power than
the average seventy-year-old. By the late 1980s, the average seventy-
year-old had 18 percent more to spend than the average thirty-
year-old. In 2000, the median net worth of households where the
head was over age sixty-five was twice the median net worth of all
households—and *fifteen times* the net worth of households
headed by those under thirty-five!

Because of the quirks of history and deliberate policies by
both parties, the generational divide has become a class divide.
Our grandparents are the very same generation that benefited so
magnificently from the huge government payout that was the GI

Bill. Uncle Sam helped them attend college and then buy their homes. Because of their own hard work as they lived through this country's great postwar expansion, they have the highest average net worth by far, not just of any age group now living but of any group of seniors who ever lived in America. Meanwhile, the members of this generation residing in both houses of Congress preserve their fortunes and pass the bill to their own grandchildren via tax cuts on wealth and growing budget deficits.

Even as Social Security reduces poverty to a rarity among the old, American children and young adults are more likely to be poor than the general population. I don't believe that anybody deserves to be poor, and I'm glad Social Security is there to take care of my grandparents. I do believe that America's future deserves a fairer shake. Spending on old people rewards the accomplishments of the past. Spending on the young endows the achievements of the next century.

Yet talking this way, using phrases like "fiscal responsibility," feels odd for liberals like me. After all, I'm part of the problem, a big fan of federal programs of all kinds. And I think it's going to take more government spending, not less, to improve the fortunes of my generation and of the country.

It's one thing to point out that the federal budget and tax policy favor the old and wealthy over the young and future generations. It doesn't follow, as some conservatives say, that the way out of the imbalance is to cancel all promises to everyone. If Republicans cared so much about younger workers, they'd be all about increasing the Pell Grant, extending state health insurance programs to cover young adults, student debt relief, and raising the

minimum wage. In fact, they're on the opposite side of all these issues. So why should we believe what they say about Social Security and its impact on us?

The people arguing most vociferously that Social Security is
doomed are the very ones who want to doom it. They hate Social
Security because it's a huge government antipoverty program,
created and expanded by Democrats, that is also incredibly popular. Starting in the 1970s, conservatives have created well-funded
institutions like the Cato Institute and the Heritage Foundation,
all dedicated to gutting the program.

Then again, the people who want to save Social Security by
not touching it aren't saying much about the disproportionate impact it will have on younger workers, the likelihood that we'll be
paying far more than we get out. This lack of representation on
both sides is to our detriment no matter what the future brings.

Sorting through the claims and counterclaims about the true
nature of Social Security and Medicare, their cost, and their relationship to the rest of the federal budget is not for the faint-
hearted. Reasonable economists, not just foaming-at-the-mouth
partisan advocates, disagree strenuously on facts and interpreta-
tions. The basis for this disagreement was built into the program
from the very beginning.

I don't intend to evaluate every statement out there about Social Security, Medicare, and the budget. I simply want to lay out
some of the basic issues on the table, and identify the special concerns of workers now under thirty-five.

Social Security is our nation's oldest, largest, and most popular welfare program, and the only one funded with a dedicated tax. How did this anomaly come to be, and how has it lasted through seven rocky decades of American history?

The Great Depression fell heaviest on the weakest members of society. Banks failed; millions lost their life savings. More than half of older people became penniless and dependent on their families, and unrest was growing. Senator Huey P. Long of Louisiana was drawing crowds all over the country extolling his Share Our Wealth plan. He proposed to seize personal fortunes and dole out enough cash to allow every family to buy a house, a car, and a radio. The great populist demagogue was well known to have his eye on the presidency as a third-party candidate in the 1936 election.

Besides the moral imperative, President Franklin Roosevelt and many in his government feared that if they did not respond to the epidemic of misery, socialist revolution would convulse the country.

So Roosevelt instituted his own bit of homegrown socialism—Social Security. He signed the Social Security Act on August 14, 1935. Roosevelt's advisers crafted what looked like a defined-benefit retirement program. Once an American puts in at least ten years of eligible work, or marriage for ten years to an eligible employee, he can keep collecting a monthly check at retirement as long as he lives. To fund the program, a special tax on wages, the payroll tax, is collected from employers and employees. The first set of amendments, enacted in 1939, included unemployment, disability, and survivor insurance, as well as old age insurance. It put in place the financing system Social Security was to have for the next seven decades.

. . .

The New Deal was a revolution in the mission of American government. For the first time, economic rights were enshrined in the
law. Yale legal scholar Bruce Ackerman identifies three "constitu-
tional moments," when American freedoms were fundamentally
expanded and redefined: the Founding, the Civil War and Recon-
struction, and the New Deal. As part of the New Deal, alone of
the three, the Social Security Act didn't change the text of the Constitution directly, but it forever altered public expectations of what
it meant to be an American. For the first time, the government
promised to protect people from unpredictable misfortune and
the poverty of inevitable old age.

Roosevelt linked Social Security explicitly to consensus American values of freedom and safety. "Fear and worry, based on
unknown danger, contribute to social unrest and economic
demoralization," he proclaimed in 1935. "If, as our Constitution
tells us, our federal government was established, among other
things, to 'promote the general welfare,' it is our plain duty to
provide for that security upon which welfare depends." In an important 1937 decision, as described in Cass R. Sunstein's book
The Second Bill of Rights, a conservative Supreme Court upheld
the constitutionality of the Social Security Act. Justice Benjamin
Cardozo, writing the opinion, agreed that economic security was
indeed part of "general welfare."

This moral revolution could not be pushed through without a
little fast talking. From the beginning, Social Security was called
"contributory old-age insurance." It looks like a pension plan,

and that's how most people have always thought of it. Checks go only to workers, their spouses, or dependent survivors. "Contributions" from wages, split between employees and employers, fund the program. Workers receive statements from the Social Security Administration each year showing their earnings and estimated benefits, just as if their earnings were being invested. Benefits correspond to salaries: if you earn more during your working life, you collect more in retirement. Unlike other welfare programs, Social Security benefits are not just for the poor—even Paul Newman collects his check. But there is a minimum benefit level, meant to ensure that even low earners will receive enough to live decently in retirement.

The contributory principle underpins the broad political acceptance of Social Security. The program has thrived even as proposals for large-scale poverty relief and national health care fail over and over. The payroll tax gives even the most conservative, anti–big-government, free-market capitalist the feeling that she has earned her benefits. Roosevelt knew this well. "With those taxes in there," he famously said of the payroll tax, "no damn politician can ever scrap my Social Security program."

Critics of Social Security, however, have never hesitated to point out that the program does not work exactly like insurance. Private companies with pension plans are supposed to build up reserves, invest them, and pay benefits out of the returns. (The government bailout of hundreds of underfunded private pension plans over the past decade shows that this structure does not always work perfectly.) Social Security, on the other hand, began paying benefits two years early, in 1940. Ever since then, current workers' taxes have funded current retirees' benefits, in a pay-as-you-go system, or pay-go for short. Critics also know it as "the largest Ponzi scheme ever created."

Charles Ponzi was a scam artist in 1920s Boston. He made up a phony investment opportunity, collected cash from a round of investors, and then paid them "profits" from the money of new investors. One day he ran out of new investors and the scheme collapsed. Everybody ended up fine except for the last round of investors—they lost everything.

The first Social Security beneficiaries, like Ponzi's early investors, collected fat returns on a small initial investment. Take Ida May Fuller, the first person to receive a Social Security benefit check. Ida May, a legal secretary in Vermont, paid one percent of her income into the system from age sixty-three to age sixty-five, for a total of $24.75 in payroll taxes. She retired in 1940, lived to be one hundred, and collected a grand total of $22,888.92 in Social Security benefits, almost a thousand times return on her "investment."

All those Ida Mays add up. According to the Congressional Budget Office, Americans born between 1876 and 1937 are projected to receive a total of $8.1 trillion more out of the Social Security system than they paid into it. To make up that shortfall, some of us in future generations will be getting back less than we put in.

Because it effectively reduced poverty among older people, because benefits go to the middle class as well as the poor, and because older people tend to vote more than everybody else, Social Security has grown into one of the most popular government programs ever. Every president from Roosevelt through Carter signed legislation to increase benefits, expanding the program and hastening its day of budgetary reckoning.

Up through the mid-1960s, Social Security benefits stayed so low that the elderly were still more likely to be in poverty, and had far lower assets, than working-age people. In 1975, benefits were tied to the growth in average wages for the first time, creating a measure called the Cost of Living Adjustment (COLA). Wages have tended to go up faster than prices, so benefits have been well protected from inflation since COLA was introduced. Retirees thus share in our nation's rising standard of living. But the COLA means we can't grow our way out of Social Security funding shortages. In order for payroll tax receipts to go up, employment and wages have to go up. But when wages rise, so do benefits.

Yet another obscure rule limits the program's revenues. The 12.4 percent payroll tax, for some reason, is not collected on salaries above a certain ceiling, now $90,000 a year. When this ceiling was last raised substantially, in 1983, it covered 90 percent of all earnings. Since then, the rich have grown richer by leaps and bounds. If we readjusted payroll taxes to reflect today's distribution of income, that by itself would go a long way to cover Social Security's projected shortfall over the next seventy-five years.

Pay-as-you-go has worked up to now because each generation has been larger and earned more in real terms than the last. Right now, the program still runs annual surpluses, taking in more payroll taxes from the Boomers and Gen X than it pays out to the smaller generation of war babies and Depression babies.

This pattern will soon reverse itself. Gen X and Gen Y are each smaller than the Boomers. We post-Boomers are earning less. And a cluster of demographic factors is rapidly lowering the ratio of workers to retirees.

As journalist Phillip Longman describes in his 2004 book *The Empty Cradle*, this country's, and the world's, demographics are tilting toward the white-haired end of the scale for the foreseeable future. Life expectancy has grown by several years. At the same time, American fertility has declined to just below replacement rates.

Since about 1960, the labor force has expanded at a steady rate, even as the percentage of men working has declined, because more and more women have been going to work. Roughly half of the economy's growth for the past forty years is due to women's entry into the labor force.

In the past decade, however, the percentage of working-age women in the job market has plateaued at about 60 percent. Without major lifestyle changes, America doesn't have too much more capacity to expand the workforce, and thus the economy, in coming decades.

Together, these demographic trends mean more elderly people supported by fewer workers. In 1945, there were 41.9 workers for every Medicare or Social Security beneficiary. By 2030, when today's young people should be at the peak of their earning power, there will be one elderly check collector for every two of them.

. . .

Didn't anyone see the Boomer bust coming? Sure. In the late '70s, Social Security was under pressure because of the generally dismal economy. Inflation was going up faster than wages, so benefit checks were getting squeezed. Unemployment was high, so payroll taxes were down. The demographic transition to smaller families had begun with a "birth dearth," intimating shrinking generations in the future. There was a round of amendments, including a big payroll tax hike, under Carter in 1977, but it didn't go far enough. Finally, with the Social Security system only days away from running out of cash, a package of amendments was passed, with bipartisan support, in 1983. The adjustments were evenly split between higher payroll taxes and benefit cuts.

After the 1983 amendments, Social Security, considered as its own self-contained program, started building a sizable annual surplus. Around 25 percent of current revenues are stored up in a trust fund. Now over $1.5 trillion, this surplus is designated to pay for the Boomers' retirement.

The trust fund is a sticking point in the Social Security debate. The federal government hasn't kept it in gold bars or even in cash. Since they wouldn't be using it for several decades, they lent the money back to themselves by issuing special securities, and spent it. Confusingly, the government's accountants subtract the trust fund from the national debt, even though the money has already been lent and spent again. Without counting the Social Security surplus, the 2005 deficit would be $675 billion instead of $521.

The people beating the drum of Social Security crisis call the special-issue bonds "worthless IOUs" that shouldn't be counted to

Social Security's credit. Others point out that the bonds are interest-bearing government securities, just like the ones issued when we borrow money from foreign governments. It's true that in order to make good on those bonds, the government will have to either borrow or raise taxes, just as if we didn't have the fund in the first place. Yet defaulting would mean trashing the United States's credit rating, which wouldn't exactly be good for our economy.

So, okay, the trust fund thing is pretty slippery. But the basic idea is simple. Too little money coming in, more and more money going out: that, in a nutshell, is the Social Security problem. The Social Security Administration's 2005 report states it clearly:

> Social Security's current annual cash surpluses will soon begin to decline and will be followed by deficits that begin to grow rapidly toward the end of the next decade as the baby-boom generation retires. . . . We do not believe the currently projected long run growth rates of Social Security and Medicare are sustainable under current financing arrangements.

"Not sustainable" means we'll need higher taxes, smaller benefits, borrowing, or all three to bring the program back into balance.

The Social Security "crisis," or "countdown," refers alternatively to the date at which we'll need to start cashing in the bonds in the trust fund and to the date that money will run out. There are disagreements about these projections, as they extend for decades and rest on a bunch of different assumptions: The rate of growth of the economy. Unemployment. Life expectancy. Fertility.

Health care costs. Immigration. The likelihood of a meteor hitting the earth. (Just kidding about that last one.) The estimates of just when the trust fund will run out vary from 2042 to 2052 or even later, and they get readjusted every few years. In fact, just since 1997, government accountants have pushed back the date of the projected insolvency of Social Security from 2029 to 2041. Slightly more optimistic assumptions of economic growth actually put the program in the black for decades to come. As the nonpartisan Century Foundation states, "What we face is a possible shortfall almost four decades in the future, not an immediate crisis or impending collapse."

Nevertheless, hoping we grow our way out of Social Security's problems sounds to me like a criminally passive response. We have to raise taxes and cut benefits to bring the Social Security and Medicare programs back into balance, and furthermore, the burden will be divided much more fairly among the generations if we do it sooner rather than later. Timing is everything when dealing with giant, federal-budget-sized messes. The government's accountants reported in 2003 that bringing Social Security into balance starting in 2017 would require either cutting average monthly benefits from today's $1,185 to $995, or raising the payroll tax to 14.9 percent. If we wait until 2041, the year before we exhaust the trust fund, the average monthly benefit would need to be slashed to $818 in today's dollars, or the payroll tax would need to go up to 17.69 percent.

Back in 1998, in an address to the students at Georgetown University, President Bill Clinton explained that waiting to address the situation will hurt young people and future generations. "If you don't do anything [to fix Social Security]," he told the crowd of now thirty-year-olds, "one of two things will happen—either it will go broke and you won't ever get it; or if we wait too long to fix it, the burden on society of taking care of our generation's Social Security obligations will lower your income and lower your ability to take care of your children to a degree most of us who are your parents think would be horribly wrong and unfair to you and unfair to the future prospects of the United States." No matter how you slice it, Bill was gently letting us know, we're the generation that stands to get fleeced.

Young people have responded to all the talk of a crisis. Polls over the past few years have consistently shown that young adults are the least likely of any age group to believe that Social Security will be there for them. Josh Brown, a twenty-one-year-old undergraduate at the University of Georgia, captured that attitude in an op-ed in *The Atlanta Journal-Constitution* in November 2004 calling the pay-as-you-go system "flushing money down the drain." "It is naïve for college students like me to think Social Security will be around to support us when we retire in four decades," he wrote. "It is vital that we begin investing now for our retirement."

The young people I've been talking to express a more nuanced view of Social Security, private investment, and public promises than the polls can show. But many are limited in what they, personally, can do about it.

Michael, thirty-two, displays a typical combination of support for and distrust of Social Security's promises. After working in business for seven years in the Midwest, where he grew up, he quit his job, sold his house, and moved to New York City to pursue a Ph.D. in media studies at NYU. His new bride, a freshly minted lawyer, joined a large firm and started to pay back their combined debt: first the $10,000 on credit cards, then the $75,000 in his-and-hers student loans.

"I don't think Social Security will be there when I'm ready to retire, at least not in its current form," Michael says. "I think the best thing to be done to help fix the funding problem is to reduce benefits—an unpopular move, for sure. Social Security should be conceptualized as 'insurance,' not a 'pension.'" Michael has $40,000 in a retirement account from his former career; at the moment, he and his wife are focused on paying back their debts and then buying a home rather than on saving further for retirement.

"Dan," thirty-three, has a similar, but murkier, outlook on Social Security. He grew up in Michigan, graduated from college in 1993, and dropped out of a Ph.D. program in anthropology after two years. He lived in Phoenix for most of his twenties. His work history is a succession of crap jobs, including stints behind the counters of a drugstore and a camera store, doing tech support for a software company, tutoring for the Princeton Review, and selling home security systems door-to-door. Finally, mounting credit card debt sent him back to his parents' house in January 2003.

Dan's two younger brothers, married with kids, live several states away. His fifty-five-year-old father is legally blind and took medical early retirement, and his fifty-two-year-old mother is suffering from mobility impairments after a stroke, making Dan something of a caregiver. Between temp agency assignments, he drives his mother to appointments and helps around the house.

Unlike his father, who is collecting Social Security disability payments and a private pension and has his house paid off, Dan has no savings, no assets, and no faith in Social Security. "I know the demographics of this country are changing. I have an anthropology degree. I still have a stack of public health textbooks warning that too many old people and not enough oil is not really good for the economy."

But Dan has little recourse to ensure his own security. "I'm willing to work my entire life," he says. "If I ever get a steady, good-paying job, I'll move to a cheap apartment and throw a lot of money into a retirement fund. But that's a big if."

Megan, the job switcher from Minneapolis, feels the same way. At twenty-eight, she's pretty much expecting an impoverished old age. "My greatest financial concern is retirement," she says. "Am I ever going to have a chance to retire? I don't have a 401(k). I have no faith that Social Security will be there. I'm going to be working into my sixties. Especially if I stay here in L.A., I'm certainly not buying a house. I might be the crazy old lady in the apartment with eighty cats. I'm coming to terms with the fact that we have this American dream that not everyone fits into."

In early 2005, President Bush introduced the topic of Social Security reform in a series of press conferences and staged "town hall" meetings featuring students and young workers. While he would not be nailed down to a specific proposal, he floated the idea of private retirement accounts, funded with points taken from the payroll tax. In this way, Social Security would go from a defined-benefit plan to defined-contribution. Instead of the money of today's workers going to support today's retirees, your own personal money would one day pay for your own retirement. In Bush's preferred phrases, it's a "market-based" solution, designed to create an "ownership society."

The privatization scheme, however, had glaring structural problems that were quickly pointed out by everyone from Democratic senators to *The New York Times* to independent economists. If the government let current workers keep more of their own money, it would then have to borrow quite a bit to pay the benefits of current retirees: $2 to $3 trillion over the next decade. That's a transition cost almost as much as the entire seventy-five-year shortfall!

In January 2005, *The New York Times* printed excerpts from an internal memo written by Peter Wehner, an aide to Karl Rove, the president's top political adviser. The memo established Bush's plan to take apart Social Security.

"The current system is heading for an iceberg," Wehner wrote. "The notion that younger workers will receive anything like the benefits they have been promised is fiction, unless significant reforms are undertaken."

Fair enough. Then the guy shows his true colors: "For the first time in six decades, the Social Security battle is one we can win—and in doing so, we can help transform the political and philosophical landscape of the country. We have it within our grasp to move away from dependency on government and toward giving greater power and responsibility to individuals."

The battle he's talking about is not the battle to "save" Social Security, which worked remarkably well for most of the past six decades. It's the battle to destroy it, for ideological reasons. That battle is likely to continue throughout our working lives, as a raging partisan conflict over just what the government owes to its citizens.

Consider this measure of the current administration's priorities: According to the Center on Budget and Policy Priorities, the tax cuts for the top one percent of households alone, if extended indefinitely, will cost 80 percent as much as the Social Security gap. From a generational-accounting perspective, a tax cut for high earners today is really a massive tax increase for those whose careers are largely ahead of us.

Privatization wouldn't restore freedom, control, or intergenerational balance for younger workers. Instead, it would be another step like the shift from government-funded education grants to student loans. In both cases, we reduce the government's obligation toward the "general welfare" while increasing individual risk. In both cases, the cost is felt disproportionately by those with the least power to speak up: the young, minorities, and low-income citizens. And in both cases, society as a whole is shortchanged when we shortchange the future.

Those who don't want to destroy Social Security in order to save it talk about the program's current successes. Today, 96 percent of workers pay Social Security taxes, and almost 50 million Americans collect benefits. Benefits also go to millions of disabled workers and dependent survivors. Less than 10 percent of the elderly now live below the poverty line; without Social Security, it would be 40 percent. Social Security does all this with administrative costs that are around 1 percent of all revenues.

With the political death of Bush's reform proposal, entitlement reform is likely to go on the back burner for several more years. This is a shame, because the sooner we act, the better for young workers. We can't afford to have Social Security remain the untouchable third rail of politics.

The public debate over our nation's unfunded liabilities has been all about retirement income payments. Barry Bosworth, a senior fellow at the Brookings Institution, is an expert on Social Security finances. Yet when I ask him about the big crisis, he says that Social Security isn't really the problem.

"The focus has been on Social Security reform when in fact the problems with Social Security are pretty minor. It will run out of money in the future, around 2030 or 2040, and so either you have to cut benefits or increase taxes. That problem is not very large. The real problem with aging costs is in health care, where the cost increases are much larger, and no one talks about what they're going to do about that."

Medicare is the largest health insurance program in the United States, and the fastest-growing federal benefit program. It pays for one out of every five dollars spent on health care in the United

States, and currently makes up 12 percent of the federal budget. Medicare Part A, hospital insurance, has its own payroll tax, an additional 2.9 percent of wages. It also has its own trust fund, which is projected to be empty by 2019. Medicare Part B, supplemental medical insurance, is paid for out of regular tax revenue. (Medicare Part C is a partly outsourced managed-care alternative to A plus B.)

The Government Accountability Office, the central budget control office, agrees with Bosworth. In 2003 testimony before the Senate on Social Security's problems, the nation's comptroller general, David Walker, interrupted himself to point out, "Medicare presents a much greater, more complex, and more urgent fiscal challenge than does Social Security. . . . Medicare growth rates reflect not only a burgeoning beneficiary population, but also the escalation of health care costs at rates well exceeding general rates of inflation." While the government can cut Social Security benefits simply by signing a piece of paper, regulating health care spending is much harder.

Bosworth sees a psychological block at work in the emphasis on Social Security over health care for the aged. "I think people like to talk about Social Security reform because they say, Oh, I could have an individual account and play on the stock market. The options seem attractive. But with Medicare the options we face are all very unattractive. Denying health care to somebody, some system of rationing—Americans don't want to talk about that."

Decency forbids cutting off care for the old and frail. But it's funny how no one wants to talk about "denying health care to somebody," even with 46 million uninsured Americans. The free market creates inequities we would never consciously condone.

. . .

In 1965, when President Lyndon Johnson signed the act creating Medicare, he explicitly linked protection for the elderly to the security of younger people. "No longer will older Americans be denied the healing miracle of modern medicine," he proclaimed. "No longer will illness crush and destroy the savings that they have so carefully put away over a lifetime so that they might enjoy dignity in their later years. *No longer will young families see their own incomes, and their own hopes, eaten away simply because they are carrying out their deep moral obligations to their parents, and to their uncles, and their aunts*" (emphasis mine).

That was then. Today, rising health care costs, especially for Medicare and Medicaid, are the biggest single engine driving state and federal budgets over the edge, increasing tax burdens on young workers and squeezing out programs for young families.

My grandfather's recent passing brought this issue home for me. In the past few years, I have seen grandparents and other older relatives fall victim to the health crises that await us at the end of life: strokes, heart disease, cancer, hip replacements, Parkinson's, Alzheimer's. Watching them cope with their new limitations is unutterably sad. It drives home the truism that you can't put a price on good health.

On the other hand, the cost of good health, for my own older family members and everyone else their age, is a major driver of the risk shift. As our country ages, Medicaid is taxing state budgets, health care plans are overloading employers, and medical bills are overwhelming families.

My grandfather came home from fighting in World War II to a

twenty-year-old wife with baby twin daughters. He worked six or seven days a week to support them and the three sons who came later. He deserved the absolute best care that money could buy. As does everyone else's grandfather. So who is going to pay for it? And who is going to decide who gets what, if we can't pay for everyone to get it all?

My thinking on this issue is admittedly unresolved. I'm far from an expert, and it's hard to keep emotions from overwhelming the facts. It does seem to me that our health care system is constructed so that everyone tries to push the costs onto everyone else, administrative costs are multiplying, and no one seems able to rein anything in. Health care, especially care for the aging with chronic conditions, is crowding out every other item up for public investment. Yet for all we spend, we're still not covering everybody. Much as in the arena of higher education, there's little space on the agenda to even talk about what a fair distribution of health care resources would look like. Both markets share the characteristics of spiraling costs, increasing demand, and widening inequities.

With costs on the rampage, many private employers are scaling back or canceling their health coverage for new retirees, or passing more costs on to the patients. Among large employers, according to the Kaiser Family Foundation, 38 percent offered retiree health plans in 2003, compared with 66 percent in 1988. This only passes the buck to government programs and to individuals. *The New York Times* reported in February 2005 that many retirees are headed back to work to supplement their health coverage.

Many point to the rising cost of prescription drugs, including marketing as well as research, as a central factor in the cost of health care. In December 2003, in response to years of lobbying by the AARP and the pharmaceutical industry, Bush and the Republican-controlled Congress—the same guys so worried about the cost of Social Security—signed a giant prescription drug bill, Medicare Part D. At the beginning, they projected $400 billion in new spending between 2004 and 2013. By early 2005, the new estimate was $724 billion between 2006 and 2015, and it will almost certainly continue to grow. Of this money, $71 billion is going to companies as an enticement not to cancel their own drug benefit plans; other provisions protect the profits of drug companies. The Social Security trustees project the cost of the Medicare drug benefit alone to be at least double the size of the Social Security shortfall in the next seventy-five years.

One of the most pressing, and depressing, issues in health is long-term care. About one and a half million Americans, 4.5 percent of the elderly population, live in nursing homes today. Medicare pays for specialized care only after someone is released from the hospital. Medicaid, the program for the poor, pays for about half of all nursing home care, kicking in after all the Medicare benefits and almost all of the individual's own assets are exhausted.

The rate of disability among the elderly is declining modestly. On the other hand, the oldest old, those over eighty-five, are the fastest-growing segment of the entire population, as well as the sickest and frailest. The obesity epidemic may accelerate the need for elder care, as people with diabetes, heart disease, and impaired mobility age. By 2020, the number of elderly individuals using paid long-term care, both inside and outside traditional nursing homes, is expected to triple to 12 million, according to the Health Insurance Association of America. Nursing homes, assisted-living facilities, and home health care are all on the rise.

Who will pay for this care? Young people, as families and as taxpayers. Private long-term-care insurance, one of the only ways the nonrich can personally underwrite their nursing home stays, is still uncommon among today's retirees. Less than 10 percent of the elderly had purchased it as of 2002. Because families are smaller and more scattered than in previous generations, aged Boomers will be less likely to have a child or other relative willing to care for them at home. Instead of having three or four siblings to help care for two aging parents, the typical adult caregiver of my generation may be a divorced mom with four elderly parents and step-parents to tend to, not to mention a grandmother, a widowed aunt, and a bachelor uncle. Just as LBJ said, repaying our deep moral obligations threatens to eat away our income and our hopes.

Ultimately, the Social Security and Medicare debate, and the debate over federal deficits in general, are moral, not purely economic. As Roosevelt said, a civilized society has a "plain duty" to alleviate fear and worry for as many of its citizens as possible. Only with a basic level of economic security can people be truly free.

I agree with Roosevelt that the government, the most powerful institution in our society, should carry out our collective obligation to protect the most vulnerable. I also happen to believe in the justice of taxes that are more progressive and higher in order to accomplish this. At the same time, the realities of poverty and disadvantage in America today are very different from what they were when New Deal programs were first designed. We have discovered in the intervening years that the government pie is not all-you-can-eat. Extended deficit spending can actually stunt economic growth, leaving everyone worse off. The budget needs to reflect a more fair division of national resources between the young and the old, the poor and the well-off, the past and the future.

I'm not just talking about more investment in higher education, job training, and family support. National solvency is going to entail some sacrifices by the young, too. For example, those I've talked with accept the idea of lower Social Security benefits, and I agree, as long as the poor are protected. Postponing retirement makes the most sense to me as a means of cutting benefits. For people my age, the official retirement age is now sixty-seven. I think that, like Michael and Megan, most of us should expect to work several years beyond that.

This will require a major paradigm shift—back three generations. In 1950, workers started collecting Social Security at a median age of sixty-eight. Back then, far more jobs were physically demanding than is the case now. Yet today a majority of retirees opt for reduced early benefits at age sixty-two.

Even though our parents are looking forward to two decades on average of government-supported retirement, the present scene looks very different for us. On the downside, the new norm is several years of underemployment during and after school. On the upside, experiences like travel and volunteer work have become far more common for young people. Our whole approach to careers implies we will need more time to reach full productivity.

Finally, we can expect longer lives than generations before us, and it's only fair that we should work for a greater portion of those lives. In fact, evidence suggests that work itself can lead to a longer life, by keeping older people engaged with the world. The age requirement could easily contain exemptions for those doing hard physical labor.

Medicare, like health care in general, is a whole other mess. Short of a national single-payer plan, I don't have any bright ideas. Twenty-somethings should probably prevail on our Boomer parents to buy long-term-care insurance instead of writing us birthday checks, as it will benefit both parents and kids more in the long run. And make sure Mom makes it to power-walking class.

I wish I knew what will really happen to Social Security, Medicare, and the federal budget in the next half-century. I do think young people need to wake up. We are earning and saving less than previous generations, we're less likely to have a pension, and we're going to be supporting the retirement of the Boomers one way or another. If we want to protect ourselves and keep a shred of security in the face of these fiscal realities, it seems likely that we'll have to rally at least as strongly as the blocs of elderly voters who have strengthened Medicare and Social Security lo these many years.

A 1994 nationwide survey by Third Millennium, a now defunct youth advocacy group, leaves a bad taste in my mouth. When retirees were asked whether they would accept a slower rate in growth in their benefits in order to prevent a tax increase on their grandchildren, 58 percent said no. Then they were asked, "Some experts say that America's young people will be facing a major financial crisis because of government spending on your generation. Do you feel guilty about this?" Three-fourths said no, not at all.

Since civilization first got organized, children and parents have depended on each other for care in turn, a relationship that moves across time and generations. In order to return to the vision of intergenerational and social reciprocity that Roosevelt saw in the Constitution, parents and children must give more thought to each other's needs. If we don't work together for a positive solution, the breakdown of guarantees provided to workers and retirees has the potential to drive families apart.

SEVEN

Family Troubles:
Love and Independence

SHARON: CHRIS!!!!

CHRIS: Yeah.

SHARON: Let me just say this as precisely as I possibly can.

CHRIS: Okay.

SHARON: You're thirty years old.

CHRIS: Yes.

SHARON: You still live with your parents. You're losing your hair. And you're stupid. Yee-uh. I think that about covers it.

—*GET A LIFE*, FOX, 1990

CHARLOTTE: I've been dating since I was fifteen. Where is he?

—*SEX AND THE CITY*, HBO, 1998

As a nineteen-year-old college sophomore, I fell in love with a man five years older than I was. After graduation, in May 2002, I moved into his apartment in New York City. In June 2005, while I was completing this book, we got engaged. Sliding that ring onto my finger unexpectedly popped

me down a rabbit hole into a fantasia of fears and hopes, arche-
types and unexamined assumptions. As I explained it to a close
friend not long ago, "Over here is the shaky bridge between family expectations and independence. Here lies the mucky swamp
of gender roles and heterosexual privilege. There be the poison-
green forest of consumerism and class striving—starting with the
china registry and moving quickly into real estate. And finally, a
vast uncharted territory before us, which may or may not contain
children and zero to seventy-five years of bliss."

The difficulties my generation is facing can't help but be felt in
the most basic unit of society—the family. Our relationships with
parents are changing, and so are the intimate relationships we
form. One fact is immediately evident: This generation is taking
longer to get married than any generation before us. The median
age at first marriage was 20.8 for women and 23.2 for men in
1970. In 2004, it reached a historic high of 25.8 and 27.4. Divorce
is down slightly over the past two decades, but the marriage rate
is declining, too.

I will be twenty-six when I marry; my groom will be thirty-
one. It's obvious to us why Americans are waiting to walk down
the aisle. We've been happily living together for over three years at
this point. Our friends, straight and gay, are all in different places,
from casual dating to cohabitation, long-distance romances to a
series of flings. We don't have censorious relatives to drop ominous hints about "living in sin." His parents have been divorced
for almost twenty years; before I went off to college, my father
quoted to me the lines, "Learn to change partners while dancing,
and give but a kiss for a kiss."

If I were to look to the broader culture for guidance, I would currently be enjoying my Me Years as part of an Urban Tribe of carefree friends while having constant, and inventive, Sex in the City with near-strangers. All the while, I would follow the Rules™: If He's Just Not That Into You, drop him immediately. This choreographed mating dance calls for abundant disposable income: like a good Bachelorette, I should be auditioning an endless series of rose-bearing hunks while indulging in Brazilian waxes, Italian shoes, cosmopolitans, and *Cosmopolitan*, sorting through all the Average Joes to find an American Idol, or at least a Millionaire. Then I would try to avoid becoming a Bridezilla while planning my ultimate dream Wedding Story, and my glamorous husband and I would indulge in the Chaotic pleasures of Newlyweds before quickly shifting into a future ruled by a Supernanny and Monster House makeovers.

Beyond the silliness, it's painfully true that there aren't many consistent messages out there for young people trying to plan their futures. Ever the good student, I thought that researching the sociological and economic aspects of changing families for this book would help me make my own decisions. Yet what I have learned about the dilemma called work-life balance only fills me with trepidation.

As my own experience suggests, intimate configurations are more and more left up to the individual, without community input. What may not be immediately evident is that this is another component of the risk shift, the increased uncertainty engulfing members of Generation Debt. Today's young people, already struggling, will soon be called on to simultaneously parent a new generation of workers, care for a growing population of elders, and redouble our commitment to the labor force in order to raise overall productivity and support our own children. Women especially, who still shoulder most of the burden of caregiving, are facing a major time bind.

This generation as a whole is experiencing a deficit between the careers we aspire to and prepare for and the jobs and paychecks that are actually out there. For women, the contrast is even more glaring. We now make up the majority of undergraduates and graduate students and half of professional school students. We do better in school all the way through. Among those under thirty, the number of women in the workforce nearly equals the number of men. Women under forty-five are more highly educated than men.

Yet three decades after women first appeared in law school, business school, and Ph.D. programs in large numbers, they are still grossly underrepresented at the highest levels of American business, politics, science, technology, and academics. It's hard to see how the younger generation is going to catch up when it's treading water furiously just to stay afloat.

A 2002 national survey found that 53 percent of single young women are living paycheck to paycheck, compared with 42 percent of single young men. More young women than young men reported having credit card debt. In 2002, young women with a college degree still earned 78 cents to the educated male's dollar.

. . .

The women I talked with for this book generally experience the question of marriage and children as a looming dilemma. "In the Bay Area everyone is single," says Catherine, twenty-eight. She is the granddaughter of Mexican immigrants and grew up in a small town in central California with a single mother, who remarried when she was in high school.

Catherine was the first in her family to go to college. In high school, she walked a mile, rain or shine, to her six A.M. shift at McDonald's, which paid for most of her books, clothes, and school supplies. To limit her debt, she started her education at junior college, before jumping through the hoops required to get herself declared independent for the purposes of financial aid and graduating from the University of California. Now she works in finance in San Francisco, earning around $65,000, and is midway through paying off what started as $26,000 in student loan debt.

Catherine sees a husband and kids as part of her ideal "total package" of happiness. "I would love to start a family, possibly sooner rather than later," she says. Yet she sees how her other goals, especially that of earning an MBA, might conflict with marriage. "If I want to start a family at a moderately young age, I'll have to go to graduate school in the next few years," she says in logical tones. "If I wait till I'm thirty, I'll get out at thirty-two. I'll take on tremendous debt over my head, so that I could not afford to not work." When I got back in touch with her eight months after our first conversation, she had recently reunited with her college boyfriend, and reported via e-mail, "I'm in the midst, RIGHT NOW, of determining my path. It is made even more complicated by the idea of taking on the debt of TWO graduate school educations and trying to afford a home and family in the expensive Bay Area."

What all this adds up to is that women my age are finding that the feminism of the 1970s is an unfinished revolution. While opportunities and dreams have expanded, social structures have not fundamentally transformed. Nor is the public debate on the subject particularly engaging to younger women. Instead of a real movement for change, I hear our mothers either berating themselves for their failures or engaging in internecine warfare between the homemakers and the career-focused. Much-hyped books like *I Don't Know How She Does It* or *Creating a Life: Professional Women and the Quest for Children* plumb the depths of these neuroses. *The New York Times Magazine* puts highly educated stay-at-home moms on its cover and calls it "The Opt-Out Revolution," ignoring the fact that most mothers have no choice economically but to work. Women like me, who grew up with working mothers, already see that there are no perfect choices here, only trade-offs. Female high school seniors in the '00s are less likely than the boys to believe that marriage will make you happier, 30 percent versus 39 percent. The percentage of girls in a large national survey agreeing with this statement has declined nine points since 1976.

I happen to believe that my marriage to this particular man will contribute to lasting happiness for both of us. But it doesn't mean I'm sanguine about taking on the lifelong roles of wife and, especially, mother. Right now I'm putting in late nights and weekends toward my career goals. It makes me queasy to think of swallowing back my full potential to parent full-time. My partner is equally ambitious and equally hardworking, and at the moment, still completing a Ph.D. Neither of us will be able to work this much while rearing the children we absolutely want to have. Having made a conscious choice to have children, I want to be there to care for them. Nor do I want to wait so long to have kids that I risk health complications or expensive fertility treatments and lose the energy of a young mother. I don't see how there's going to be time for everything. I don't see what I can give up.

Harvard University president Lawrence Summers ignited a firestorm in early 2005 by suggesting publicly that discrimination is the least important among common explanations for persistent sex differences in recognized achievement. Yet Summers also posed some good questions in that speech. The most prestigious, highest-paying jobs these days, he said, are the ones where people are expected to show up eighty hours a week, and think about work 24/7. Whether you're trying to make partner or win tenure, the most intense effort is demanded at the beginning of one's career, during the prime childbearing years. "Is our society right to have familial arrangements in which women are asked to make that choice and asked more to make that choice than men?" Summers asked.

This problem, my problem, is far from just an individual one. Just as with higher education and health care, family policy in America represents a choice of private over public and the past over the future. Nearly all the cost of supporting the elderly is borne by the public in general. Yet as economist Nancy Folbre argues in her 2001 book *The Invisible Heart*, the rising costs of having children and preparing them to be contributing members of society fall almost entirely on individuals who are not rewarded commensurately with the valuable work they do. Day care workers are overwhelmingly female, teachers are mostly female, and both are underpaid. Even pediatricians, also disproportionately women, earn less than other medical specialists. Parents, above all, bear the greatest burden in income and time. Ann Crittenden, in her book *The Price of Motherhood*, publicized the finding that motherhood will cost the average college-educated woman nearly a million dollars in lifetime earnings. Recall that that million-dollar difference is the same as the gap between the earnings of high-school-educated people and college graduates.

Human capital—our next generation—is our most valuable national resource, yet it is overwhelmingly cultivated using private money, time, and love. It's as if we expected private citizens to maintain the national highway system from their own pockets.

It's no wonder many members of Generation Debt conclude that they can't afford young motherhood; the average age of women at the birth of their first child rose from twenty-one to almost twenty-five between 1970 and 2000. Becoming a mother at a traditional age often means coming down in the world. Rebecca, twenty-three, grew up middle-class. She is white; her boyfriend is from Trinidad. She got pregnant in college after they had been dating for six months. They both managed to graduate from the University of Massachusetts while accepting significant financial

help, around $20,000 from his mother and a family friend. Then
Rebecca went to work full-time to support herself, her infant
daughter, and her boyfriend. "I just buy everything that my
daughter needs as soon as I get my paycheck—formula and dia-
pers, wipes. Whatever's left over we eat with and we pay what we
can on our credit cards." Parenthood has forced Rebecca to re-
define her priorities, although her boyfriend has been lagging behind. "It's been this endless struggle—does he do what he wants
to do or what he has to do?" she says. The young couple carries
$3,000 in credit card debt, $10,000 in student loans, and the debt
to her boyfriend's mother. When asked whether she is thinking
about getting married, Rebecca answered, "Yes, in the very dis-
tant future, once we're financially stable. We feel like we don't
want to rush anything or make decisions on the fact that we have
a kid. We want to base it on the fact that we want to be together."
The number of unmarried couples living with a child was 8.5
times higher in 2002 than in 1960.

Just as young people finding real estate too expensive are forced
to rent, they are also choosing a less permanent form of relationship. Between 1960 and 2002, the number of cohabiting unmarried
couples in America increased by over 1,100 percent. Living together is most common among young couples. Few scholars have
looked systematically at this huge social transition; there isn't
even a word in common circulation for loving partners who share
a home.

Many have come to see living together as a necessary prelude
to marriage, to find out if you are really compatible with another

person. For others, living together is all they need. "I've been with my boyfriend for seven years, so it seems like we're already married," says Daphne, who owns a house with her boyfriend.

Gay couples, of course, cannot legally marry, and they vary in how they view cohabitation. "In my community it's almost like polar extremes," says "Leon," thirty, a gay man living in Oakland, California. "There are young guys who jump into a live-in relationship, leave, jump into another. Then there are those who wait, because it means a lot more to them." Leon and his partner Cris moved in together three years ago. They are registered as domestic partners with the State of California and are saving money for a down payment on a house. Still, like many if not most cohabiting couples, they keep their day-to-day finances separate. "I was previously partnered for six years," Leon says. "And with my first partner everything was joint. When that ended it was so difficult, it was just like a divorce." Leon, who earns about $55,000 as a manager at a PR firm, has been working full-time since he was eighteen and didn't finish college; financial independence is important to him, especially since he is paying off credit card debt from his younger days.

It's a catch-22. As long as their relationships lack the stamp of permanence, members of Generation Debt have trouble making plans for the future. But as long as our financial houses are not in order, it's hard to conceive of marriage. For my partner and me, getting engaged has only sharpened the questions of where we are going to live, how we can afford to buy a home, and how to invest for and pay for our retirement.

However positive a choice it may be for individuals, remaining

unmarried is bad for your wealth. The Smug Marrieds, as Bridget
Jones called them, are more likely to buy houses, invest, and save.
They get tax breaks. They also receive more money from family
members than the unmarried do, including cohabiting couples.
According to the National Marriage Project at Rutgers University, people who never marry have 75 percent less wealth at retirement, and those who divorce and don't remarry have 73 percent
less, compared with those who are married continuously throughout their adult lives. Dallas Salisbury of the American Savings
Education Council cites statistics estimating that about 60 percent of single women and 40 percent of single men end up with
inadequate resources at retirement to cover basic expenses. That's
compared with just 10 percent of married couples. A glance at incomes and savings rates shows that cohabitants resemble single
people more than married people. It's little wonder that gay
Americans are fighting for marriage rights as an issue of economic
equality.

Even if this generation does eventually tie the knot, and history suggests it will in large numbers, marriage itself may no
longer provide the same guarantee of security that it did in the
postwar era. The single-breadwinner marriage once formed a
two-person insurance system against life's misfortunes; if something happened to Dad, Mom frequently went to work. As Elizabeth Warren and Amelia Warren Tyagi argue in *The Two-Income
Trap,* middle-class family life has moved to a new, less stable economic model. Without the entry of women into the workforce,
real family incomes would have fallen for the working class in the
past twenty-five years and stagnated for the middle class. Whereas

the typical middle-class family needed only one salary in the 1960s, it now relies on both incomes to maintain an adequate standard of living. The dual-income lifestyle is doubly vulnerable to illness or downsizing, another way in which people are exposed to more risk. Divorce, meanwhile, is the outcome for half of marriages. Warren and Tyagi point to the huge growth in bankruptcies among the middle class, especially women, as a direct result of these increased risks.

Considering the many new economic threats to families, I find the prevailing cultural and political attitudes toward marriage wrong in their emphasis. Gallons of ink have been expended on the sad downfall of commitment and romance. When the debate focuses on college-educated single young women (hardly ever men), it turns distressingly superficial and prefeminist. When it turns to lower-income people, it takes on racist overtones. If only all those welfare mothers would force their men to behave, the Rush Limbaugh argument goes, they wouldn't have to collect checks from the government.

In time with the presidency of a Christian conservative, a political "marriage movement" has taken shape. A common marriage-movement gambit is to quote how much lower the child-poverty rate would be if all children grew up in two-parent families instead of with single mothers. These pundits never seem to wonder what would happen if those single mothers earned a living wage, or received parental subsidies like those in the many European countries where child poverty is almost unknown.

Three dozen states have instituted education and public relations campaigns to encourage marriage. As part of a "Healthy Marriage Initiative," starting in 2002, the Bush administration redirected federal funding from the Temporary Assistance to Needy Families program toward often faith-based "marriage education," promoting unions for low-income people. As this book went to press, there were bills before both houses of Congress to make this spending a permanent part of welfare programs. Louisiana, Arizona, and Arkansas have introduced "covenant marriage," a kind of beefed-up legal category that makes divorce more difficult. None of these policies has yet had measurable effects on marriage or divorce rates.

I see different reasons to panic from those that frighten the self-described champions of family values. To me, the rising child poverty and bankruptcy rates are much better predictors of the health of our society than the leveling-off divorce rate. Those who want to coerce personal responsibility in young men by placing gold rings on their fingers are putting the (baby) carriage before the horse. I met BJ, a twenty-eight-year-old from the San Francisco Bay area, at CET, the job-training program. He had graduated from public high school, taken a few community college classes, and been out of work for over three years. BJ, whose own parents were never married and who lives with his retired father, describes his dilemma in simple and compelling terms: "If I can't be responsible for myself, how can I have a wife or child?" he asks. "I would like to have a family at some point, when I'm financially stable." This is true not just for practical but also for emotional reasons, he explains. "In order to be able to communicate and have a strong relationship, you need to have things in order for yourself." Dr. Laura couldn't have said it better.

BJ is Native American, African-American, Mexican, and working-class, a member of nearly every group of young men maligned for a failure to commit. He has avoided fathering any children thus far. BJ thinks the problem is that the labor market refuses to commit to men like him, not that the men are reluctant to commit to a settled-down life. "Not one of my friends has had a job for five years, or even three years. They've all transferred from job to job, because of the economy in the Bay area." On the opposite coast, a much-publicized study found that the unemployment rate for black men in New York City approached 50 percent in 2003. A more direct way to strengthen relationships and protect families would surely be to provide better opportunities for young men like BJ, rather than try to dictate what they should do in their personal lives.

Financial pressures and the work-life balance are not the only reasons my generation is skittish about marriage and family. If I can get in the psychologist's chair for a minute, our relationships with our parents have a lot to do with it.

Because of the massive economic imbalance between our generation's straits and the financial status of our parents and grandparents, dependence has become the biggest issue in Generation Debt's filial relationships. Too many of the young people I've talked with express betrayal or resentment toward their folks about money. Some parents bankrupt themselves to try to shore up their kids' lives. They worry, they advise, they cajole, they bribe, they threaten, they blame themselves. Some families manipulate young adults through lavish gifts, cut them off on a whim, or give them inconsistent messages from year to year. Other parents, saddled with their own economic problems, can't or won't help as kids borrow themselves into oblivion. Teenagers often ignore family finances until they graduate from high school and realize there's nothing put aside for their college education.

As Jennifer, the mother of twenty-eight-year-old Amelia, points out, to parent a young adult in these times is to be torn between indulgence and teaching responsibility. "I don't know what we should have done to prepare our children" to be economically independent, she says. "Parents would just stand on their heads for their kids. You try not to give them too much money, even though you want to, because you want to make things work for them."

Parents awash in the new middle-class debt don't make the best economic role models. In a 2001 national survey, parents with kids over ten at home mostly rated themselves as "fairly" or "very" good at understanding financial matters. Yet only four in ten paid off their credit card bills every month, 36 percent had less than $10,000 in savings, and only one-third had a tuition savings account. More worryingly, it seems that often parents don't recognize their role as financial educators. In a 1999 survey by the same researchers, 94 percent of those sixteen to twenty-two years old said they turn mostly to their parents for financial advice. Yet more than half of parents could think of only one example of something they had taught their kids about financial management.

After talking for a while to Seth, the would-be Zen millionaire,

I discovered how his conflicted attitude toward spending was tangled up in his family relationships. His father had died a few years before and left Seth $25,000, a sum he blew through in just one year. "It was shocking," he says now. "That kind of money is hard to control. I spent so much partying and drinking. I was going out every night, trying to make myself feel better. My father showed his love through gifts, so it felt natural for me to spend like that." Now Seth has thousands of plans and no savings.

You can't blame millions of struggling families for not having a trust fund socked away for when the kids turn eighteen. Nor can you blame parents for the bad choices their adult offspring continue to make. Yet clearly, many young people could benefit from a more open dialogue about money, instead of either indulgence or lectures.

Conflicts over dependence play out dramatically when young adults move in under the folks' roof. The "boomerang" phenomenon is real, if slightly exaggerated. Sixty percent of new college graduates said in a 2005 national survey that they were planning to move back home. On the other hand, the 2000 U.S. Census showed only 10.5 percent of those twenty-five to thirty-four years old living with their parents, up from a low of 8 percent in 1970, so presumably those grads aren't planning to stay too long.

Studies find that parents are on balance happy to have their adult offspring close. Although the arrangement is stigmatized in the United States, it prevails throughout southern Europe, Latin America, and Japan. Fred, twenty-six, who has lived with his family for the past three years while in college, says he's lucky that in his Filipino culture it's the expected thing to do. "As long as I'm in San Francisco I have a place to stay."

But some boomerang kids clash with families or face depression over landing back at home. "Dan," thirty-three, has been living with his parents for over two years in Michigan, recovering from a string of bad job luck and credit card debt. He asked me not to talk to his parents because his underemployment and his living there is such a sore issue. "I like the temping and the freelancing," he says. "I'm perfectly willing to go through my life as a sort of half-assed bohemian, with no steady job. That freaks my parents out, because they don't understand how the job market has changed. My dad's been a union guy his entire life, so he never had to do a real job search. My parents think you answer a classified ad and you show up and dazzle them with your personality and get hired on the spot."

Amelia, Jennifer's daughter, who was downsized after September 11, moved back home to Tennessee at the age of twenty-six for fourteen months and went through treatment for depression. "It's so not like *Get a Life,* that show with a narcissistic, infantile person who thinks that it's wonderful to live in his parents' basement," she says of her time at home, which ended when she moved across the country to Los Angeles and eventually found a higher-paying job. "My parents are great and I love being around them, but it was difficult emotionally to be back at home." While her parents were supportive, they were worried, too. Both her mother, Jennifer, who works at a company that records textbooks for the blind, and her husband, Jim, a recently retired insurance agent, always encouraged their children to get an education.

"Our biggest disappointment and upset has been that her college degree has not netted her the salary that we thought it would," Jennifer says, voicing the frustration of millions of tuition-check-writing parents. "We spent our whole lives telling our children to go to college, and it didn't work out the way they planned."

Divorce is probably the single most important factor affecting how Boomers support their children, or don't. As the cultural dispute over the long-term effect of divorce on children rages on, my generation has grown up defined by the facts on the ground. The divorce rate reached a historical peak in 1980, with 22.6 per 1,000 women; it has fallen slightly since then, but half of all marriages are still projected to break up. In the 1980s, the percentage of all children under eighteen living with a single parent, overwhelmingly the mother, reached one-quarter for the first time. By 2004, it was 27 percent.

All my life I've had good friends whose parents were divorced and who grew up to be wonderful, successful people. Whatever the emotional result is, though, growing up with Mom alone puts the family at risk economically. Just over half of all families living in poverty in 2001 were headed by a single mother. Divorced and never-married parents, overwhelmingly fathers, owed an estimated total of $96 billion in unpaid child support in 2003, according to the federal government.

"For me, up until the divorce, we had no more and no less than anyone else as far as I could tell," says Christopher, the thirty-one-year-old Minnesota librarian. Money was extremely tight after his father left, and Christopher became his mother's confidant at the age of thirteen. "My mother was very open with me about the family budget and sacrifices we had to make. For me now, money is always on my mind. It's something that has to be managed and I never get quite to a place of comfort with it."

Too many divorced and blended families clash over support for teenagers and young adults. My interviewees say that noncustodial parents who may have started new families, as well as stepparents, are less willing to foot the ever-pricier bills for college, and more likely to withdraw assistance over some disagreement. While the federal government may calculate an expected family contribution for college that includes both Mom's and Stepdad's income, Stepdad may have his own kids to worry about and often refuses to write that check. Money fights in divided families can be as dramatic as the stepmother of Seth kicking him out of their expensive Florida home at age eighteen, or a more subtle matter of gifts, loans, resentment, and guilt.

"My parents owed my father's mother money when my parents were married. My grandmother demanded that money from my mother at the divorce. Basically it was used as leverage in a scheme for manipulation," Christopher says. "My father, not surprisingly, then tried to use that dynamic on me. I was very angry that he was not willing to help me beyond the minimum mandated by the court, for example with my college expenses."

Besides its economic effects, the divorce revolution has inevitably shaped our generation's attitudes toward forming our own families. Even in families that did not go through a split, kids like me grew up with the fear that it could happen anytime. Some young people have responded with an avoidance of long-term unions that mirrors the impermanence of jobs, living situations, and other aspects of their lives. Others, like my fiancé, went through their parents' divorce and grew up to value commitment all the more. When I asked him why he decided to propose, the first thing he said was that he was ready to have kids and wanted them to grow up in a stable home with two parents.

We of Generation Debt may have experienced more than our share of abandonment and rejection, from parents as well as the president. But we haven't entirely thrown off the bonds of love, honor, and obligation. We still grow up wanting to create loving, happy homes for ourselves, whether that includes a till-death-do-us-part marriage, singlehood, cohabitation, a family of friends, or some combination. You can look at the decline and delay in marriages as a threatening dissolution of the social order, or as a necessary lag as we figure out what to do next.

In either case, we are going to continue to need our families more than ever. With the breakdown of guarantees from government and private employers, families are our last refuge for mutual support as well as love and affection. In his book *The Empty Cradle,* Phillip Longman suggests that a return to a nineteenth-century historical model, "three-generation households united in common enterprise," could be a way out of the economic bind caused by changing demographics. I thought this was a little outrageous until I saw a financial expert on CBS's *The Early Show* in June 2005 recommending to parents that they offer their debt-ridden graduating seniors a job in the family business if there is one—or if not, maybe hire them to do lawn care. Even if we don't all go into business together, young adults priced out of the housing market and aging Boomers facing exorbitant costs for long-term care may increasingly find that a full nest is the best solution for everyone.

In May 2006, *The New York Times* featured Boomers remodeling their homes to take in both elderly parents and adult sons and daughters. Multigenerational households, they reported, are growing faster than any other type of living arrangement.

In the meantime, one of the most helpful things our parents can do is to try to understand what's really changed for us, what we're up against right now. Jennifer, Amelia's mother, is coming to see this. "My husband and I compare sometimes, but times are real different, too. You can't necessarily draw on your own youth as a model for what your children should do."

"I think they have all done just fine," says Doris, the mother of twenty-nine-year-old Miriam, of her four adult children, with compassion that we might all hope the older generation would show us. "There is never an easy comparison of lives. Time and circumstances, history and culture are different and keep changing."

EIGHT

Waking Up
and Taking Charge

*We aren't particularly interested in "rocking the vote." ...
We're here to represent our generation because decisions are
made by the people who show up.*

—*VIRGINIA21*,
THE FIRST STUDENT-LED
STATE POLITICAL ACTION COMMITTEE, 2004

One night during the summer of 2005, a friend of my
fiancé's came over for dinner and we got to talking
about this book. "Tim" could definitely relate to the
topic. Like many of our friends, he had gone to grad school in his
mid-twenties once he figured out what he wanted to do with his
life: design environmentally sustainable buildings. Then he had
served a low-paid internship for several months with a German
firm until they hired him for real. Now he was thirty-one, putting
in long hours at a job where he was expected to prove himself
quickly, with no savings or investments, and earning a real salary
for the first time in his life.

I was into my usual spiel about the lack of political guarantees and our generation's new exposure to risk. Tim pushed back his plate and stopped me with a question: "What should I do?"

It was simple enough, but it served to remind me that while members of my generation do have a certain need for commiseration and recognition of our plight, what we really need is answers— a way out of this mess.

I told Tim that in my opinion, there were two things to do. First, live within your means and save as much money as you can starting now, and do what you can to make sure your parents are going to be okay in their own retirement. Second, fight to redistribute our nation's resources more fairly.

If you're like me, you're a little impatient with the political sphere of action. Spend months and years supporting local candidates? Send blast faxes to your congresspeople? Actually read those endless e-mail alerts?

Well, look, if 35 million people over fifty can band together to demand respect from Congress, so can we. Unless we're willing to continue being typecast as passive "adultescents," unless we really want to get "rolled over by greedy middle-aged and older people who have been expropriating our earnings for generations," as the economist Laurence Kotlikoff says, it's the only way. Young people urgently need a strong national generational movement— for higher education funding, fairer credit laws, a better-designed school-to-work system, justice system reform, worker protections, a living wage, health care, saving programs, support for young families and homeowners, entitlement reform, and a million other issues.

As college gets ever more out of reach, there are signs of a nascent movement. At my alma mater on a freezing day in February 2005, fifteen students sat in at the admissions office until removed by police. The undergraduates were demanding changes to Yale's financial aid policy to bring it in line with several other Ivies, including Harvard, Princeton, and Brown. In the past few years, these schools have all dipped into their multimillion-dollar endowments to make it easier for families to afford college without heavy loans. One week after the sit-in, Yale, too, announced that it would no longer expect any tuition contribution at all from families earning less than $45,000 a year.

By all accounts, the financial aid reform issue galvanized the campus. One in five Yalies signed on to the reform platform, including the president of the Yale College Republicans and other campus conservatives. "This is self-interested organizing in a positive way," Phoebe Rounds, a sophomore on financial aid who organized for six months leading up to the sit-in, told me. "The campaign has made people realize the extent to which their individual struggles are shared by a large number of students."

The Yale action also demonstrates, however, that without a unified voice, individual protests can make only small ripples. Tuition discounting is possible only at a tiny percentage of well-endowed private schools serving a tiny percentage of students. At selective colleges in 2004, only 10 percent of students came from the bottom half of the income scale.

An effective student movement should be organized state by state, to pressure the governors who make decisions about public schools where the vast majority of students are enrolled. When it comes to the broader problems facing young people, only national political organizing will do.

The student loan debt explosion could potentially be more amenable to lobbying than any of the other problems facing Generation Debt. The federal government gives out most student financial aid. They say how much you can borrow in guaranteed student loans and how high an interest rate the banks can charge. Given a true reordering of our national priorities—a big given— a few amendments to the Higher Education Act could immediately bring student borrowing down to a manageable level and lower the barriers to access. Increasing the maximum Pell Grant, and making the grant an entitlement that rises automatically from year to year, are obvious first steps. In the words of the National Association of Student Financial Aid Administrators, "If we are serious about reducing student loan debt . . . making the Pell Grant Program a true entitlement, divorced from the vagaries of the appropriations process, is the only way."

As this book was going to press, the eighth reauthorization of the Higher Education Act was finally getting under way, a few years overdue. The Bush administration assigned the lion's share of spending cuts for the purpose of deficit reduction to the House and Senate Education committees, and they turned around and passed the pain on to student aid, proposing $15 billion in cuts and new fees—the biggest cuts since HEA programs were created.

Even if legislative reform is years in coming, a vocal activist campaign about the dangers of student loans could accomplish a lot. After all, excessive student debt is not measured by a fixed number of dollars. It's a function of each person's income, other debts, financial management skills, ability to persist in college, and expectations about the value of a diploma. Raising awareness about the long-term dangers of high debt could help all those kids who "just sign on the dotted line as an eighteen-year-old and you don't know what you're getting into," as one interviewee put it.

Youth activism could effectively address credit card debt, too. It would be great to reinstate usury laws nationwide and end 29 percent annual interest rates, so that twenty-somethings earning $12,000 a year are no longer profitable customers for $10,000 lines of credit. That would require a morally high-fiber Congress willing to take on one of the fastest-growing profit areas in financial services. Failing that, returning to the norms of the 1980s, when college students without incomes needed a parental cosigner for a card, would keep eighteen-year-olds from charging down that path before they realize the consequences.

With credit card debt, just as with student loans, a vocal activist movement could bring the problem out into the open, making kids think twice before signing up for the free Frisbees and key chains. Universities have a role to play, too, in limiting their students' exposure to credit card marketing. Just as Stella, the thirty-one-year-old debtor in Chapter Two, says, the next time you see the Discover Card table, RUN the other way!

Where is our national student antidebt crusade? Over the past four decades, college students have gained a reputation as the most engaged political activists in the country—except on issues directly affecting them. Each year, for example, *Mother Jones* magazine recognizes the top ten activist campuses in the nation. From 2001 to 2005, the list featured left-wing campaigns on free speech, the war in Iraq, AIDS, the drug war, and living wages. Missing were bipartisan student issues like mounting debt burden, aggressive credit card marketing, the lack of health insurance, and the dearth of solid entry-level jobs.

Standing up for world peace is utterly admirable, but the social safety net in this country was woven by people lobbying for their own lives, not fighting for causes a world away. American college students need to experience that "click" moment, as the feminists of the 1970s called it, and realize that our personal problems are also political. If we young people don't march on our own behalf, who will march for us?

In other countries, students get it. Many EU and Latin American countries have overwhelmingly public, centralized university systems, making organizing easier (and education cheaper). Around the world, national undergraduate student unions have lobbied forcefully for decades. They address issues like diversity and date rape, along with tuition, books, housing, health care, debt, and jobs. They win battles for their constituencies, keeping young people on the social agenda.

The UK's National Union of Students claims 5 million members, nearly all the country's higher education students. In October 2003, an estimated 31,000 of them rallied in London against higher school fees.

After huge national budget cuts in the '90s, Canadians' student loans are comparable to Americans', at an average $22,520 ($19,143 U.S.) in 2001. Educational access is worsening for lower-income Canadians, although not quite as badly as in the United States.

Canada's two national student lobbying organizations boast combined memberships of 750,000, nearly half the nation's college students. James Kusie, a 2002 university grad from Manitoba, served from 2003 to 2005 as the elected national director of the Canadian Alliance of Student Associations (CASA). His group, founded in 1995, represents 300,000 students at nineteen universities across Canada. Member associations fund CASA's full-time staff of five, which drafts policy in the nation's capital and builds relationships with lawmakers, both elected representatives and bureaucrats. "You can be rallying outside and shouting through the window, and that's an important piece of building public support," Kusie says. "But you also need to be at the table with them, engaging them on the issues."

Each year, the presidents and vice presidents of each student council in CASA come to the national capital, Ottawa, and meet in person with their elected representatives. They also hold media stunts. In November 2003, they built a 120-foot Wall of Debt out of foam blocks, bearing the signatures of 20,000 students along with the debt burdens of each.

Throughout the 1990s, Canadian student organizations won tuition freezes and even cuts in several provinces. Kusie glows as he describes the accomplishments of his term as CASA's chair. In 2004, the federal government adopted their proposal for a new grant to low-income students, up to $3,000, modeled on the Pell Grant. They also changed the formulas for expected parental contributions, making up to 50,000 more students eligible for financial aid. These victories came during comparatively good economic times for Canada, but after more than a decade of deep budget cuts that shrank the size of the federal government by a third and while the country was experiencing the same increases in health care and pension costs as in the United States. CASA and the Canadian Federation of Students work to ensure that a government tending to the needs of an aging population does not forget young people.

"When Parliament begins a new session following an election, the government gives a 'throne speech,' setting out its priorities for the legislative session," Kusie says. "When it came to the section on education, chunks of it seemed to have come word for word from our pre-budget submission. . . . We were very happy to see that our work had paid off."

The United States Student Association, this nation's oldest and largest student organization, contrasts poorly with the muscle flexed abroad. Its exact membership is not available on its seldom updated website. Most students have never heard of it, and the media tend to pass it over. Its lobbying clout is dwarfed by that of the big student loan companies—it spent just $20,000 on lobbying in 2000, compared with $1.5 million spent by Sallie Mae.

The 80 percent of students who attend public schools are pitted against the immovable object of state budgets. In the past few years, community college and state university students from California and New York demonstrated against big tuition hikes coupled with budget cuts. Ten thousand students from California's community colleges marched to Sacramento in 2003 to protest a 120 percent rise in fees and budget cuts in the hundreds of millions. They carried paper effigies representing an estimated 200,000 students priced out of the community college system. Public college students backed by the New York Public Interest Research Group rallied strongly against tuition hikes throughout the '90s, marching 561 miles across New York State in 2003. In both cases, despite temporary responses, the budget cuts and tuition increases continued.

There is a model here in America of what students could be doing to focus legislators' attention on education. A state political action committee, as powerful and well organized as the student unions in other countries, has taken root in, of all places, placid suburban Virginia.

In 2002, students at the public College of William and Mary formed Students PAC to help pass a $900 million state bond issue for higher education. In the summer of 2003, the coalition, now called Virginia21, went statewide. It now boasts over 14,500

members at all fifteen public four-year colleges and universities in
the Commonwealth.

VA21, the first student-led state PAC, addresses voters between
eighteen and twenty-four on economic issues like tuition, book
costs, and education budget cuts. They reject the popular approach of relying on mass media or celebrity to sell young voters
on civic involvement. Jesse Ferguson, the twenty-four-year-old executive director, notes that voters of all ages tend to be motivated
by concrete self-interest, not abstract ideals.

"We're trying to find a way to support mainstream, bipartisan,
middle-of-the-road issues that affect all of us on a day-to-day basis," Ferguson says. He cofounded Students of Virginia PAC as a
college student. Now he and a small staff work full-time in Virginia's capital to drive home their message about budget priorities.
At their website, you can check the status of all the legislation
they're working on, from cutting textbook prices, to increasing
student financial aid, to reforming absentee voting so college students have an easier time getting to the ballot box. Their rhetoric
strikes a determined but not angry note; they remind legislators
that education is an investment in Virginia, and they remind
students that they don't deserve to be priced out. In June 2004,
Virginia21 celebrated passage of a state budget with $275 million
more for higher education than the year before, the first such increase in years.

VA21 draws on its members for letter-writing campaigns,
e-mail blasts, and rallies. They collected and trucked 200,000 pen-
nies to the state capitol in 2004 in support of a one-cent sales tax
for education. Meanwhile, Ferguson and his team haunted the

halls of the capitol during their first legislative session just as all the other power players did.

In a bow to the realities of American politics, VA21, unlike the Canadian groups, depends on corporate contributions. Their 2003–2004 budget was $100,000. Donors included America Online, Bank of America, and Philip Morris's corporate owner. With this backing, it's hard to imagine VA21 addressing issues like unfair credit card marketing. Still, they're getting results, and lawmakers are taking them seriously.

Jesse Ferguson says he would seize the chance to take VA21 national if offered the funding. He calls his group a young, wired equivalent of the AARP, for its focus on issues that affect everyone of a certain age, and for its pragmatic, even insider, approach. "There's a change you can see in recent years in eighteen- to twenty-four-year-olds—they would rather have a seat at the table than a rally outside," Ferguson told me, echoing James Kusie of CASA. "It's got to be not just student activism but effective student activism."

Caught between their roles as students and teachers, Ph.D. students have taken a very different approach from that of undergraduates to high tuition, student loans, and the dismal job market. Across the country, they are channeling their frustrations with the changing academy into a growing movement: graduate student unionization.

Graduate unions date from 1969, when the University of Wisconsin struck the first grad student contract. Today there are twenty-three graduate unions nationwide, representing over sixty campuses. More than half have been recognized since 1990. All but one, the Graduate Student Organizing Committee at NYU, is at a public university. Many of these unions include adjuncts, part-time instructors who are likely to be recent postdocs.

Graduate student and adjunct unions typically demand health care benefits and higher pay or stipends, which are usually less than $20,000. They also ask for more autonomy in the classroom, and tokens of respect such as access to office space on campus. When a union manages to be recognized, as at NYU, conditions improve and stipends get higher. But getting there can take years, even decades, of painstaking organizing, cycling through several generations of teaching assistants (TAs) and part-time teachers.

Universities, for their part, maintain that TAs are fundamentally students, not employees. "The Union seeks to distort the educational nature of those teaching and research experiences by contending that students who teach and research, while simultaneously receiving generous financial aid that enables them to attend graduate school in the first place, are Penn employees," testified John Langel, a lawyer for the University of Pennsylvania, in one student union case before the National Labor Relations Board (NLRB). Langel argued that Penn's academic freedom would be infringed if the school was made to bargain with a union. Universities scored an important victory in the summer of 2004 when the Republican-controlled NLRB ruled 3 to 2 that grad students at private universities have no right to organize. The decision in the case of Brown University overturned a ruling four years earlier, when Democrats led the board, in favor of the NYU grad student union, and threatened all union campaigns at private schools.

Ph.D. students may be escaping a bad job market. Yet they face the same dilemmas as contingent workers in the real world. Their employer insists it is not their employer. Their work is not a real job. Pay is low and benefits are elusive. There are no promises.

Jon Curtiss, who maintains the website of the Coalition of Graduate Student Unions, compares the enthusiasm among graduate teaching union members favorably with the hard times for America's manufacturing unions. But the parallel has an unfortunate side: All the strikes in the world are not going to revive our manufacturing base. Similarly, even if graduate and other part-time teachers succeed all across the higher education sector in getting better prevailing terms for themselves, each hard-won victory acknowledges that the old, genteel academic apprenticeship system is disappearing forever.

Nationally, the union movement is in bad, bad trouble. Union membership declined from a high of 35 percent of the workforce in the 1950s to hardly 10 percent today, and union political influence has gone right along with it, most obviously in the Democratic Party's loss of national power. In the summer of 2005, seven large unions split from the AFL-CIO, the worst crisis organized labor has seen since the Great Depression, to form a coalition called Change to Win.

Old-school trade unions have the weakest penetration in the same growing sectors that young people are most likely to join: retail, temporary, and contingent work, as well as "new economy" areas like technology. The current AFL-CIO split is widely viewed as a struggle between Andrew Stern's Service Employees International

Union (SEIU), which recognizes the need to radically scale up organizing efforts and reach low-wage and immigrant workers, and John Sweeney's AFL-CIO, more focused on consolidating power.

The union movement, especially SEIU and its fellow coalition member, UNITE HERE!, did reach out to young people in the 1990s—but as students, not workers. The unions' organizing institutes and their Union Summer internship program have strengthened ties between campus activists and labor, producing a new generation of young college-educated organizers.

But there has been little success among these same unions in reaching young workers themselves, toiling out there in the Wal-Mart economy. Workers under twenty-four are the least likely to be members of a union—just 5 percent hold a union card.

So why even look to this embattled, seemingly antiquated approach to bettering the lives of the millions of youth stuck in bad jobs? Well, as I looked for examples across the country of young people working on their own behalf, I kept meeting a new generation of labor organizers and advocates. They are on the margins for now. Their victories so far are scattered, but they are at least addressing problems for young workers and proposing solutions where precious few exist.

Marcus Courtney, thirty-four, tested software for Microsoft in the 1990s, just out of college. He was an Orange Badge, a temp agency employee making $18 an hour with no benefits—an official crap job. "It was a scam," he says now. "I had a college degree, the economy was booming, I was working in this exciting industry. I was supposed to be making all this money. You'd apply to full-time jobs and you realized that working as a contractor was a mark against you. It was a caste system. There was amazing frustration there."

The Microsoft permatemp class-action suit had already been filed by the time Courtney quit and made the transition to organizing full-time in 1998. He and former tech coworkers realized they wanted a permanent bargaining force for workers, not the one-time payoff the suit represented. They further realized they'd have to start without union backing. "We did outreach to unions, but most unions weren't interested in organizing high-tech workers. The concept was foreign. Even among unions there was a perception that tech people made $300,000 a year and were loaded with stock options."

So Courtney and his friends went their own way, organizing for improved benefits and starting a letter-writing campaign for better overtime rules. Eventually, they received backing from the Communications Workers of America to form WashTech, the Washington Alliance of Technology Workers, Local 37083 of the AFL-CIO. Although WashTech has just 1,500 local dues-paying members, it conceives of itself as an industrywide union. They have called their model "open-source unionism," a term borrowed from the tech world. An open-source piece of software, such as the Linux operating system, is written and revised collaboratively, the source code made freely available to all. WashTech offers information, organizing resources, and support to every tech worker anywhere who wants to improve his working conditions.

In the Seattle area, WashTech has helped workers at IBM fight changes in their pension plan. They even elected one of their members to the Washington state legislature. WashTech's national arm, TechsUnite, has 17,000 network members in New York City, Boston, Chicago, St. Louis, Oregon, and Silicon Valley. Members collaborate online on issues like outsourcing, job security, and health care.

Courtney says that WashTech's MO differs little from the collective bargaining of the past, despite the new-economy setting. "This idea that there's no employer attachment, it's really not true. Most freelancers go into a workplace," he says. Even the newest and least formal working arrangements usually include a place of business, coworkers, and someone who signs the checks and tells you what to do. Courts are beginning to recognize the concept of a "common-law" employer that can be held responsible for obeying labor law, even when that employer has done some paper shuffling to make it look as if its workers are free agents. For example, in 1999, Harvard University agreed to pay millions in back pay and benefits to technical and clerical workers misclassified as casual employees. "It's really not a new way," Courtney says of WashTech's techniques. "It's an old way done in new times."

If you have any kind of crap job, there may be a workers' organization you can join. The North American Alliance for Fair Employment, in Boston, is an advocacy coalition with goals similar to those of WashTech, but applied to nonstandard workers across the economic spectrum, everyone from day laborers to clerical workers to janitors to people in workfare jobs. Working Today, in New York, offers information, advocacy, and group health insurance to freelancers. The Center for a Changing Workforce, in Seattle, devotes itself to the cause of permatemps. Permatemp unions have succeeded at large universities, in city and state governments, and in large corporations.

In San Francisco, another group of younger workers are trying to improve their own lot. They punch a time clock, not a keyboard, but their playbook has a lot in common with that of WashTech's members. Rather than sticking with traditional collective bargaining, workplace by workplace, they are taking on a whole industry. Rather than focusing solely on workers, their campaigns draw on the strength of entire communities, working through the streets, the courts, and the media. This broader vision distinguishes so-called new labor, or social movement unionism.

Social movement unionism is the theory, flourishing in the past two decades, that in order to achieve their goals, workers' advocates must broaden their mission and work alongside peace, immigrants', antipoverty, housing, and women's groups. Instead of focusing solely on on-the-job actions, unions adopt adversarial, activist tactics, like putting pressure on legislators, using the media, and fighting through lawsuits. Jobs With Justice—a network of forty local coalitions uniting labor, church, student, and community-organizing groups—is an example. Sometimes these coalitions are strategic, focused on a single goal, like a local election or the living-wage campaigns seen across the country in the past ten years. Other times, new workers' rights organizations are formed, taking some elements from trade unions and others from activist organizations.

Nato Green, twenty-seven, is a poster boy for old labor meets new. A proud red-diaper baby, he marched on his first picket line at three years old with his father, an active member of the San Francisco teachers' union. In 1997, he graduated from college, where he studied labor history, and moved back home to a familiar twenty-something routine: a fruitless job search, followed by a post in retail. But Nato had something bigger in mind.

"I wanted to organize young workers," he told me, "and nobody thought it was important or worthwhile or possible. I was trying to get a union or a nonprofit to hire me to do that, and no one would. So I went and got a job at Noah's Bagels [a West Coast chain] and organized a union there." As he tells it, though, the grocery workers' union he was organizing with didn't have the resources to leverage victories won at one store across the entire Noah's chain, nor did they know how to sell the union to the mostly part-time, low-wage, and young bagel slicers. "We won the union election ultimately in three stores, and then it fell apart and I got fired."

For Nato, the fight, though finally unsuccessful, exposed the need both for new unions and for new kinds of unions to serve youth. "It confirmed for me my intuition, which is that the barrier to organizing young workers is not that young workers like being exploited or don't want to be organized or are stupid but that the sectors that young workers are concentrated in are sectors that unions don't know how to build power in."

Next, Nato spent three and a half years as a salt, meaning he worked a job while simultaneously in the employ of the union, organizing his fellow workers—in this case, car and bike messengers, on behalf of the longshoremen's union. The San Francisco messengers' campaign ultimately won two contracts in September 2000, only to see their union representation dissolve from internal conflict and their industry take a dive because of the dot-com crash.

Despite the years of arduous work and setback after setback, Nato has not soured on worker organizing. "It was invaluable to me to have spent five years working low-wage jobs and organizing," he says. "There are things you learn about talking to workers and being a worker and what it takes to fight your boss that you're not going to learn in the abstract." It's just that right now, he says, young workers need both more and less than a union.

In 2002, Nato and Sara Flocks, an organizer and graduate student with the UC Berkeley Labor Center, formed Young Workers United (YWU). Their multicultural organizing crew works out of one tiny room, papered with placards and posters, in the office of Hotel Employees and Restaurant Employees (HERE) Local 2 in downtown San Francisco. YWU started with restaurants, which employ the highest percentage of young people of any business. Their target population, almost by definition, is working night and day, either going to school or just trying to survive. Turnover is high and attachment to a particular workplace is low, so the benefits of joining a traditional trade union, with its annual dues, are hard for young workers to see. Add to that the incredible diversity of San Francisco's service workforce, with many restaurants staffed by Spanish- or Chinese-speaking immigrants, and you have a truly daunting organizing task.

"We set out to build an institution that reflected the reality of people's lives," Nato said. From the start, YWU bypassed the traditional process of collective bargaining, which means slowly convincing a majority of employees at one workplace to form a local chapter of an existing union and hold an election, an approach that had ultimately failed both at Noah's and with the messengers. Instead, anyone can join YWU. Members picket, flyer, and sit in, attracting free media, all to shame business owners who deny breaks, harass, don't pay overtime, or otherwise discriminate against young workers. YWU was active in the 2003 campaign that passed an $8.50 minimum wage for San Francisco, the highest in the nation. In 2004, it pitched in to help some workers who were suing Cheesecake Factory for allegedly stiffing them on meal breaks and overtime, and withholding a total of $1 million in back pay; the company spent at least $4.5 million fighting the suit before settling out of court. The mayor and the Governator also come in for their share of heat from YWU protests.

Nato says these actions are stopgaps waiting for a stronger national labor infrastructure. "From our point of view, it's not worth the trouble to take people through the legal ordeal of collective bargaining and union recognition unless you have the juice to turn it into something sustained," he explains. "Until there are unions with the resources and strategy to win real improvements for low-wage service workers industrywide, we're trying to win what can be won through collective action and public policy. We want to build a constituency and build a presence in certain parts of the restaurant industry in San Francisco until we have a critical mass of restaurant workers who can fight for large-scale unionization." The victories may be small and fleeting, but once young people see themselves as part of an effective community, that experience of collective power can reverberate over a lifetime.

Jasmine, twenty-one, is a proud Young Workers United member. She grew up in a middle-class black family in Bakersfield, California, and has worked full-time as a waitress for the past four years to put herself through San Francisco State University. Exploitation has been routine. "What they've done for us is amazing," Jasmine says of YWU. "It's made me realize I don't have to brush this off. I'm so busy, working and going to school, but I can still fight back."

These tales of collective action in the workplace may leave some readers cold. After all, those of us in this generation are marked by little attachment to our jobs. Besides, labor organizing is predicated on a strong, clear division between employee and management, a distinction that doesn't really hold for the growing numbers of freelancers and self-employed people.

What if you're not a coder, an adjunct English professor, or a bagel shmearer? What if you don't have a boss? Is there any other way to better the lives of young people, including your own?

The growth of student loans, the bear market in opportunity, and massive budget deficits call for congressional hearings and letter-writing and 200,000-strong marches on Washington and millions of dollars in online contributions and generally the biggest collective action we can muster, if we are going to see any change.

I recommend political action wholeheartedly. I have personally thrown my hat into the ring by writing this book: I am hereby committed to talking to as many people about these issues as exhaustively as I can. There's more to this problem than calling your senator or writing articles in the paper, though. There are things each of us can do, right now, to improve our individual situations.

Like what? Give some thought to finding your calling without taking on massive student loan debt. Live on less, and save more, than you thought possible. Plan for the future even when it seems as though it's out of your hands. It can be done. I've talked to people who are doing it.

In an age when over 90 percent of high schoolers aspire to college, it's not easy to question the value of a diploma. It takes a new paradigm, or maybe a new look at an old one. *Deschooling Society,* a 1971 book by Ivan Illich, is a classic of radical educational theory. Illich argued that all school should be abolished. A truly free and democratic society is impossible, he said, as long as we continue to force our children through the authoritarian mill of organized schooling.

Illich proposed, instead, a nonsystematic system of self-directed study, alone or in pairs, of any material a person finds interesting; tutoring, including peer tutoring, for skills like math and foreign languages; and apprenticeships to learn any trade or profession. His archenemy is curriculum, which he defines as the making of decisions by another about what a person should know. Speaking from his experience teaching adult South American peasants to read, he argues that education must be made relevant to people's immediate concerns.

As the Internet speeds the delivery of almost any information to almost anyone who cares to know it, the practical barriers to Illich's ideas have been lowered. At the same time, the high-tech industry has suddenly made it feasible to forge a well-paying, intellectual, prestigious career without higher education. Bill Gates, who left Harvard to found Microsoft, may be the most famous college dropout of all time.

What would this wild idea look like in practice? A growing "unschooling" movement offers a lucky few children and teenagers—from mostly educated, middle-class families—the opportunity to escape the regimentation of our often floundering public schools and discover what they really love. By various estimates, between a million and 2 million children in the United States are home-schooled today.

"Annette," twenty-two, from Phoenix, directed her own education throughout high school. For her, this meant working as a nanny to earn money to study with a professional photographer for five years, studying Hindi and traveling to India to make a documentary, and teaching English to university students in rural China. She earned her GED and is now working her way through college, majoring in political science and Chinese. "I'm very self-directed in what I want to do," she says, with unshakable composure. "A lot of my classmates don't have the skills they need to find out what they want to know. They're not excited about learning."

I missed out on being liberated as a teenager, but I think the "unschooling" idea is tremendously empowering and brave. Ultimately, everyone is responsible for her own learning. No university program, no matter how expensive, can educate you about something that you're not interested in or prepared to absorb on your own through diligent study. The nearly half of students who start college but don't finish deserve to hear that message a little sooner.

Nick, a thirty-one-year-old native of Queens, New York, is a follower of Illich without knowing it. "My experience with school in general is that I've never been able to really learn from someone teaching me," he says. "I like doing things at my own pace. When there's a topic I'm interested in, I become obsessed and really immerse myself in it." Nick has been extraordinarily lucky, in that his obsession from the age of nine or ten was computers. When he was thirteen, in 1987, he started his own bulletin board system. A BBS, a precursor to the World Wide Web, allows local users to communicate with one another on message boards via dial-up modem. Nick's BBS had hundreds of paying subscribers.

Nick graduated from public high school and enrolled at Queens College, but he was bored, bored, bored. "I failed computer science classes because the way they were teaching didn't make any sense to me, even though I already knew [the material]." Nick dropped out of college at nineteen but ran the school's computer lab as a full-time job for four years. He was also doing consulting work and teaching himself as much as he could about programming.

"When I was trying to decide if I should continue going to Queens College, the professors I was working with told me I didn't need to go to school—look at all these idiots who graduate every year," he says with more than a trace of cockiness. "I totally felt cool about leaving without a degree." Nick saw, furthermore, that college was not a direct ticket to employment. "The computer lab was a résumé mill. Kids were just sending them out over and over again. I've never really had a résumé in my life." Nick's career in the high-tech industry, kick-started by personal connections he made with his BBS subscribers, remained buoyant throughout the dot-com bust, and his annual salary now tops $100,000.

There is a giant book published by an independent specialty press every few years called *300 Best Jobs Without a Four-Year Degree*. The book lists jobs for all interest areas, ranked by income, growth, and number of openings. At the top of the list in 2002 was registered nurse. It requires an associate's degree, paid an average of $46,410 in 2000, is projected to grow 25.6 percent through 2010, and has 140,000 openings every year.

I'm not suggesting that the shortcut to advancement is avoiding college, or even staying away from a Ph.D. program, if that's what you really love. Rather, it falls to each of us to do a realistic assessment of our abilities, interests, and goals, as well as the job market, and choose a program that will best serve us. At a certain point, we all need to deschool our minds, taking back our intellectual curiosity from the domain of papers and exams. The hardest part of finding your true vocation might be holding your head up high when the culture says you're a loser if you don't have a square hat.

Skipping higher education is just about the opposite of a guaranteed path to success, and not everyone can be a geek-genius. But there are elements of Nick's story that everyone can learn from. He works hard. He concentrates on what he loves, shutting out distractions. He seeks out mentors. He made connections to the real world of employment in his chosen field. And maybe most impressively, he has managed his own affairs with an eye toward long-term financial independence.

From the age of fifteen, Nick has saved as much money as he could. "I don't drive, I don't drink, I don't buy anything—sometimes I dress like a homeless person," he says. By 2002, after fifteen years, Nick had enough for a $140,000 down payment on a building in Brooklyn. Although the rental income alone is enough to live on, he still works a full-time tech job, putting in the hours at night so he can manage his landlord responsibilities during the day. Rather than borrow, he saves the money he needs for renovations. His goal is to make enough money from real estate investments so that either he or his future life partner has the luxury to stay home with their kids.

Nick's father immigrated from Greece and his mother from Cyprus; they owned a diner. He credits his industriousness to his immigrant background. "My father had his own business, and so did my grandfather," he says. "Right now, I'm willing to work all the time. I'm awake twenty hours a day. I don't feel like I'm working for my company to make them money. It's for my building, for my future. It's for me."

. . .

The funny coincidence of Nick's $140,000 stash is that it matches the price of four years at a private university. Many young people might benefit from getting up front the money they would have borrowed for college. They could use it to invest in real estate, as Nick did, or start a business, or support themselves while they complete an internship or apprenticeship. Maybe they'd get to college later, when they could afford it themselves or get help from their employer. Or maybe they'd take the extra time and independence to find out that for what they really want to do, they don't need college.

The stake idea has been proposed before. George McGovern campaigned for president in 1972 on a "demogrant" proposal to give every American $1,000. In their 1999 book *The Stakeholder Society*, Bruce Ackerman and Anne Alstott proposed making unrestricted grants of $80,000 to every young person who graduated high school. Their aim was to erode economic inequality by creating a nation of "free and equal economic citizens." The idea may sound outlandish, but it represents a federal commitment on a similar scale to the GI Bill for a new generation. If nothing else, $255 billion in stakeholder pledges would certainly level the imbalance between entitlements paid to the old and resources directed to the young.

In a similar vein, when I talked to young people in all kinds of situations about how they thought they could brighten their chances for success, they overwhelmingly mentioned starting their own business. "Luis" came to California from Guanajuato, Mexico, at age seventeen and has worked in restaurants ever since, moving from dishwasher to cook. He dropped out of community college when his girlfriend became pregnant; now they have a baby girl.

"My girlfriend does events planning, so she wants to get into that more. I want to open a coffee shop or a taquería," he says. "I hope it goes really well. I don't want to be poor all my life. When you work for somebody else, you just work to pay bills. I want to open a little business and make more money."

Around nine of ten new small businesses are doomed to failure. But young adults swimming in the crap-job market have little to lose on a venture that allows them to both pursue a passion and be their own boss. After all, in today's low-guarantee world, we're all self-employed to some extent.

Another type of self-reliance involves simply living on less. Julia, twenty-seven, lives in Davis, in central California. She graduated from UC Davis, her tuition paid for by a bequest from her grandparents, and got her master's in education from Mills College, financed through an assistantship and a year of teaching high school. Now she works as a preschool teacher in the public school system, earning about $1,600 a month. She also helps out in her mother's clothing store in Berkeley on the weekends for $10 an hour.

Despite an income that is a little over half the average earned by master's degree holders, Julia doesn't worry about money. She has one credit card, which she barely touches, and she puts ample money from her paycheck into savings every month. She manages to live extremely frugally because of Davis's vibrant cooperative housing community. First as an undergrad and then as a young low-income worker, she has lived in communal settings for the past seven years.

The co-op where she was living when we spoke, called Sunwise, has eight residents who each pay just $300 in rent and another $100 or so in monthly board, covering everything from olive oil to their DSL Internet service to toothpaste. The 2,800-square-foot house has solar cells, keeping energy and heating bills low. It was built on donated land in 1979 and is owned, along with two other communal residences, by a nonprofit, the Solar Community Housing Association. At Sunwise, they grow almost all their own vegetables and fruit in an organic garden. They keep chickens for eggs and bees for honey. Residents, who can't earn more than $32,000 a year, take turns cooking house meals four nights a week, and meet every other week to govern themselves.

Besides room and board, Julia's fixed expenses are a $120 monthly co-pay for her health insurance and about $800 yearly for car insurance, plus gas for the daily commute. She spends cash on little else. "You try to do the things you can do by yourself so that you don't consume that much," she says. She and her housemates make their own candles and pickles, knit their own socks and hats, and buy most of what they need used. Julia owns just three pairs of shoes, all bought for around $2 and worn until "they flap up and down," she says.

But she is no wannabe Amish. By living this way for three years, Julia saved $10,000 out of her $19,200 salary and spent it on a six-month trip around the world, traveling everywhere from Romania to Fiji to Madagascar. Her girlfriend, who lives in a similar but even cheaper situation in nearby Yuba City, California, has saved almost enough money for a down payment on a piece of property. They are thinking about starting their own co-op in Mendocino County.

This California dream is not for everybody. It requires an ideological commitment to sustainability, not to mention the patience to get along with seven housemates. Every day is filled with hours of board meetings, community work, and chores, along with the ordinary responsibilities of a full-time job. "It gives you an adrenaline rush to know you're saving the world," Julia says with a laugh, when asked how she manages it all. She and her housemates benefit from the extremely specialized community of Davis, which has over twenty-one co-ops and many organic farms nearby. For example, she trades five hours a week of work at the Artery, an arts-and-crafts cooperative, for weekly classes in hot glass art. On the weekends, she goes to community parties and festivals instead of paying for movie tickets or cover charges at clubs.

Despite the idiosyncrasies of her lifestyle, Julia maintains that everyone can learn something by getting a little distance on our culture's prevailing consumerism. "The concept of living lightly, once you're doing it, is easy to continue," she says. "You don't always have the luxury to make your own bread or make yogurt from scratch. But once you have the skills, you can always draw on them. You have the reverse snobbery that this is a better way to live. You don't need everything new."

I have been surprised by the number of people I've talked to who agreed with Julia, at least in theory. They told me they didn't want to work day and night, they didn't need to make a fixed amount of money, they'd rather be happy and love their work and family and friends than pile up a lot of material things. Of course, some of them said this while carrying thousands in credit card debt.

Home economics—cooking, buying used, making our own—is not going to solve all our problems. But it can't hurt either. The need to keep up with what it looks as though our friends are buying is one of the major drivers of excessive consumption. Keeping company with people who prefer eating in, renting movies, and buying used clothes is a good way to short-circuit that debt-producing effect. True independence starts with living within your means. If more of us could figure out ways to spend less than we make, while living richly, we would no longer be beholden to our creditors to tell us how much we're worth.

You met Miriam, twenty-nine, in the first chapter. She is neither an entrepreneur nor an idealist nor a computer genius: she's your typical student loan borrower. Her mother, Doris, a medical physicist, raised her and her three older siblings. Her father was a florist who rarely paid his child support after her parents divorced.

Just before Miriam began her junior year at the University of Connecticut, her mother was laid off from her job. Because financial aid assessments are based on the previous year's family income, Miriam didn't qualify for the additional help she needed to continue school. "I was out of luck," she says. She finished the year with emergency loans. Rather than borrow even more heavily, Miriam then dropped out of UConn and moved back to her mother's home in Hamden, where two of her siblings had also boomeranged home. Like an increasing number of middle-class students, she traded down, finishing college as a part-time student at the less expensive, and lower-ranked, regional state college. She moved out of her mother's house and into a run-down apartment in an unsafe neighborhood. To support herself, she worked part-time, and occasionally covered her basic expenses, like groceries and books, with credit cards.

Miriam's story has a happy ending. When she graduated in 2000, at age twenty-five, she came clean with her mother about her mounting credit card debt, which was then up to $5,000. Miriam's older brother, who had been through his own money problems, put her in touch with a credit counselor, who helped her negotiate the interest rate on one credit card from a 26 percent APR to a more reasonable 9 percent. She applied for and received a series of deferments and forbearances on her student loans until she had paid off her higher-interest credit card debt. She still owes around $14,500 of her original $20,000 in student loans. Her minimum payment, over $100 a month, barely covers the interest; she sends more when she can, but barring an unforeseen stroke of fortune, she will be paying off this loan for the next thirty years. "I would say that my loan obligations have had a profound impact upon my life," she says.

Still, Miriam says, she has finally taken control of her financial life. She paid off her credit cards and bought a condo with her mother's help and consolidated her student loans at a low 5 percent interest rate. On the other hand, in a small irony, getting a handle on her own debt helped Miriam discover an interest in finance. "The idea that I had to take care of myself in the future came to be at the forefront of my consciousness," she said. "I started to read and I started to invest in mutual funds. People in my office"—a law firm where she was temping—"were coming to me and asking for investment advice." She now lives in Madison, Wisconsin, and is working toward her license as a commodities broker, at a firm where she started as a temp. She currently makes $28,000, with the promise to earn much more in coming years. "It's very well rounded," she says. "There's even creativity attached to it." She hopes to move up and maybe become a licensed financial adviser.

There are debt counselors in all fifty states, and piles of self-help books to guide people out of debt. Online communities are another avenue of mutual support for people who are struggling to gain control over their debt, including many student loan borrowers. There is an advantage to being young: no matter how deep a hole you may be in, there is time to turn things around.

I hope I've made the case here that my generation is not entirely made up of shiftless, walleyed dawdlers lingering in outgrown sandboxes (as depicted on the cover of *Time* magazine). Nor are we simply passive victims of wicked, mustachioed Social Conditions.

The transition to adulthood these days may be more convoluted and difficult. The deck is stacked against us in many ways: economic, social, political, and in the court of public opinion. But it just might turn out that the most striking character trait of Generation Debt—our penchant for outsized dreams—is exactly what we need to turn things around.

Terry, twenty-two, is the younger daughter of Taiwanese immigrants. Her father works in an airport concession; her mother is a clerk in an office. "They are very, very modest people," she says. "Simple. Not professionals. They don't function the best in an English[-language] environment. They had to take the jobs they've taken."

Terry will probably take a total of six years to finish her B.A. in interdisciplinary international development studies, having taken classes at both UCLA and at a community college to save money. When I met up with her at a coffee shop in San Francisco's Richmond neighborhood, she was interning at a global culture magazine, indulging her fascination in multicultural art. She's an irrepressible girl with a nose piercing and a trendy haircut who practices the Brazilian martial art capoeira in her free time. She's considering a career as either a freelance writer or some kind of contemporary art curator. But she's aware that her passions conflict with her parents' program of "study hard, get an education, and make more money than we did."

"I should be having a better future than my parents," Terry says. "They came here and they were able to buy a house. My dad's job's secure, five days a week, unionized, steady paycheck, health care." She knows that in today's job climate, she is unlikely to find the same. And that's not even all she's looking for. "I'm not going to be happy to just have this all-right job. My generation has more desires, which complicates things."

Should Terry shelve her interests and switch her major to accounting, or ask her dad to get her into the airport concession-

aire's union? Tough questions! They might well be more practical
choices, and I've been spending this time telling people to adjust
to reality. But I'm still rooting for her to pursue her talents. To do
otherwise would be to give up on the America I love, the America
of progress and opportunity.

The direction of American history is and must be toward more
freedom, not less. Neither I nor any woman I know would want
to go back to my mother's day, when her classmates at Smith College were still said to be going for their MRS degrees. Nor do
the ethnic minorities and immigrants I have spoken with have
any desire to go back to a time when their opportunities were determined by discrimination. This country needs the energy and
optimism of young people like Terry if it's going to get things
back on track. We need more dreams fulfilled, not dreams deferred.

This book is about economic forces, impersonal as storm winds
battering a small fishing boat. I have introduced you to the people
behind the numbers: how it feels to hear your mother say she
couldn't afford to send your tuition check, or to declare bankruptcy at age twenty-four because of a life-threatening illness, or
to sit at your kitchen table and cry over a $700 car repair. No one
should have to go through times like these. No more should we
keep quiet about it.

If you feel the same urgency I do about the new economics of
being young, I have some suggestions of what to do after you put
down this book.

If you're a parent or a concerned older person:

Understand that things have truly changed, and not all your experience in work and life is relevant to ours. Be on the lookout for unthinking attitudes that condescend to young people and blame us for a lack of success or initiative, when the causes are much more complicated.

Start an adult conversation with your kids about money. They should know your hopes and fears and your own financial plans, even as you quiz them about theirs. What kind of example are you setting? Is your retirement plan in order? Is your credit card debt mounting? If you don't have the means to save for college, do you and your children have a Plan B?

Don't be afraid to let your kids take some economic responsibility from an early age. Make sure you teach them about the dangers of credit and debt.

Our government's obligation to the security of young and old alike is a matter of open debate. Understand that as members of a large, aging generation, you have a built-in advantage in this debate, and a disproportionate amount of public resources is already being diverted to your needs.

I know that parents don't need to be told to sacrifice for their children, but consider, as well, that investing in the future will benefit everyone, including you and the people who will take care of you in your old age.

If you're a member of my generation:

Begin a real adult conversation with your parents about money, security, and success. Stop being defensive and start talking positively. Usually, they want to help you and to understand what you're going through.

If you are in college, think about founding a national student PAC. Or start by lobbying your state government for a one-cent sales tax for education and a cap on tuition hikes.

If you're working, join an organization to try to improve your own working conditions and get health care, better wages, or whatever it is you need most. Or start your own.

Yes, the job market sucks. But if the job you personally have sucks, it's ultimately up to you to find something you can live on, and live with. This could mean grad school. It could also mean working hard enough to get promoted, a short course to improve your skills, an internship, an apprenticeship, studying for a real estate license, or bartending a hundred hours a week to save up money to start your own business.

Eventual success could mean adjusting your expectations now. Are you ready to change your lifestyle and exchange some of the anxiety of wanting and buying for the joy of making and doing? Can you cut up your credit cards, consolidate your debt, and start climbing out of that hole? Forget what you've been taught about money, forget placing blame, and start over.

Strike up a conversation with strangers your age, from the next cubicle or in the coffee shop. Talk about the economic problems you have in common, about your trouble getting health insurance, your worry over your credit card debt. Share your frustrations and aspirations.

Okay, so we're ready to start a movement. What should our banners read? How about more public investment in young people, supporting education, job training, entrepreneurship, and child rearing, for a start? Call it human capital development, or the Homeland Security Jobs Act, or No Twenty-Something Left Behind.

Increased government spending on young people ought to appeal to every shade of the political spectrum, because we are in a unique position to repay what we're given. To take just one example, equalizing educational opportunity among whites, blacks, and Hispanics, says Richard Kazis in the book *Double the Numbers,* could add as much as $230 billion to the gross domestic product and raise $80 billion in new tax revenues from higher earners.

Corporate responsibility for companies that both employ and market overwhelmingly to young people is another place to start. Why not ask MTV to pay the interns who give it such invaluable advice on what's "hott"? Why not make McDonald's accountable for how many of its teenage workers rise to management—or graduate high school? Why not require Citibank to offer free financial management classes on college campuses where they market their credit cards?

I want my generation to accomplish all it can, and not only for its own sake. The nation's progress depends on the productivity of the young, and our productivity depends on the education and opportunities available to us. If we get the resources we need now, supporting ourselves, our parents, and eventually our children will be a joyful responsibility, not a hardship. When the people in power today shortchange us, they are really shortchanging themselves, and the nation as a whole. It is time for all of us to start living for the future.

NINE

Looking Ahead

This chapter covers responses to and new solutions for Generation Debt—both collective and individual—that have come to light since this book's hardcover publication. At the end, you'll find a list of online resources and a personal financial freedom guide.

Unfortunately for the members of Generation Debt, the hardcover edition of this book had two perfect news hooks. On February 1, 2006, the day before the book's official publication date, the House passed over $12 billion in reductions to federal higher education aid, the largest such cuts in the forty-year history of the program, by 216 to 214 along party lines. The state Public Interest Research Group's (PIRG's) Higher Education Project calculated that 70 percent of the savings to the government would come directly from parents and students, mainly through payments redirected from lenders and higher interest rates. On July 1, 2006, the interest rates on regular federal student loans went up to a fixed 6.8 percent, a steep rise from years of record-low variable interest rates. This increase will cost the average college borrower thousands of dollars over the repayment period of his or her loan.

The so-called "Raid on Student Aid" was the biggest chunk of a $39 billion "deficit reduction package." A $70 billion tax cut, mostly for the wealthy, passed later in the spring. Wonder why they never call those bills "deficit enhancement packages"?

Then, on February 2, as *Generation Debt* hit stores, Sallie Mae's favorite congressman was elected House Majority Leader. Ohio Republican John Boehner replaced the disgraced Tom De-Lay, successfully positioning himself as the reform candidate. This was mildly ironic, since Boehner's run was underwritten chiefly by the student loan and for-profit college industries while he was directly in charge of writing legislation to benefit them. As the *Chronicle of Higher Education* reported, Boehner and his political action committee collected a total of $259,000 from the student loan industry while he was working on reauthorizing the Higher Education Act in 2003 and 2004. Boehner got more than $100,000 from Sallie Mae alone, and enjoyed multiple golf outings with then–Sallie Mae CEO Al Lord, traveling in Lord's private plane. When it looked like the planned 2006 cuts would reduce some subsidies for lenders, the compassionate congressman rushed to reassure them, remarking to a meeting of the Consumer Bankers Association in December 2005, "Know that I have all of you in my two trusted hands."

Between the cuts and the corruption, there was very little good news on the public policy side in 2006 for students and their families struggling to pay for college. However, in the court of public opinion, as opposed to the halls of Congress, young people did start to see a shift. During 2006, the student debt crisis got wider and more sympathetic notice in the mainstream media than ever before. In the first half of 2006, *USA Today*, the country's largest-circulation newspaper, ran twenty-nine stories on student loans, including a Page One story in June on 2006 grads facing six-figure debt burdens. That stacks up against thirteen stories—and zero Page One stories—in the same paper in the first half of 2004. *Fortune*, not exactly known for its left-wing politics, ran a remarkable investigative piece suggesting Sallie Mae engaged in "predatory lending." This was followed by a *60 Minutes* exposé of the lender's practices, and further denunciations from everyone from Ralph Nader to the free-market Adam Smith Society.

The new, sympathetic attention to the student loan problem led a small, but recognizable shift in the news media's portrayal of young people. This book became part of a rising tide of more serious debate on Generation Debt issues. *The New York Times Magazine*, the *Washington Post*, the *LA Times*, the *Chicago Tribune*, and the *San Francisco Chronicle* all devoted space to student loans, the Generation Debt phenomenon, and/or *Generation Debt*, the book, in 2006. So did ABC's *The View*, the *CBS Evening News* and *60 Minutes*, MSNBC, CNN, PBS, CSPAN, Fox News, NPR, Air America, ABC Radio, and the Voice of America.

Economics-focused headlines like THIRTY AND BROKE and HEY, TWENTY-SOMETHINGS, DEBT BECOMES YOU replaced the superficial "twixter" coverage of years past. Journalists reported on the burden of student borrowing, exploitation by lenders, growing consumer debt, the generational effects of housing costs and job market changes, and the greater risks faced by those hoping to enter the middle class. Even the occasional reviewers who hated this book in particular and thought I was Exhibit A for spoiled whiners conceded some basic facts that had not been part of the popular discourse before. "Today's twenty-something authors are clearly onto something," wrote one reviewer. "College is more expensive today in real terms. There's been a shift in student aid—more loans and fewer grants. The Baby Boomers, closer to retirement, are sucking up more dollars in benefits. There's more income volatility and job insecurity than there used to be." A pretty fair assessment from an overwhelmingly negative piece headlined MEET THE IT-SUCKS-TO-BE-ME GENERATION.

Still, stereotypes don't disappear overnight. One of my favorite critical responses to *Generation Debt* came from a college student in Anchorage, Alaska. She had read this book and Tamara Draut's similarly themed book *Strapped*, and compared both to the plots of a new movie and TV series. *Failure to Launch* was a romantic comedy about a hapless thirty-something child-man played by Matthew McConaughey and the life coach, played by Sarah Jessica Parker, his parents hire to get him out of the house and onto his own two feet. *Free Ride* was a Fox sitcom about a college grad boomeranging home to hang with his loser friends. Neither one connected with audiences, and Mary Lochner suggested why:

> Unlike the real-life twenty- and thirty-somethings documented in Draut and Kamenetz's books, Nate, Amber and Mark do not suffer from the machinations of greedy, government-subsidized

lending corporations, decreased job opportunities and wage buy-ing-power. They do not lament college tuition's inverse relation-ship with the dwindling amount of federal aid made available each year to students.

In *Free Ride*, the men of the boomerang generation suffer only from a lack of character and self-sabotage.

As with many other recent television series that purported to reach out to our demographic but insulted our characters and our intelligence instead, it's hard to decide whether *Free Ride* is more deplorable because it's so offensive or because it's so lame.

Dear Author

Along with the media response to *Generation Debt* came howls of recognition from readers. Emails from young people and their parents and grandparents started filling my inbox. "While reading I had to look over my shoulder," emailed someone who ran across this book at a New York City Barnes & Noble. "I felt like you've been freakishly watching me for the past decade . . . if I had the money I would buy every baby boomer I know this book." A college student in Montana who was working sixty hours a week over the summer to minimize her debt wrote that she'd been calling her parents on breaks from her job at a ceiling tile factory, "to fill them in on some of the crazy statistics you present . . . I swear your book is exactly about me." Of course there were some naysayers, who thought I was either too liberal or too gloom-and-doom or both. But the vast majority of readers who took the time to email did so because they felt someone had finally told their story.

I met even more Generation Debters when I traveled to speak
at bookstores and campuses around the country, from Maryland
to Washington State. Jake, twenty-one, came up to me after a talk
at Kalamazoo College. He was transferring from a community
college to Michigan State University, and he asked if there was any
way he could apply to receive more federal aid as an independent
student before reaching the cutoff age of twenty-four. (There is;
you have to apply to your campus financial aid office for a "professional judgment review," and show that your parents no longer
support you.) Afterward, he wrote me:

> I have been living on my own and working shitty 40, 50, and 60
> hour weeks while taking a full load of night classes at community
> college. And after two years of sweating through mandatory over-
> time and overdosing on caffeine to stay awake for three hours of
> class four nights a week, all for Uncle Sam to say I only qualify
> for 3,500 dollars for a university that costs 17,600 a year because
> my step-dad makes X amount of dollars a year. I hope I don't
> come off as a cynic, I am far from pessimistic about obtaining
> my goals (journalism) or having the impact I want to on this
> world(fix it). It's just this knee-jerk whiplash effect of finding out
> once again that everything in this system isn't as simple an equa-
> tion as my bobble-headed, perky-smiled high school counselors
> described.

I later told that story at a conference of college financial aid
professionals. In the audience was Debra Wiley, the Federal Student
Aid Ombudsman. She invited me to send along any questions that

I got from people about problems with student loans or grants—her office investigates disputes. Her contact information can be found at the end of this chapter.

One of the toughest questions I got was from a high school senior named Olabisi Sobowale. I was visiting Marble Hill School for International Studies, a small, high-performing public school housed with four others in a giant complex in the Bronx. The juniors and seniors wore uniforms and were unusually attentive, even on the first nice day of spring. I talked about how a BA isn't a golden ticket to success anymore, and that you need a master plan to match your interests with an occupation, especially if going to a four-year college means taking on serious financial risks.

After my talk, an intent young woman wearing a head kerchief raised her hand. Olabisi, who had immigrated from Lagos, Nigeria, with her family in 2001, asked me if the dangers posed by high loans meant she and students like herself, from less wealthy backgrounds, should give up on college. And if not, how much debt is too much? She had brought along financial aid letters from two selective colleges, one higher-ranked than the other. The in-state, public college had offered her a package with $6000 a year in loans, while the out-of-state private school's package included $20,000 a year in loans. I didn't have any easy answers for her, so I invited her to continue the conversation over email. She wrote:

> Many have advised that I choose what is best for me. Well, the question now is, How do you know what is best for you? Others said just go for it, many people in America are in debt. Making it seem like it's "An American thing to do."

Your book made me think about my future further. I want to
be able to have a family of my own and someday have my own
children. Can I do that with lots of loans and debt following me
around? I advised my mom to invest her money for her retirement
and she promised to fill her 401K just like it was mentioned in
your book.

Your book has definitely got into me by explaining why it's important to save and buy things you really need. It will help me
while I am in college. I am glad I took the time to finish the book.
While reading your book, I asked myself if I really want to attend
college because of the outcome of the people that had shared
their college experience. Now I realize that I can learn from them
and avoid making similar mistakes.

Olabisi's story had a happy ending. She was accepted to Middlebury, her top choice, and the elite liberal arts college offered her a
far more generous financial aid package than either of the other
two universities. Like many well-endowed private colleges, including Princeton and Dartmouth, Middlebury has a rule limiting
family loan burdens—in their case, to a total of $4000. Olabisi
graduated as her class valedictorian, bound for Middlebury in the
fall. But I kept mulling over her questions.

Looking at such a smart and conscientious student, it's clear
that for her own good and that of the country she should invest in
her future by going to college, even if it means taking on loans.
But it's less clear to me that it would have been the best decision
for her to borrow $80,000 instead of $24,000 to go to a marginally
higher-ranked institution. Do you tell students like her to give up

on college? Unconscionable. Do you tell them to borrow away, because that's what Americans do? Irresponsible. The way our system is set up right now, there are no good answers.

What You Can Do: Laws

Most of the people who contacted me wanted to share their own stories of getting by, and a lot, like "Charles," wanted to know what they could do to fight back. Charles called in to a radio show where I was being interviewed. Later that day, he wrote me:

> My wife and I have around $80,000 of student loan debt (she has a master's, and I have two bachelor's) and we are working hard to get back into the middle-class for ourselves and our two kids. We ARE steadily paying down our debt, but it's a tremendous burden that keeps us from really moving forward as a family. We're already 30 and it'll likely be four or five years before we can get a starter home that may not even be as good as the house we're currently renting.
>
> As you articulate so well, we as a society have decided that it's just not important enough to invest in educating our people. We expect those who wish to educate themselves (as we're told we MUST do in this global age) to take on an amount of debt that will severely delay the time before they can even begin to pursue our so-called American dream. This is even more pronounced in a situation like mine, where both members of a marriage bring this burden of student loan debt. This is not how I remember life with a college degree being described . . . So, is there anything we

can do? I mean for average people who aren't writing books and who obviously don't have a lot of money to spare?

I wrote back that he could support several politicians—all Democrats—who are speaking out right now on student loan issues:

• On May 26, 2006, Senator Hillary Clinton, after several months of consultation with student advocates, introduced a comprehensive "Borrower's Bill of Rights" in the Senate. The new protections include income-contingent repayment plans, the possibility of full debt forgiveness, and caps on the total amount that lenders can load on in interest and penalties on student loans in default or delinquency. Financial aid policy experts I talked to gave the bill a poor chance of passing in its entirety, but agreed it was an important strategic step.

• On June 14, 2006, House Minority Leader Nancy Pelosi pledged that if the Democrats took back Congress in November, they would cut student loan interest rates in half to 3.4 percent—a simple, yet appealing, proposition.

• On June 28, 2006, Senator Ted Kennedy and seven Democratic cosponsors (Clinton, Dodd, Durbin, Harkin, Lieberman, Mikulski, and Schumer) introduced the Student Debt Relief Act. This act includes the same language as the Student Aid Reward Act from 2005, which would save billions from the federal higher education budget by rewarding schools that switch to the direct lending program, which is far more cost-efficient for taxpayers. The savings would be redirected to grant aid.

The bill includes a substantial increase to the Pell Grant and more loan repayment options.

· And on July 19, 2006, the Democratic Leadership Council proposed a package of $3000 tuition tax credits, $150 billion in performance-based grants to states, and incentives to colleges, all aimed at producing one million more college graduates by 2015.

With all of these possible reforms in the pipeline, a bit of well-timed citizen communication could go a long way toward creating more sensible and equitable student aid policies.

What You Can Do: Activism

Although no generational Superman showed up to save the day in 2005–2006, the year did see more examples of students acting on their own behalf. One member of the new breed of Generation Debt activists is Nathan Dickerson. Tall, blond, and whip-smart, he grew up on a small cattle farm in western Kentucky near the Indiana border, and was the first in his family to go to college. He scored a full merit scholarship to the University of Kentucky at Louisville. Yet he saw his friends struggling with huge debt burdens as his state university went through double-digit tuition increases. "The ideal of social mobility inspired me to work hard in school," he said, yet without the luck of his scholarship, college would have been out of reach. "If I hadn't had this scholarship, I doubt I would have made it even to the state university. It would have been a technical school or community college. I would just like to think that anyone who works hard should be able to achieve a middle-class lifestyle, and it seems like a college diploma is the primary vehicle to get that." So Nathan started thinking more about the threat to the American Dream posed by the high cost of college. On campus, he helped organize students to phone bank and travel to the state capital in order to protest the Kentucky state legislature's decisions to raise tuition by 14.5 percent in 2005 and 12 percent in 2006.

I first met Nathan at the first Campus Progress conference in 2005, a summertime gathering in Washington, D.C., attended by more than eight hundred college students. Progressive publications like *The Nation* and *Utne Reader* have cited Campus Progress, part of the Center for American Progress, as the prime example among several new organizations helping shape the new generation of politically educated, motivated young people, preparing to swing the pendulum back from years of conservative rule. Campus Progress Director David Halperin is a former speechwriter for Bill Clinton who led the youth division of the Howard Dean campaign in 2004. With a $1.25 million budget, the group established a presence on over four hundred campuses nationwide in one year, sponsoring hundreds of lectures and events (including some *Generation Debt* events), underwriting dozens of progressive student publications, and maintaining an active website and blog. Student loan debt, credit card debt, economic inequality, health care, and job insecurity are all on their agenda.

Nathan invited me to his campus to speak about *Generation Debt* in the spring of 2006. The next summer, he interned in DC at Mobilizing America's Youth (MAY), another new progressive political youth advocacy organization, founded in 2002 by UC Berkeley students. MAY has a presence on hundreds of campuses and hopes to position itself as an AARP for youth. Nathan spent the summer of 2006 working on their college affordability campaign, getting students to lobby their Congressional representatives, just as they had at the University of Kentucky.

Even more youth and student mobilization efforts either got off the ground or received more notice in 2006. The Raid on Student Aid was one impetus. Another was the Federal Secretary of Education's Commission on the Future of Higher Education, appointed in 2005 to make recommendations on issues of reining in soaring costs, improving quality, and lowering barriers to access. Beyond these, however, was a growing awareness of the potential political power of Generation Y, a theme that is bound to develop more fully in the 2008 presidential election.

The PIRG's Higher Education Project partnered with the Project on Student Debt, a brand-new organization based at the University of California at Berkeley, to set up a website called the Student Debt Yearbook. Hundreds of students from campuses all around the country submitted testimonies about their experiences with student loan debt. Congressman George Miller, the ranking Democrat on the House Education and the Workforce Committee, also organized an online forum with testimony from students and parents on the toll of student debt.

The PIRG organized rallies at various meetings of the Commission on Higher Education around the country, trying to get leaders to listen to students' concerns. They were partially rewarded with a Commission report that recommended a complete overhaul and simplification of the federal student aid system while increasing the Pell Grant to 70 percent of the cost of a public institution.

A different activist response to the student loan situation, less focused on youth, came from a renegade-sounding group called Student Loan Justice. Alan Collinge, a thirty-five-year-old former aerospace engineer in Washington State, originally borrowed $38,000 in student loans from Sallie Mae to complete three degrees at the University of Southern California. In 2001, after making about $7,000 in on-time payments, he left his engineering post at Caltech on the promise of a government job that evaporated after 9/11. He was underemployed for two years, barely making ends meet as a short-order cook in Alaska; his student loans went into default. "When I got back from Alaska, I got a bill for $85,000 and it pretty much blew me away. That's when I realized that somebody is making a lot of money around this deal." Today, Collinge owes $105,000 to the Department of Education. His credit ruined, he can't get security clearance for a government job or qualify for a regular home mortgage.

Collinge focused his personal anguish on the big lenders, especially Sallie Mae and their former CEO Al Lord. "I lose hours of sleep because of my personal situation," he told me. "So I spend my time on this." He pores over SEC filings to find out how much student loan executives earn in bonuses and stock options, and he uses sites like fundrace.org and opensecrets.org to find out how much cash they give to politicians. He started studentloanjustice .org in the spring of 2005, and by the spring of 2006 he had collected thousands of stories from people all over the country suffering in situations similar to his. Student Loan Justice is the place to turn if you are several years out of school with severe student loan problems.

Since student loans are not dischargeable in bankruptcy, lenders and their collection agents are unlikely to accept settlements for less than what they say is owed. In cases of long-term delinquency or default, they often demand three, four, or five times as much as the original amount borrowed. I have reviewed some of these cases and found migraine-inducing mazes of paperwork, with individual loans bought, resold, and reconsolidated over decades.

Student Loan Justice grabbed the attention of journalists and politicians alike. Collinge was featured in the *60 Minutes* segment about Sallie Mae and got the ear of Senator Hillary Clinton's office. Ultimately, Student Loan Justice is seeking a federal amnesty for student loan borrowers who have loans they could never hope to repay.

The National Tuition Endowment is yet another student aid policy solution proposed by the students, the people most directly affected. Matan Ariel grew up in Israel and served three years in the army there before coming to Columbia University, where he is a political science major. Nate Walker is a candidate for the Unitarian Universalist ministry from Nevada completing a doctorate in education at Columbia's divinity school. What they have in common is a mountain of student loan debt—approaching $100,000 for Walker—and a desire to find new solutions to the problem of paying for college. In the spring of 2005, Walker and Ariel started poring over the Department of Education's federal student aid budget. They produced a detailed legislative proposal to trim excess lender subsidies and redirect program profits back to students, saving around $30 billion from the federal education budget. This money, they proposed, should go to create an annual endowment for grant aid. The two students and some classmates then spent over a year gathering the endorsements of hundreds of student governments, the United States Student Association, and the state PIRGs. In the spring of 2006, they took their proposal to Capitol Hill, meeting with several sympathetic legislators. One of their proposals, eliminating a loophole that allowed student lenders to collect 9.5 percent interest from the government on certain loans, was actually enacted as part of the Raid on Student Aid, but the savings were directed to the treasury, not to students or families.

The Tuition Endowment Fund takes a moderate, market-friendly approach to financial aid reform. The big lenders would lose their special privileges, allowing a truly open market in student loans, with local credit unions perhaps playing a greater role. Streamlining the program would help students better understand the system so they can take full advantage of available aid. And eliminating corporate subsidies leaves more federal funds for student grants. *Mother Jones* magazine honored the effort as one of the top twelve campus activist accomplishments of 2006.

On a related market-based front, MyRichUncle, a finance
company founded by two twenty-something Stuyvesant High
School grads to make both private and federal student loans, offered a new commercial alternative in 2006. They became the first
student loan company to offer large across-the-board interest rate
discounts on federal student loans, of 1.5 to 2 percentage points.
They also used a two-page ad in the Sunday *New York Times* to
tell students and families how lenders market themselves to
schools, offering special deals and discounts (which MRU called
"kickbacks" and "payola"). The goal was to sell their loans to students directly, making sure students know that they have a right to
choose a lender beyond their school's "preferred" list. The *Chronicle of Higher Education* reported that the ad ruffled feathers
among financial aid officers, but prospective students immediately took notice of the good deals. I don't think market responses
are the whole solution, especially looking further ahead. But anything that gives students more choices, more information, and
maybe better prices, is a good idea in the short term.

So there has been a lot of recent activity on student loans, and
many proposals for improvement. What should we look for next?

An effective end to the higher education aid crisis must address
all parts of this dysfunctional system: colleges, students, business,
and government. The reforms currently before Congress are encouraging, but not nearly comprehensive enough.

First, the federal government must restore the buying power of
need-based grants to help close the yawning gap in college
attendance between the neediest and richest students. Restoring

the Pell Grant to its 1970s buying power of about three-fourths of the bill at an average public university, as the Secretary's own commission recommended, would be a good place to start. Nathan Dickerson's right—the American Dream is at stake here.

At the same time, we can't let tuition continue to outrun student aid. As conservatives argue, state governments and colleges together need to find ways to limit tuition increases over time. As in the Democratic Leadership Council proposal, states and campuses that increase productivity and efficiency without compromising educational goals should be rewarded. And communities and students should have more input into their colleges' budget decisions. This was brought home to me when I spoke at the University of Maryland College Park, at a brand-new student center that looked like a Marriot. I asked the students if they'd have traded their 10 percent tuition increase for a rec hall with a couple of old pool tables instead, and they rousingly agreed. Many community colleges are good models of cost-efficient institutions that respond to community demand.

And what of student loan debt? I'm not a free-higher-education absolutist—I'll leave that to the Young Democratic Socialists (whose conference I spoke at last spring). It seems fair for students and families to share some of the cost of a valuable degree, either through work or borrowing. The question is how to make that share bearable.

I still think the first order of business is to eliminate the guaranteed student loan program in favor of direct loans. This is true for both practical and political reasons. The direct loan program has shown itself over thirteen years to be much cheaper for tax-payers and more efficient in its use of government funds than the guaranteed loan program. Even more detrimental are the corruption and inherent conflicts of interest in the current system. Student advocates will have a hard time being heard as long as a lucrative industry feeds off growing student debt and lobbies Congress to the tune of hundreds of thousands of dollars a year to keep it that way.

For new ideas in student aid, lots of higher education experts are suggesting we look abroad. A September 2005 report from the international Educational Policy Institute, "Global Debt Patterns," compared student loan policies in Australia, Canada, Germany, the Netherlands, New Zealand, Sweden, the UK, and the U.S. Usher concluded, "In the worst-case scenario of having low income and high debt, the U.S. is clearly the worst place to be."

That's because other countries have better provisions for debt relief, automatic cancellation, and income-contingent repayment—people pay a fixed percentage of their disposable income until their loans are made good. In Australia, if you're earning below 35,000 Australian dollars ($26,640 U.S.) you don't pay; above that, you pay 4 to 8 percent of your income on a sliding scale. Income-contingent repayment functions like a social tax; it is sometimes administered by the equivalent of the IRS. Those who have reaped the greatest economic benefits from higher education repay their loans faster, thus subsidizing the teachers, social workers, and those whom fate has simply dealt a bad hand. In the U.S., income-contingent repayment is available only to borrowers with direct loans and low incomes who specially apply. Applied across the board, it would be a great step toward making our system both fairer and simpler.

Grandfathered Health Care

Behind student loan debt, health insurance got the most traction as a Gen Debt issue in 2005 and 2006. In fall 2005, New Jersey passed a law requiring that all employers extend health care coverage to employees' offspring up to age thirty, as long as the young adults remain single and childless. Twenty-five more states have also raised or are considering raising the dependency age limit for coverage under a parent's policy, generally from twenty-three to twenty-five or twenty-six.

The New Jersey bill has the potential to cover 100,000 of the state's uninsured, who altogether cost taxpayers $600 million a year in charity care. Private individual insurance in the state can be $7,000 a year, a price few are able or willing to pay. These new adult dependent policies cost between $1,200 and $2,000 annually, a sum close to the actual annual average medical costs incurred by relatively healthy under-thirty-year-olds. Employers don't shoulder any extra cost, since young adults or their parents pay the premiums. Neil Cohen, the State Assemblyman who introduced the law, called it "a home run for everybody."

The idea of twenty-somethings staying on their parents' plans is a less than perfect solution. First of all, low-wage young people who are not attending or have not attended college are the most likely to be uninsured, and their parents are less likely to be insured themselves. Grandfathering mostly middle-class kids into an old, disintegrating employee benefit system is, unfortunately, nothing more than a stopgap on the way to comprehensive reform. Still, in the short term, it means more young people can go to the doctor, and that's nothing to sneeze at. For a comprehensive state-by-state list of alternative sources of affordable health care, go to the website http://www.ahirc.org.

These laws are an example of a new state approach to the health care crisis. In the absence of federal action, states are reaching out to chronically underinsured populations. In 2006, Maryland passed a law, targeted at Wal-Mart, requiring very large employers who pay less than 8 percent of their payroll in health benefits to pay the difference in taxes. The law was struck down months later by the State Supreme Court, but still hailed by advocates as a model. In April 2006, Massachusetts' Republican governor Mitt Romney gained wide recognition for his bill requiring every state resident to purchase health insurance by July 2007. The practical details are still being hammered out, but they include a special low-cost state-subsidized plan for eighteen-to-twenty-six-year-olds. These are all encouraging intermediate steps toward the national health care plan we need.

What's Next?

2006 was not a banner year for most other issues affecting Generation Debt. Republicans killed an increase to the minimum wage, again. Consumer debt grew. Social Security reform died. The ceiling on the national debt was officially raised to $9 trillion. The Medicare drug plan was unofficially pronounced a disaster.

But on the activist side, there have been some increasingly exciting developments. It always surprises me when people trot out the old clichés about "youth today" not being as politically active as they were in the 1960s. "Young people today are voting, protesting, and volunteering in record numbers," counters Heather Smith of the registration and mobilization group Young Voter Strategies, and she has the research to back it up. February 15, 2003, is generally considered to be the largest single day of political protest (against the war in Iraq) the world has ever seen, and youth were out in force. And I was lucky enough to be in New York City for the Republican National Convention in 2004, standing outside the NYPD's makeshift jail at Pier 57 on the Hudson River, when Tom Hayden himself, the hero of Chicago '68, pointed out, "There have never been so many people protesting a political convention of the eighty in our history, and there have never been so many people arrested." Youth included.

Even if getting arrested isn't your thing, there's a lot you can do right now as a young person to make your voice heard nationwide. Students can join groups like the PIRGs, Campus Progress, or MAY. Tent State University is another option, an informal national movement at campuses from U Michigan to Rutgers where students hold multiday teach-ins to promote campus democracy— the idea of having a say in their own affairs from tuition hikes to teaching.

Generation Engage, founded in 2005 by Justin Rockefeller (son of Senator John D.) and Adrian Talbott (son of Strobe), is a nonpartisan civic-engagement group that holds high-tech town hall events with speakers like Spike Lee and Bill Clinton. It has the distinction of being one of very few groups with a long-term focus on engaging non-college youth in politics.

Energy Action is one of the more exciting developments in youth activism today, engaged on a front not at all covered in the first edition of my book. Billy Parish, twenty-four, dropped out of Yale University in the fall of 2003 in order to focus on youth and student environmental organizing. His focus is arguably the single most dire problem facing our future: global warming. "I thought that the revival of an aggressive, dynamic, hopeful youth movement could have a real, strategic impact," he said. "We are one of the constituencies with special moral authority on this issue. We'll be impacted the most."

Parish's Energy Action coalition joins thirty youth and student environmental and social justice organizations with a presence on 1,500 campuses nationwide. Their biggest campaign, the Campus Climate Challenge, started in the fall of 2005. Their goal is to get five hundred campuses in the U.S. and Canada to make clean energy commitments by 2008. By the summer of 2006, they were more than halfway there. The thinking goes that colleges can build markets for renewable energy, serve as moral examples, innovate, and shape the thinking of young leaders. If every campus in the U.S. converted to 100 percent clean energy, the market for renewable energy would quadruple.

Moves inspired in part by the campaign so far include a commitment by California State University, the world's largest four-year university system, to purchase 20 percent renewable energy by 2010. The University of Iowa saves $500,000 a year by using biomass—oat hulls—to replace coal in its onsite power plant. St. Olaf College in Minnesota is building a wind turbine to meet one-third of its energy costs. And the list goes on.

In the summer of 2006, I saw Parish speak on these and other victories at Take Back America, a big progressive political conference in Washington, D.C. Parish made an explicit connection between economic issues like student debt and the ecological debt that has been run up by previous and current generations. In both cases, elders are suffering from a potentially terminal case of short-term thinking, and it is up to the young to imagine and work for a different, sustainable future. The room erupted in applause when he said, "You need to listen to young people."

After a couple of years of hard work nationally and internationally, Energy Action received a major funding boost in the spring of 2006. They were able to hire several full-time staff, open a real office in Washington, D.C. instead of working out of borrowed space, and gain some high-profile strategic partners like MTV. Given that Hurricane Katrina and Al Gore's film *An Inconvenient Truth* have finally put global warming near the top of the political agenda, where it belongs; given that climate experts like James Hansen say we have less than ten years to right the ship or face irrevocable global consequences; I think it's safe to say that we'll be hearing a lot more from groups like Energy Action.

Ballot Boxing

All of these stirrings of a youth movement, on student loans, the
environment, and other economic and social issues, have a chance
to be felt in a serious way in the 2008 election. The eleven-point
spike in the vote among eighteen-to-twenty-four-year-olds in 2004
caught some serious attention from political strategists, as did the
54–45 split for John Kerry. Young Voter Strategies, a mobilization
and education group funded by the Pew Charitable Trusts, is investing $3 million on a bet that those results can be topped in
2008. Democratic pollster Celinda Lake has been among the foremost voices predicting the importance of Millennials, born between 1982 (some say 1978) and 2000. They are currently 25
percent of the voting population and are seen as a potentially
strong voting bloc in 2008. According to a July 16, 2006, article in
the *Washington Post*, "Lake said she has told Democrats they have
'a major opportunity' to nurture the future of the party. 'The
long-term studies show that if you capture a cohort in their youth
three times in a row, then you hold their party identification for
the rest of their life,' she said." The article tied this wisdom to the
decision by Democrats to put college affordability at the top of
their fall 2006 agenda.

Of course, neither party automatically deserves youth alle-
giance if they're not acting on issues that matter to us. This must
include economic opportunity for both the one-third of people
with bachelor's degrees in their futures and the majority without.
And it is even more important that we ask our leaders to take on

crises like global warming that affect all of us. That's what it means to make common cause as a generation—across racial lines, across class lines, over and above issues of self-interest, in the interest of the future.

Appendix: Let's Save America!

The challenges facing our generation demand action in both the collective and personal spheres. The personal side boils down to managing your own financial future better. In April 2006, I found myself in the beautiful lakeside resort town of Coeur d'Alene, Idaho, lecturing to a high school economics class. I was in this unlikely place because a man named Brad Dugdale had invited me to be part of the first annual Kootenai County Financial Literacy Week. Mr. Dugdale is a vice president at the largest investment and financial services firm in the Pacific Northwest. His main interest— a passion, really—is financial literacy. He founded the nonprofit Let's Save America! and has self-published several books and audio CDs on subjects like the magic of compound interest, and the Rule of 72 (a rule of thumb that bankers use to figure out how soon a lump sum will double at a given rate of interest). He created a Financial Literacy Week as part of a larger campaign to get his state to adopt a standard public school curriculum on financial literacy. "Financial literacy is not an elective," he likes to say.

Mr. Dugdale seemed pretty kooky to me at first. A passion for financial literacy is like a passion for oral hygiene—a good idea, sure, but nothing to get too excited about. Yet the more time I spent with him, the more I came around to his point of view. Maybe the only sensible counter to our country's consumer-debt insanity is a little saving fanaticism.

So there I was, in Idaho, explaining to several classes of slack-jawed teenagers that the stock market returns an average of 8 percent over the long term. Sometime toward the end of the day, I finally connected with them. A girl in the back raised her hand and said, "So, like, is there any reason to wait or can we start an IRA right now?"

Nope. And yup. So here's a quick guide—the least you need to know right now to make major improvements in your financial life. You can find even more information and resources at anyakamenetz.com.

1) Get organized.

The number-one obstacle people face in managing money is a lack of insight into their current situation. The good news is that we young folks have technology on our side. Stuff you will need on hand in order to stop crumpling up bills and tame your financial madness: A credit report (get it free at annualcreditreport.com), three previous bank statements (available online at your bank), account statements for your credit card (ditto), a couple months of pay stubs, and student loan account information (available from your lender or at the National Student Loan Data System: http://www.nslds.ed.gov/nslds_SA/).

First, go over the information and check for errors. Jot down a quick balance sheet: total assets, total debt, monthly income, and

monthly recurring expenses (rent, transportation, groceries, insurance, cell phone/Internet.)

2) Attack debt first.

Keeping in good standing with your student loans is even more
important than paying down credit cards, because of the massive
penalties and fees that student loan companies can assess. The
difference is that student loans can be put off. If you have to, get a
deferment or forbearance before you fall behind.

Now, rethink your use of plastic. If you're carrying credit card
debt at 15 percent interest, it's actually counterproductive to save.
The rate you could earn in a safe investment, minus inflation, is
less than the rate at which your debt grows. That's a major way
that Generation Debt is hobbled in the attempt to build a secure
future. So you need to dedicate your extra resources right away to
both lower the interest rates and pay that debt off.

You can lower your interest rates by transferring balances to a
zero-percent-introductory-rate card. Or call the bank to negotiate
the rates down by threatening to switch. A payment calculator,
like the one at Bankrate.com, (http://www.bankrate.com/brm/
calc/creditcardpay.asp), will help you figure out how fast you can
get debt-free. You must pay over the 2.5 percent minimum balance
each month to have any hope of closing out the cards in this lifetime. Quick example: Let's say you're carrying $4088 on your
credit cards, the average balance for twenty-five-to-thirty-four-
year-olds. If you made that 2.5 percent minimum payment, it
would take you over twenty-seven years to erase the debt, and

you'd pay more in interest than in principal. Instead, pay the same amount each month until the balance is gone. Get a windfall like a tax refund or birthday present? Spend half on yourself, half to pay off the cards.

3) Get health insurance.

You can't afford not to. A large medical expense was the number-one cause of bankruptcy for people who filed in the 1990s.

If you have a plan at work, sign up unless the rates are terrible. Otherwise, group-rate insurance typically costs $200–$250 a month. The group Access to Health Insurance/Resources for Care lists possible alternative group-rate health insurance programs for every state at the website http://www.ahirc.org. You may be eligible under a state program for low-income adults, or to purchase a group policy intended for freelancers, writers, artists, musicians, or technology workers. And there are some provisions in twenty-five states to cover young adults as dependents. These are listed by the National Conference of State Legislatures at http://www.ncsl .org/programs/health/dependentstatus.htm.

If you absolutely can't afford a monthly fee of $200-plus, then your second choice should be catastrophic or "major medical" health insurance. You pay a monthly fee as little as $15. The plan won't shell out for day-to-day care, but if something expensively terrible happens, you'll be covered. You can compare different plans and get quotes from sites like http://www.healthinsurance

.org/ or http://www.ehealthinsurance.com/. You should look for a plan that covers you above $5000.

4) Start the saving habit.

You need at least two months' income socked away so the next car breakdown doesn't go on the Visa card. Saving 10 percent of monthly income is a good benchmark (that would mean putting away $212 a month after taxes if your annual salary is $30,000). To earn more, try a money-market account instead of a regular savings account. The good news for savers, as opposed to borrowers, is that interest rates are currently trending up. With most major banks, you can go online and arrange recurring transfers from checking to savings or money-market accounts, making your saving routine automatic. Last year, Bank of America introduced a program that rounds up each bankcard purchase you make and puts the change in your savings account. Every little bit helps!

5) Save for the long haul.

Once you have a cushion of a few thousand for unexpected expenses and are in the saving habit, open a tax-free retirement account. The sooner you start, the less you'll need to salt away overall to be secure in a world where private pensions and Social Security are both at risk.

If you happen to have a 401(k) with employer matching, use it! This is the number-one advice I have gotten from several financial advisers. You should fill your 401(k) before you put money in emergency savings and even contribute while paying off credit cards, because that 50 percent or 100 percent matching is the best rate you can earn on your money, anywhere.

If you don't have access to a 401(k), the best choice for most people in their twenties and thirties is a Roth Individual Retirement Account (IRA). You can open one at any time, with any amount of money, through a bank or directly with a brokerage. The maximum annual contribution is $4,000 for 2007 and $5,000 for 2008. The smart, simple thing to ask for when setting up your IRA is no-load mutual funds. "Mutual fund" just means you're buying a mix of stocks and/or bonds. "No-load" means no commission fees, which translates into higher returns for you. Vanguard (www.vanguard.com) offers a number of no-load mutual funds.

Despite all I've said about the obstacles facing Generation Debt, one factor all young people have on our side is time. Remember, when it comes to saving, time really is money. What Brad Dugdale calls "the magic of compound interest" can work for you or against you.

I started my own retirement planning midway through writing this book by putting $3,600 in an IRA at age twenty-five. If I continue to save the same amount for the next fifteen years and earn 8 percent each year, I will have invested a total of $54,000. If I then forget all about that account and continue to earn that 8 percent and cash out when I'm seventy-one, I'll have $1.5 million. Again, I saved for only 15 years and I have almost enough to retire on. But if I had waited until I was thirty-nine to start saving my $3,600 a year, and saved right through to retirement at seventy, and earned that same 8 percent, I'd have invested twice as much money—$108,000, and ended up with less than one-third in the end—$450,000. The difference is the number of years that my cash had to grow.

Run through these numbers for yourself, and a funny thing will start to happen—you'll actually start to get excited about saving. I promise.

6) Spend in balance.

Most money guides for young people start with condescending and obvious advice about tightening spending. Did you know that if you just stopped washing your hair with Starbucks coffee you could save $70,000 a year? I think that's a superficial way to approach money management. For most people, once you follow the steps above, taking a good hard look at your status quo, setting financial goals and following them, tedious budgeting is unnecessary. To put it another way, if you're paying the bills and meeting your savings and investment goals, personally I think the rest of your earnings are for you to spend as you like without necessarily tracking every cent.

On the other hand, if you go into the details and discover that your basic cost of living—rent, phone, food—actually exceeds your income, if you're paying overdraft or late fees month after month, then yes, you have to track these expenses more closely and get back in balance, by spending less or earning more or both. Some money experts would tell you to sell your car, others to get a second job delivering pizza. You could take in another room-mate, or set up a home-based business. Balance is the key.

Can you pay the bills, but can't seem to save? Anything you can do to keep aware of the money you have flowing in and going out will act as a natural check on regrettable shopping. For example, limiting ATM visits to once a week or every other week helps a lot of people I know—when you're out of cash, you're out of cash. If you want to get a little more specific, a friend of mine, Jake Schwartz, who is a certified financial adviser, recommends sub-tracting all your recurring expenses, from the Sallie Mae payment to the cell phone bill, from your monthly income, and dividing the remainder by thirty. Presto: you have issued yourself your own "per diem" discretionary spending allowance. Pack a peanut butter sandwich Monday and you'll have enough cash for sushi on Friday.

Over the last three years, I have developed great confidence in this generation's abillity to turn things around personally and po-litically. Time is on your side, if you only realize the power you al-ready have.

ACKNOWLEDGMENTS

A person at my stage of her career does not produce a book like this without the strong help and encouragement of many, many people. First of all, I owe a debt to the people across the country who bravely and honestly shared their stories with me. This is your book.

Much credit is due my *Village Voice* editor, Laura Conaway, who originally conceived the idea of a feature series on "the new economics of being young," and who has always been both a generous mentor and a reality check. I must also thank Don Forst and everyone else at the *Voice* for giving me a chance. Throughout this process, my parents and teachers, Moira Crone and Rodger Kamenetz, somehow managed a perfect balance of familial affirmation and expert advice on matters of argument and style. I have been so lucky to draw on the expertise of my wonderful agent, Katinka Matson, and my incredible editor, Cindy

Spiegel, and Susan Ambler, Charlotte Douglas, and everyone else at Riverhead Books. Jaclyn Delamatre, Gabriel Freiman, Yuka Igarashi, Daniel Kurtz-Phelan, Linda Rosenbury, Alan Schoenfeld, Alexander Southgate, Arielle Zibrak, and many other accomplished friends offered thoughtful readings, comments, and feedback. Countless experts took the time to share their insights with me; particularly helpful were Dr. Laurence Kotlikoff, Dr. Michael Males, Jerry Davis, Dr. Sara Collins, Dr. Donald Heller, Dr. Richard Fossey, and Dr. Stuart Tannock. Among the many people who also helped with the research, Timothy Killikelly opened up his classes at City College of San Francisco to me, and Art Gonzalez did the same thing at the Center for Employment Training. Stephen Dubner and Susan Orlean, with kindness, set me on this path and showed me how a book is written. Thanks to Eryn Leavens for her research assistance. And more than anything, thanks to Adam Berenzweig for his ideas, his encouragement, his unique talent for listening, and for always, always being there.

The complete endnotes for each chapter are available online at anyakamenetz.blogspot.com.

PREFACE

p. xi. Not only am I one of just 28 percent of the young population with a bachelor's degree:

Two of the crucial facts in this book are subject to some dispute. The first is the educational attainment of the U.S. population. The Census Bureau reports, based on the annual Current Population Survey—a sampling, not a full census—that 27 percent of adults over twenty-five, and 28 percent of adults twenty-five to twenty-nine, had completed a bachelor's degree in 2003, and that 87 percent of adults twenty-five to twenty-nine were high school graduates.

According to the full 2000 U.S. Census, only 24.4 percent of the population over twenty-five has a B.A., and 80.4 percent are high school graduates. Paul Barton, of the nonprofit Educational Testing Service, which administers the SAT, reported in February 2005 ("One-Third of a Nation: Rising Dropout Rates and Declining Opportunities") that official estimates of the percentage of high school graduates were too high, and that four recent independent estimates had put the figure between 66 and 71 percent. The 2004 book *Double the Numbers,* authored by three leaders of the research and policy organization Jobs for the Future, uses the 25 percent figure for college graduates and the 67 percent figure for high school graduates.

While the exact numbers may be elusive, the trend lines are clearer. The Current Population Survey report ("Educational Attainment in the United States: 2003"), while putting the best face on the data, clearly shows that young people's educational attainment rose between 1950 and 1970 yet has remained essentially flat since the mid-1970s.

CHAPTER ONE. WHY GENERATION DEBT?

p. 6. Statistically, the typical college student today:

These characterizations of students come from the National Center for Education Statistics (NCES), a government agency that is part of the U.S. Department of Education. They are valid for the 1999–2000 school year. The average age of all U.S. undergrads is twenty-six; their median age is twenty-two; 50.7 percent of students attend part-time for some period of their enrollment; 42.1 percent are enrolled in public two-year community colleges; 80.1 percent of all students work while enrolled, averaging 31.6 hours per week.

Persistence and completion of college programs is a notoriously difficult statistic to track, as students increasingly drop out, stop out, transfer schools, or go from full-time to part-time enrollment. Of first-year students in 1995–96, according to another NCES study, 46.6 percent had completed any degree (bachelor's or associate's) five years later; 37.2 percent had dropped out.

The credit card information comes from student lender Nellie Mae, which conducts annual national analyses based on both surveys and data provided by banks. According to its May 2005 survey, 76 percent of all undergraduate students carry credit cards; 72 percent reported using credit cards for food, 72 percent for textbooks, 68 percent for clothing, and 24 percent for tuition; 79 percent carry a balance forward each month.

p. 10. When I talked to Shaffer, she backpedaled:

Shaffer offered clarification: "Many [twenty-somethings] feel a sense of entitlement because we tended to do so much for them. This should be a time for exploration when their responsibilities are more limited. If we (as parents) continue to hinder their development into adulthood, by doing for them rather than mentoring them to do for themselves, then we can expect to be their personal concierges."

CHAPTER TWO. COLLEGE ON CREDIT

p. 18. the average student loan debt for graduates:

The second major fact in this book that remains elusive is the average student loan burden. Again, there is no official figure for the full amount the average student owes on graduation day. The Department of Education's yearly budget tables do show the average federal loan made per student each year; that figure was $4,194 in 2005. But to get the cumulative student loan burden, you can't merely add the averages of four consecutive years; with the spotty enrollment pattern of many students, and with the growth of private loans, that total is getting more and more difficult to track. One of the most commonly cited recent figures is $19,200, according to a 2005 analysis by the State Public Interest Research Group. The Center for Economic and Policy Research found in September 2005, by analyzing NCES numbers, that the average indebted graduating senior was $17,600 in debt in 2004. The highest credible estimate I have seen, $23,785, comes from an online survey in October 2004 by another student lender, Collegiate Funding Services, and is based on a sample of 668 recent four-year graduates who had not yet paid off their loans.

CHAPTER THREE. LOW-WAGE JOBS

p. 73. The next time we spoke:

The third time I caught up with Jerman, his fortunes had changed again; he had landed a job as a medical administrative assistant, just what he had trained for. The job paid more than he had ever made in his life, and he was thinking about going back to school to become a certified nursing assistant or maybe even a registered nurse.

p. 79. McDonald's alone has provided a McJob:

The BLS *Monthly Labor Review* issued an article in May 2001 titled "Do Some Workers Have Minimum Wage Careers?" that found that while minimum-wage jobs are temporary for most, working for low wages as a teen can affect the chances that someone will continue to do so, and some stay at that level throughout their lives.

CHAPTER FOUR. TEMP GIGS . . .

p. 97. A large amount of recent research has found young people in the '90s and '00s doing worse:

In characterizing the reports of various economists this way, I am doing some simplification and making some assumptions. The longitudinal data required to definitively state that young people in 2005 will do worse on average throughout their lifetimes than their parents did is not yet available. I am assuming, based on educational data and economic trends, that people coming of age in the mid-'00s have more in common with those coming of age in the mid-'90s than with those in the mid-'70s.

p. 103. **Manpower, the nation's largest temp agency, has more American workers:**

Manpower placed 2.5 million people on temporary and contract assignments in 2004, according to its website, manpower.com. Wal-Mart had 1.2 million employees nationwide in 2004, according to a June 2004 article by Liza Featherstone in *The Nation*.

p. 122. **Then they lovingly passed that wisdom down to us:**

See, for example, the Montessori school, home-schooling, Waldorf school, and attachment parenting movements:

www.montessori.edu/method.html

http://psychcentral.com/psypsych/homeschooling

www.awsna.org/welcome.html

www.attachmentparenting.org

p. 127. **It might make us anxious college kids feel better:**

Thanks to my father, Rodger Kamenetz, for having suggested the reference.

Chapter Five. . . . Without Benefits

p. 129. **We live in an age of what political scientist Jacob Hacker:**

Thanks to Alan Schoenfeld for the reference.

p. 133. **we are much more likely than any other age group to visit the emergency room:**

Car crashes are the first leading cause of death for Americans ages three to thirty-three, according to a June 2005 report by the National Highway Traffic Safety Administration. Homicide is the second leading cause of death for youth ten to twenty-four, according to the Centers for Disease Control and Prevention.

CHAPTER SIX. FEDERAL RIP-OFFS:
DEFICITS, SOCIAL SECURITY, MEDICARE

p. 156. **The total national debt:**

On August 26, 2005, the public debt was $7,932,175,772,551.98, according to the Treasury Department's "The Debt to the Penny" website. Federal Budget outlays for 2005 were a third of that, $2,343,000,000,000, according to the Office of Management and Budget.

p. 186. **A 1994 nationwide survey by Third Millennium:**

This same survey is the original source for one of the most often quoted factoids about young people and Social Security: the notion that young people are more likely to believe that UFOs are real than to believe that Social Security will be there for them. President George W. Bush referred to the survey in one of his "town hall" Social Security events in May 2005, eleven years after it was conducted.

Set aside the fact that the survey did not ask respondents to compare directly the likelihood that these two things were true; it merely asked them, in separate questions, whether they believed in each. My question is why there are so few youth advocacy groups operating in Washington today to update this kind of research. Research groups like Third Millennium and the 2030 Center received national attention in the mid-1990s. There is only one such group dedicated to generational policy issues that I have come across in two years of reporting on the subject, the little-known 18to35.org.

CHAPTER SEVEN. FAMILY TROUBLES: LOVE AND INDEPENDENCE

p. 191. **they are still grossly underrepresented:**

As of 2005, there were fourteen women in the Senate. Women made up 16.9 percent of the boards of Fortune 100 companies in 2004. Women were 21 percent of the science and engineering faculty at four-year colleges and universities in 2004, and 10 percent of all employed engineers in 2001. (Sources: senate.gov; The Alliance for Board Diversity, 2005; Current Population Survey, 2001; National Science Foundation, 2000.)

p. 191. **In 2002, young women with a college degree:**

The pay gap is often misunderstood or dismissed. The most commonly cited figure, 76 cents to the dollar in 2003, comes from the Department of Labor. In 2003, real median earnings for women working full-time and year-round were $30,724. For men, the figure was $40,668. The 78-cent figure compares the earnings of college-educated women aged twenty-five to thirty-four. It comes from the National Center for Education Statistics.

As Heather Boushey, an economist for the progressive Center for Economic and Policy Research, explained in a 2004 editorial: "Economists have sliced the data every imaginable way, and found no other explanation for the difference in earnings by gender than this simple one: discrimination. Even when women and men have the same levels of education, fall in the same age range, and work in the same profession, the data show that women earn less than men."

p. 196. **Few scholars have looked systematically:**

In the words of the director of the Center for Marital and Family Studies at the University of Denver, Howard J. Markman, found on his organization's website, cohabitationresearch.org: "Even though close to 70% of couples in the U.S. will live together before or instead of marriage, we know very little about these relationships."

CHAPTER EIGHT. WAKING UP AND TAKING CHARGE

p. 212. **only national political organizing will do:**

For example, see the National Tuition Endowment (tuitionendow ment.org), announced at Columbia University in November 2005.

p. 226. **Nato Green, twenty-seven, is a poster boy:**

Green left Young Workers United in the summer of 2005. Sara Flocks is still with the group.

p. 241. **There are debt counselors in all fifty states:**

Things to watch for when choosing a counseling agency: It should be accredited by the National Foundation for Credit Counseling and/or the Association of Independent Consumer Credit Counseling Agencies. Nonprofit agencies may be a red flag. They are not subject to the same state regulations as for-profits.

BIBLIOGRAPHY

Aaron, Henry J., and Robert Reischauer. *Countdown to Reform: The Great Social Security Debate.* New York: Century Foundation Press, 2001.

Ackerman, Bruce. *We the People.* Cambridge, MA: Harvard University Press, 1991.

————, and Anne Alstott. *The Stakeholder Society.* New Haven, CT: Yale University Press, 1999.

Adams, Jane. *When Our Grown Kids Disappoint Us: Letting Go of Their Problems, Loving Them Anyway, and Getting On with Our Lives.* New York: Free Press, 2003.

Advisory Committee on Student Financial Assistance. *Empty Promises: The Myth of College Access in America.* Report to the U.S. Congress. Washington, DC, June 26, 2002.

American Bar Association. "Lifting the Burden: Law Student Debt as a Barrier to Public Service." The Final Report of the ABA Commission on Loan Repayment and Forgiveness, 2003.

American Council on Education. "Federal Student Loan Debt: 1993 to 2004." ACE Issue Brief, June 2005. Accessed August 25, 2005. www.acenet.edu/AM/Template.cfm?Section=CPA&Template=/CM/ContentDisplay.cfm&ContentID=10733

Andrew, John A. *Lyndon Johnson and the Great Society.* Chicago: I. R. Dee, 1998.

Anrig, Greg, Jr. "Ten Myths About Social Security." January 26, 2005. The Century Foundation. Accessed August 25, 2005. http://www.socsec.org/publications.asp?pubid=507

Arnett, Jeffrey Jensen. *Emerging Adulthood: The Winding Road from the Late Teens Through the Twenties.* New York: Oxford University Press, 2004.

Arnone, Michael, et al. "Ronald Reagan Remembered." *Chronicle of Higher Education,* vol. 50, issue 41. June 18, 2004, p. A24.

Bartlett, Donald L., and James B. Steele. *Critical Condition: How Health Care in America Became Big Business—and Bad Medicine.* New York: Doubleday, 2004.

Barton, Paul E. "One-Third of a Nation: Rising Dropout Rates and Declining Opportunities." Educational Testing Service Policy Information Center, February 2005.

Berker, Ali, and Laura Horn. "Work First, Study Second: Adult Undergraduates Who Combine Employment and Postsecondary Enrollment." August 2003. National Center for Education Statistics. Accessed August 20, 2005. http://nces.ed.gov/pubsearch/pubsinfo.asp?pubid=2003167

Berkowitz, Edward D., ed. *Social Security After Fifty: Successes and Failures.* New York: Greenwood Press, 1987.

Berkowitz, Elana. "Eyes on the Fries." March 31, 2005. Accessed July 31, 2005. http://www.campusprogress.org/features/217/eyes-on-the-fries

Bernhardt, Annette, et al. *Divergent Paths: Economic Mobility in the New American Labor Market.* New York: Russell Sage Foundation, 2001.

Bernstein, Jared. "The Job Market for Young College Graduates: A Difficult Start Amidst a Jobless Recovery." Economic Snapshot, Economic Policy Institute, May 13, 2003.

————, and Karen Kornbluh. "Running Faster to Stay in Place: The Growth of Family Work Hours and Incomes." Work and Family Program Research Paper, New America Foundation, June 2005. Accessed August 31, 2005. http://www.newamerica.net/Download_Docs/pdfs/Doc_File_2437_1.pdf

Boehner, John A., and Howard McKeon. "The College Cost Crisis: A Congressional Analysis of College Costs and Implications for America's Higher Education System." U.S. Congress, September 4, 2003.

Bonczar, T. P. Prevalence of Imprisonment in the U.S. Population, 1974–2001. Washington, DC: Bureau of Justice Statistics, August 2003.

Boushey, Heather. "Student Debt: Bigger and Bigger." Center for Economic and Policy Research, September 2005.

Carrington, William J., and Bruce C. Fallick. "Do Some Workers Have Minimum Wage Careers?" Monthly Labor Review, vol. 124, no. 5 (May 2001).

Cauchon, Dennis, and John Waggoner. "$84,454 Is the Average Household's Personal Debt . . . ," USA Today, October 4, 2004, page A1. Accessed August 30, 2005. http://www.usatoday.com/printedition/news/20041004/1a_debtcovxx.art.htm

CBS News, The Early Show (Vera Gibbons, guest), June 2, 2005. Accessed August 31, 2005. http://www.cbsnews.com/stories/2005/06/02/earlyshow/living/money/main699181_page2.shtml

Center for Information and Research on Civic Learning and Engagement. "Young Americans Support Civil Unions, Marriage, and Protections for Gays and Lesbians: New Survey Finds Youth Overwhelmingly Support Equal Protection on Housing, Employment, and Hate Crimes," February 5, 2004.

Centers for Disease Control and Prevention. "American Women Are

Waiting to Begin Families." December 11, 2002. Accessed August 31, 2005. http://www.cdc.gov/nchs/pressroom/02news/ameriwomen.htm

Collins, Sara R., et al. "Rite of Passage? Why Young Adults Become Uninsured and How New Policies Can Help." The Commonwealth Fund Issue Brief, May 2004.

Colvin, Geoffrey. "Is America the World's 97-lb Weakling?" *Fortune,* July 25, 2005. Accessed August 22, 2005. http://www.fortune.com/fortune/articles/0,15114,1081269,00.html

The Condition of Education 2004. National Center for Education Statistics. Accessed August 21, 2005. nces.ed.gov

"Contingent and Alternative Employment Arrangements." February 2005. Bureau of Labor Statistics. Accessed August 15, 2005. http://www.bls.gov/news.release/conemp.nr0.htm

Cross, Coy F. *Justin Smith Morrill: Father of the Land-Grant Colleges.* East Lansing: Michigan State University Press, 1999.

Csikszentmihalyi, Mihaly, and Barbara Schneider. *Becoming Adult: How Teenagers Prepare for the World of Work.* New York: Basic Books, 2000.

Cubanski, Juliette, and Janet Kline. "In Pursuit of Long-Term Care: Ensuring Access, Coverage, Quality." Issue Brief #536, Commonwealth Fund, April 2002. Accessed August 29, 2005. http://www.cmwf.org/usr_doc/cubanski_inpursuit.pdf

"Decisions Without Direction: Career Guidance and Decision-Making Among American Youth." May 2002. Ferris State University's Career Institute for Education and Workforce Development. Accessed August 25, 2005. http://www.californiacareers.info/download/Ferriseport.pdf

"The Disposable Worker: Living in a Job Loss Economy." *Work Trends,* vol. 6, no. 2 (June 2003). John J. Heldrich Center for Workforce Development at Rutgers University. Accessed August 25, 2005. http://www.heldrich.rutgers.edu/Resources/Publication/100/WorkTrends XIVDisposableWorkerPressReleasePDFFinal.pdf

Draut, Tamara, and Javier Silva. "Generation Broke: The Growth of Debt Among Young Americans." Borrowing to Make Ends Meet Briefing Paper #2. Demos, October 2004.

Eliot, Thomas. *Recollections of the New Deal.* Boston: Northeastern University Press, 1992.

Ellis, Abraham. *The Social Security Fraud.* New Rochelle, NY: Arlington House, 1971.

Emerson, Ralph Waldo. "Self-Reliance." *Essays by Ralph Waldo Emerson.* New York: Dover, 1993.

"Employer Health Benefits: 2004 Summary of Findings." The Kaiser Family Foundation. Accessed August 25, 2005. http://www.kff .org/insurance/7148/upload/2004-Employer-Health-Benefits-Survey -Summary-of-Findings.pdf

"EPI Issue Guide: Minimum Wage." March 2005. Economic Policy Institute. Accessed August 22, 2005. http://www.epi.org/content.cfm/ issueguides_minwage_minwage

"Financial Aid Awards and Services to Graduate/Professional Students in 2002–2003: Reports from the 2003 Survey of Graduate Aid Policies, Practices, and Procedures." June 22, 2004. National Association of Student Financial Aid Administrators. Accessed August 1, 2005. http://www.nasfaa.org/AnnualPubs/2003Sogapppfinal report.PDF

"Fiscal Year 2005 President's Budget Loan Volumes. Policy: Net Commitments by Fiscal Year." U.S. Department of Education. Accessed August 31, 2005. http://www.ed.gov/about/overview/budget/index .html?src=ln

Florida, Richard L. *The Rise of the Creative Class: And How It's Transforming Work, Leisure, Community and Everyday Life.* New York: Basic Books, 2002.

Folbre, Nancy. *The Invisible Heart: Economics and Family Values.* New York: The New Press, 2001.

Fossey, Richard, and Mark Bateman, eds. *Condemning Students to*

Debt: College Loans and Public Policy. New York: Teachers College Press, 1998.

Friedman, Thomas L. *The World Is Flat.* New York: Farrar, Straus & Giroux, 2005.

Fronstin, Paul. "The Impact on Employment-Based Health Benefits of the Shift from a Manufacturing Economy to a Service Economy." Employment Benefit Research Institute. *EBRI Notes,* vol. 25, no. 6 (June 2004).

Froomkin, Dan. "Exploiting a Misconception." May 20, 2005. washingtonpost.com. Accessed August 31, 2005.

Galbraith, James K. *Created Unequal: The Crisis in American Pay.* New York: Free Press, 1998.

Gladieux, Laurence. *The College Aid Quandary.* Washington, DC: Brookings Institution Press, 1995.

Gordon, Linda Perlman, and Susan Morris Shaffer. *Mom, Can I Move Back In with You?* New York: Penguin, 2004.

Greenstein, Robert, and Richard Kogan. "Analysis of the President's Budget." March 5, 2004. Center on Budget and Policy Priorities. Accessed August 28, 2005. http://www.cbpp.org/2-2-04bud.pdf

Grossman, Lev. "Grow Up? Not So Fast." *Time,* January 24, 2005, p. 1.

Gustman, Alan L., and Thomas L. Steinmeier. "Retirement Effects of Social Security Reform." Prepared for the Fifth Annual Conference of the Retirement Research Consortium "Securing Retirement Income for Tomorrow's Retirees," May 15–16, 2003.

Hacker, Jacob. "The New Insecurity: Families Are Slipping off the Economic Ladder." *The Boston Globe,* April 24, 2005.

Harding, Sarah, and Christian Weller. "Retirement Made Riskier." Issue Brief 189. April 9, 2003. Economic Policy Institute. Accessed September 9, 2005. http://www.epi.org/content.cfm/issue-briefs_ib189

Heller, Donald E., and Patricia Marin, ed. "Who Should We Help? The Negative Social Consequences of Merit Aid Scholarships." Accessed August 23, 2002. Harvard University Civil Rights Project.

August 18, 2005. http://www.civilrightsproject.harvard.edu/research/
meritaid/merit_aid02.php

Hewlett, Sylvia Ann. *Creating a Life: Professional Women and the Quest for Children.* New York: Miramax Books, 2002.

Hine, Thomas. *The Rise and Fall of the American Teenager.* New York: William Morrow, 1999.

Holden, Sarah, and Jack VanDerhei. "Can 401(k) Accumulations Generate Significant Income for Future Retirees?" Investment Company Institute, November 2002.

Illich, Ivan. *Deschooling Society.* New York: Harper & Row, 1971.

Jorgensen, Helene. "When Good Jobs Go Bad: Young Adults and Temporary Employment in the New Economy." 2030 Center, 1999.

Kazis, Richard, Joel Vargas, and Nancy Hoffman, eds. *Double the Numbers: Increasing Postsecondary Credentials for Underrepresented Youth.* Cambridge, MA: Harvard Education Press, 2004.

Kerr, Clark. *The Uses of the University.* Cambridge, MA: Harvard University Press, 1963.

King, Jacqueline E., ed. *Financing a College Education: How It Works, How It's Changing.* Westport, CT: Oryx Press, 1999.

King, Tracey, and Ellynne Bannon. "The Burden of Borrowing: A Report on the Rising Rates of Student Loan Debt." The State PIRGs' Higher Education Project, March 2002.

King, Tracey, and Ivan Frishberg. "Big Loans Bigger Problems: A Report on the Sticker Shock of Student Loans." State PIRGs. March 2001.

Kogan, Richard, and Robert Greenstein. "Official Treasury Report Shows Fourth Year of Deficit Growth, Despite Economic Recovery: This Marks First Time Since World War II That Deficit Grew for Four Straight Years." Press release. October 14, 2004. Center on Budget and Policy Priorities. Accessed August 29, 2005. http://www.cbpp.org/10-14-04bud.htm

Kogan, Richard, and Robert Greenstein. "President Portrays Social Security Shortfall as Enormous, but His Tax Cuts and Drug Benefit

Will Cost at Least Five Times as Much." Center on Budget and
Policy Priorities. January 4, 2005. Accessed August 25, 2005.
www.cbpp.org/1-4-05socsec.pdf

Kogan, Richard, and David Kamin. "New Congressional Budget
Office Estimates Show Continued High Deficits and Further Fiscal
Deterioration." Press release. October 1, 2004. Center on Budget
and Policy Priorities. Accessed August 29, 2005. http://www.cbpp
.org/9-7-04.bud.htm

Kollmann, Geoffrey, and Carmen Solomon-Fears. *Social Security:
Major Decisions in the House and Senate, 1935–2000.* New York:
Novinka Books, 2002.

Koss, Andrew. *No-Collar: The Humane Workplace and Its Hidden
Costs.* New York: Basic Books, 2002.

Kotlikoff, Laurence. *Generational Accounting: Knowing Who
Pays, and When, for What We Spend.* New York: The Free Press,
1992.

——— and Scott Burns. *The Coming Generational Storm.* Boston,
MA: The MIT Press, 2004.

Lee, Linda. *Success Without College: Why Your Child May Not Have
to Go to College Right Now—and May Not Have to Go at All.*
New York: Broadway Books, 2001.

Levitan, Mark. "A Crisis of Black Male Employment: Unemployment
and Joblessness in New York City, 2003." Community Service Society, February 2004.

Llewellyn, Grace. *The Teenage Liberation Handbook.* Eugene, OR:
Lowry House, 1991.

"Long-Range Fiscal Policy Brief: How Pension Financing Affects
Returns to Different Generations." A series of issue summaries from
the Congressional Budget Office. No. 12. September 22, 2004. Accessed August 25, 2005. http://www.cbo.gov/showdoc.cfm?index=
5822&sequence=0

Longman, Phillip. *The Empty Cradle.* New York: Basic Books, 2004.

Lopez, Mark Hugo, et al. "The Youth Vote 2004." Center for Information and Research on Civic Learning and Engagement, July 2005.

Losing Ground: A National Status Report on the Affordability of American Higher Education. The National Center for Public Policy and Higher Education, 2002. www.highereducation.org

Lowenstein, Roger. "A Question of Numbers." *The New York Times Magazine,* January 16, 2005, p. 19.

Lubove, Roy. *The Struggle for Social Security, 1900–1935.* Pittsburgh: University of Pittsburgh Press, 1986.

Males, Michael A. *Framing Youth: Ten Myths About the Next Generation.* Monroe, ME: Common Courage Press, 2000.

Manning, Robert. *Credit Card Nation.* New York: Basic Books, 2000.

Marshall, Ray, and Marc Tucker. *Thinking for a Living: Education and the Wealth of Nations.* New York: Basic Books, 1992.

Meier, David. "Sallie Mae Goes Solo." *The Motley Fool.* December 31, 2004. Accessed July 1, 2005. www.fool.com/News/mft/2004/mft04123109

Michel, Lawrence. "No Boom in the Need for College Graduates." Economic Snapshots. July 21, 2004. Economic Policy Institute. Accessed August 21, 2005. www.epinet.org/content.cfm/webfeatures_snapshots_07212004

———, Jared Bernstein, and Sylvia Allegretto. *State of Working America 2004–05.* Economic Policy Institute. Ithaca, NY: Cornell University Press, 2005.

Mitchell, Daniel. *Pensions, Politics, and the Elderly: Historic Social Movements and Their Lessons for Our Aging Society.* Armonk, NY: M. E. Sharpe, 2000.

Morris, Charles R. *The AARP: America's Most Powerful Lobby and the Clash of Generations.* New York: Times Books, 1996.

"Motor Vehicle Traffic Crashes as a Leading Cause of Death in the U.S., 2002—A Demographic Perspective." National Highway Traffic Safety Administration, June 2005.

"National Population Estimates." July 1, 2002. U.S. Bureau of the Census. Accessed July 31, 2005. http://www.census.gov/popest/archives/2000s/vintage_2002/NA-EST2002-ASRO-01.html

Newman, Katherine. *Declining Fortunes: The Withering of the American Dream*. New York: Basic Books, 1993.

―――. *Falling from Grace: Downward Mobility in the Age of Affluence*. New York: The Free Press, 1988.

―――. *No Shame in My Game: The Working Poor in the Inner City*. New York: Alfred A. Knopf, 1999.

Occupational Outlook Handbook 2004–2005. U.S. Department of Labor. Bureau of Labor Statistics. Accessed August 31, 2005. www.bls.gov/oco/home.htm

"Occupations with the Largest Job Growth, 2002–2012." *Monthly Labor Review*, February 2004. Bureau of Labor Statistics. Accessed July 31, 2005. http://www.bls.gov/emp/emptab4.htm

Oeffinger, Kevin C., M.D., et al. "Health Care of Young Adult Survivors of Childhood Cancer: A Report from the Childhood Cancer Survivor Study," *Annals of Family Medicine,* vol. 2 (2004): 61–70. DOI: 10.1370/afm.26.

Oldman, Mark. *The Internship Bible*. New York: Princeton Review Publishing, 2004.

Orman, Suze. *The Money Book for the Young, Fabulous & Broke*. New York: Riverhead Books, 2005.

Orzechowski, Shawna, and Peter Sepielli. "Net Worth and Asset Ownership of Households: 1998 and 2000." May 2003. Household Economic Studies. U.S. Census Bureau, Current Population Reports.

Osterman, Paul, et al. *Working in America: A Blueprint for the New Labor Market*. Cambridge, MA: The MIT Press, 2002.

Palladino, Lenore, and Heather McGhee. "Paycheck Politics: Young Workers Are Fighting Back." Around the Kitchen Table Commentary. Demos. December 8, 2004.

"Parents, Youth and Money Survey." 2001. American Savings Education Council (ASEC), the Employee Benefit Research Institute (EBRI), and Mathew Greenwald & Associates. Accessed August 25, 2005. http://tiaa-crefinstitute.org/Data/surveys/pdfs/2001hlights.pdf

Paulin, Geoffrey, and Brian Riordan. "Making It on Their Own: The Baby Boom Meets Generation X." *Monthly Labor Review,* vol. 121, no. 2 (February 1998). Bureau of Labor Statistics. Accessed August 18, 2005. http://www.bls.gov/opub/mlr/1998/02/art2abs.htm

"Pay Rates for Freelance Journalists." June 1, 2002. National Writers Union. Accessed August 25, 2005. www.nwu.org/journ/minrate.htm.

Pearson, Alison. *I Don't Know How She Does It.* New York: Alfred A. Knopf, 2002.

"Pension Coverage from 1979–1998: The Shift From Defined Benefit to Defined Contribution Plans." Accessed September 9, 2005. http://www.epi.org/issueguides/retire/charts/dbdc_600.gif

"People Average 8.6 Jobs from 18 to 32." *Monthly Labor Review.* October 13, 1998. Bureau of Labor Statistics. Accessed July 31, 2005. http://www.bls.gov/opub/ted/1998/Oct/wk2/art01.htm

Peterson, Peter G. *Running on Empty: How the Democratic and Republican Parties Are Bankrupting Our Future and What Americans Can Do About It.* New York: Farrar, Straus & Giroux, 2004.

Philippe, Kent A., ed. *National Profile of Community Colleges: Trends & Statistics.* Washington, DC: Community College Press, 2000.

Pipes, Sally. *Miracle Cure: How to Solve America's Health Care Crisis and Why Canada Isn't the Answer.* San Francisco: Pacific Research Institute, 2004.

Pollin, Robert, and Stephanie Luce. *The Living Wage.* New York: The New Press, 1998.

Porter, Eduardo, and Mary Williams Walsh. "Retirement Turns into a Rest Stop as Benefits Dwindle," *The New York Times,* February 9, 2005.

Pozen, Robert C. "A Win-Win Proposition," *The Wall Street Journal*, May 3, 2005, p. 12. Accessed August 31, 2005. www.opinionjournal .com/editorial/feature.html?id=11000639

Price, Derek. *Borrowing Inequality: Race, Class, and Student Loans.* Boulder, CO: Lynne Riener, 2004.

"Projections of Education Statistics to 2013." National Center for Education Statistics, October 2003. Accessed August 16, 2005. http:// nces.ed.gov/programs/projections/ch_2.asp#3

Redd, Kenneth E. *Discounting Toward Disaster: Tuition Discounting, College Finances, and Enrollments of Low-Income Undergraduates.* USAGroup Foundation New Agenda Series, vol. 3, no. 2 (December 2000).

Reich, Robert. *The Future of Success.* New York: Alfred A. Knopf, 2000.

———. *The Work of Nations.* New York: Alfred A. Knopf, 1991.

"Report of the Working Group on the Benefit Implications of the Growth of a Contingent Workforce." Advisory Council on Employee Welfare and Pension Benefit Plans, U.S. Department of Labor, November 10, 1999. Accessed September 7, 2005. http:// www.dol.gov/ebsa/publications/contrpt.htm

"Retirement Planning: Do We Have a Crisis in America?" Hearing before the Special Committee on Aging, U.S. Senate, 108th Congress, 2nd Session, Washington, DC, January 27, 2004.

Rosenbloom, Stephanie. "It's the Kids: Lock Up the China!" *The New York Times,* July 28, 2005.

Samuelson, Robert J. "Off Golden Pond: The Aging of America and the Reinvention of Retirement." *The New Republic,* April 12, 1999, p. 36.

Schieber, Sylvester J., and John B. Shoven. *The Real Deal: The History and Future of Social Security.* New Haven, CT: Yale University Press, 1999.

Schlosser, Eric. *Fast Food Nation.* New York: Houghton Mifflin, 2001.

Schneider, Barbara, and David Stevenson. *The Ambitious Generation: America's Teenagers, Motivated but Directionless.* New Haven, CT: Yale University Press, 1999.

Schor, Juliet. *Born to Buy: The Commercialized Child and the New Consumer Culture.* New York: Scribner, 2004.

————. *The Overspent American: Upscaling, Downshifting, and the New Consumer.* New York: Basic Books, 1998.

Schottland, Charles I. *The Social Security Program in the United States.* New York: Appleton-Century-Crofts, 1970.

Schrammel, Kurt. "Comparing the Labor Market Success of Young Adults from Two Generations." *Monthly Labor Review,* 3-48 (1998).

Schulman, Bruce. *Lyndon B. Johnson and American Liberalism: A Brief Biography with Documents.* New York: Bedford/St. Martin's, 1994.

Settersten, Richard A., Jr., Frank F. Furstenberg, and Ruben J. Rumbaut, eds. *On the Frontier of Adulthood: Theory, Research, and Public Policy.* Chicago: University of Chicago Press, 2005.

Shipler, David. *The Working Poor: Invisible in America.* New York: Alfred A. Knopf, 2004.

Shulman, Beth. *The Betrayal of Work: How Low-Wage Jobs Fail 30 Million Americans.* New York: The New Press, 2003.

Sinetar, Dr. Marsha. *Do What You Love, The Money Will Follow: Discovering Your Right Livelihood.* Mahwah, NJ: Paulist Press, 1987.

"65+ Survey." Conducted by the Luntz Research Companies/Mark A. Siegel and Associates for Third Millennium. September 1994. Accessed August 29, 2005. http://www.18to35.org/thirdmil/publications/surveys/surv7.html

Skidmore, Max. *Social Security and Its Enemies: The Case for America's Most Efficient Insurance Program.* Boulder, CO: Westview Press, 1999.

Social Security Reform: A Century Foundation Guide to the Issues, revised ed. New York: Century Foundation Press, 2002.

"Social Security: Analysis of Issues and Selected Reform Proposals."
Statement of David M. Walker, Comptroller General of the United
States, Testimony Before the Special Committee on Aging, U.S. Sen-
ate. January 15, 2003. Government Accountability Office. Accessed
August 25, 2005. http://www.gao.gov/new.items/d03376t.pdf

"The State of Our Unions 2004: The Social Health of Marriage in
America." The National Marriage Project at Rutgers University,
June 2004.

"Status of the Social Security and Medicare Programs: A Summary of
the 2005 Annual Reports." Social Security and Medicare Boards of
Trustees. Accessed August 31, 2005. http://www.ssa.gov/OACT/
TRSUM/trsummary.html

Strauss, William, and Neil Howe. *Generations: The History of America's Future 1584 to 2069.* New York: William Morrow, 1991.

Sullivan, Teresa, Elizabeth Warren, and Jay Lawrence Westbrook. *The
Fragile Middle Class: Americans in Debt.* New Haven, CT: Yale
University Press, 2000.

Sunstein, Cass R. *The Second Bill of Rights: FDR's Unfinished Revolution and Why We Need It More Than Ever.* New York: Basic
Books, 2004.

Tannock, Stuart. *Youth at Work: The Unionized Fast-Food and Grocery Workplace.* Philadelphia: Temple University Press, 2001.

Tierney, John. "2004 in a Word: Adultescent," *The New York Times,*
December 26, 2004.

Uchitelle, Louis. "College Degree Still Pays, but It's Leveling Off." *The
New York Times,* January 13, 2005.

"Undergraduate Students and Credit Cards in 2004: An Analysis of
Usage Rates and Trends." May 2005. Nellie Mae. Accessed August 25, 2005. http://www.nelliemae.com/library/research_12.html

Warren, Elizabeth, and Amelia Warren Tyagi. *The Two-Income Trap:
Why Middle-Class Mothers and Fathers Are Going Broke.* New
York: Basic Books, 2003.

Washburn, Jennifer. *University Inc: The Corporate Corruption of Higher Education.* New York: Basic Books, 2005.

Williamson, John B., Diane M. Watts-Roy, and Eric R. Kingson, eds. *The Generational Equity Debate.* New York: Columbia University Press, 1999.

Wolanin, Thomas R., ed. "Reauthorizing the Higher Education Act: Issues and Options." Institute for Higher Education Policy, March 2003.

"Youth Violence Fact Sheet." National Center for Injury Prevention and Control. Accessed August 25, 2005. http://www.cdc.gov/ncipc/factsheets/yvfacts.htm

Higher Education Policy

Public Interest Research Groups: www.pirg.org/highered
Student Debt Alert: www.studentdebtalert.org
Project on Student Debt. http://projectonstudentdebt.org
U.S. House Committee on Education and the Workforce-Democrats:
http://edworkforce.house.gov/democrats

Financial Aid Information

The Department of Education's financial aid website: http://studentaid
.ed.gov/PORTALSWebApp/students/english/index.jsp
Financial aid guidance from FastWeb scholarships: http://finaid.org/
about
National Student Loan Data System: www.nslds.ed.gov/nslds_SA
The Ombudsman at the Office of Federal Student Aid:
www.ombudsman.ed.gov/about/about.html

Activism and Voting

18to35: Innovation Deliberation Participation: www.18to35.org
Campus Progress: www.campusprogress.org
Energy Action: www.energyaction.net
Mobilizing America's Youth: www.mobilize.org
Student Loan Justice: www.studentloanjustice.org
Tent State University: www.tentstate.com
Tuition Endowment Plan: www.tuitionendowment.org
Young Voter Strategies: www.youngvoterstrategies.org

Personal Finance

Jumpstart Coalition for Personal Financial Literacy:
www.jumpstart.org
American Savings Education Coalition: www.choosetosave.org/asec
Let's Save America Financial Literacy Campaign:
www.letssaveamerica.com
Bankrate—compare credit cards and savings products: www.bankrate
.com/brm/default.asp
Moneypants—track your spending: http://moneypants.com

My website: www.AnyaKamenetz.com

ABOUT THE AUTHOR

Anya Kamenetz grew up in Louisiana and graduated from Yale University in 2002. She is a columnist for *The Village Voice* and a freelance writer. She lives in New York City.